Eye of the Beholder

AN ILLUSTRATED ANTHOLOGY

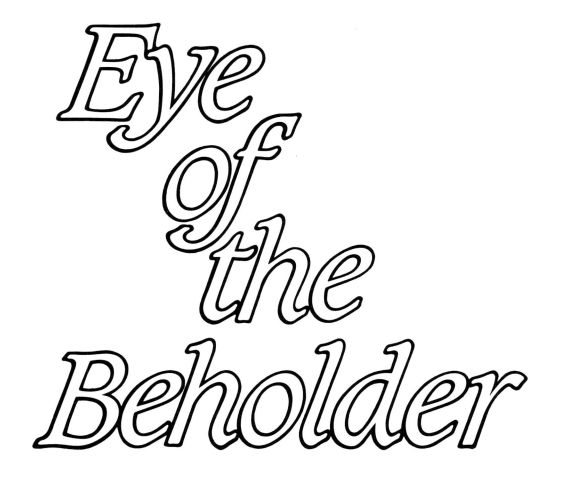

Eye of the Beholder

Richard Jefferies

Introduction by
Colin Laurie McKelvie

Illustrations by
Esdaile Hudson

Ashford Press Publishing
Southampton
1987

Published by Ashford Press Publishing
1 Church Road
Shedfield
Hampshire SO3 2HW

British Cataloguing in Publication Data

Jefferies, Richard
    Eye of the beholder : an illustrated
    anthology.
    1. Country life—England   2. Natural
    history—England   3. Hunting—England—
    History—19th century   4. Sports—
    England—History—19th century
    I. Title
    942.07'3'0924   S522.G7
    ISBN 1-85253-037-5

Designed and typeset by Jordan and Jordan, Fareham, Hampshire

Printed and bound in Great Britain by Robert Hartnoll (1985) Ltd., Bodmin, Cornwall

Contents

List of Plates

Introduction

The eye is for ever drawn onward,
and knows no end.

Richard Jefferies: *Wild Flowers (1885)*

Richard Jefferies was an author of the physical senses, and pre-eminently an author of the *eye*. Closely observed visual images and experiences were the forces which informed almost all his writing, and he could see things with an unusually sustained power of quiet concentration and intense perception, skills which were partly innate and partly self-taught. Henry Williamson, in an Introduction to the 1966 Everyman Library edition of Jefferies' *Bevis*, said that 'Jefferies had wonderful eyes. He saw what other men did not see, or were too preoccupied by the problems of earning a living, to bother about. Clear sight is the base of all good writing, as it is with painting and other arts. The true artist sees clearly and with wonder'.

Williamson claimed Jefferies had been an inspiration to him in his writing: '...I believed that the spirit of Richard Jefferies was helping me in my early struggles to write. I thought about him most of my waking hours. He was with me in my solitary walks in the country south of London'. That spirit in his writing which Williamson acknowledged is what distinguishes Jefferies' essays and longer works alike, for they combine intimate and closely observed descriptions of landscape, animals and men with a powerful sense of what is hidden beneath external appearances, the immanence and inner life which lie behind the outward and visible images. The awareness of what Wordsworth called 'something far more deeply interfused' became more and more powerful in his later writing and is most evident in the reflective and often mystical pieces he wrote in his last years, before his death at the early age of thirty-eight, on 14 August 1887.

Seeing, watching, observing and scrutinising, with stealth, minute care and in the most intimate detail, was the starting point for Richard Jefferies' writing. His skill as a descriptive writer about landscape and the natural scene has always tended to invite comparisons with other writers who stretch in a long line from Virgil in the *Georgics* to Gilbert White, John Clare, Francis Kilvert and many others. They belong to that large and disparate group of literary figures whom we tend to find slotted together in a comprehensive, convenient but rather vague literary pigeon-hole - 'country writers'. Jefferies' contemporaries at Coate did not know quite what to make of 'moony Dick' and later readers have also been at something of a loss. To describe him as a country writer will do, perhaps, but only as the loosest and most obvious assessment. By turns he was a social commentator, agronomist, anthropologist, chronicler of railway history, naturalist, storyteller, field sportsman, an authority on the making and use of sporting guns, an aspiring novelist, a prophetic visionary, a political polemicist, silviculturist, jobbing journalist, writer of pleasing *belles lettres* and a tortured mystic. The critics' professional inclination to categorise and label writers like Jefferies is perhaps inevitable, but it is only when we read writers closely and grasp their discrete and unique ways of seeing and writing that we begin to do justice to them individually.

John Richard Jefferies – he never used his first name – was born on 6 November 1848 at Coate, a small hamlet in north Wiltshire, just south-east of Swindon on the road to Hungerford. He was the eldest son of James Luckett Jefferies, a thirty-two year old farmer and small landowner who, in September 1844, had married Elizabeth Gyde. In 1896, at the age of 80 and within weeks of his death, he sent a letter from his home in Bath to Dr. Alfred Theodore Rake of Hampstead. With cramping fingers and by the light of a candle he wrote with ill-concealed impatience, if not anger, of his son's description of the family home: '...how he could think of describing Coate as such a pleasant place and deceive so I could not imagine... he styled it Coate Farm, it was not worthy of the name of Farm it was not forty acres of land'. It appears, however, that Jefferies had a reason for doing this, as we can see in his 'Wiltshire Labourers' letters to the *Times* in November 1872, which are reprinted in this selection (pp115-126) and which he signed as from 'Coate Farm, Swindon'. He simply wanted those letters to be perceived as coming from a spokesman from among that community of small farmers.

Coate Farmhouse (as it was later, formally, to be called) was a difficult and often unhappy household for the young Jefferies. His parents' marriage was fundamentally unhappy. Elizabeth was a town girl, never fully at home in the countryside and ill-suited both by temperament and by her London upbringing to life as a farmer's wife. The half-concealed but profound bitterness which developed between James Jefferies and his wife must have been apparent to their children. The difficulties of the marriage were exacerbated by James Luckett Jefferies' erratic, complex character. He seems to have been an inefficient, sometimes downright feckless farmer, whose impractical approach to farming at a time of general agricultural uncertainties meant eventual failure for the farm. In his father's personality Jefferies saw some of the perennial strengths and the self-destructive weaknesses which he regarded as typical of the Wiltshire farm labourer, and which he was to write about at length in those important letters to *The Times* in 1872 (pp115-126). His father was a temperamental man, given to angry outbursts, but he was also something of a gentle dreamer, well-informed in local history and with a wide but random and undisciplined knowledge of classical literature, picked up through his extensive, desultory reading. Charles Jefferies, Richard's younger brother, born in 1858, said that 'our parents were related to some London publishers who regularly stocked us with all sorts of books, while my father always manifested a love of reading, which he early instilled into us as boys. ... Richard early in life emulated my father's pleasure in reading.'

There was indeed a bookish, literary background to the Jefferies family on both sides. James Luckett's father had worked as an assistant to a Fleet Street publisher and printer before leaving London in 1816 to take over the management of a bakery in Swindon. Although the Gyde family's roots originally lay in Painswick in rural Gloucestershire, Elizabeth had been brought up in London. Her parents lived in Islington and her father, Charles Gyde, was in business as a bookbinder in Red Lion Court, off Fleet Street. Hints of both these pieces of family background emerge in *Amaryllis at the Fair* (1887), in which Alere Flamma is portrayed as living a chaotic, semi-bohemian and richly intellectual life in a book-filled house in Fleet Street, close to his printing business, 'the House of Flamma in Red Lion Court'. Grandfather Iden has a collection of books, 'Shakespeare and Boccaccio and Addison...all very finely bound in the best style of hand-art', and his treasured 'peel', the traditional long-handled wooden spatula of the master baker, for placing loaves in the oven: 'Grandfather Iden, being proud of his trade, in his old age had his favourite peel ornamented with silver'. Here are unmistakeable echoes of the Fleet Street connections of the Jefferies and Gyde families and of Richard's grandfather's transition from apprenticeship in the Fleet Street printing house to taking over the Swindon bakery.

The great central figure in *Amaryllis* and arguably the finest and most fully realised character in the whole corpus of Jefferies' fiction is Farmer Iden. A magnificent, powerful and ultimately fated man, he invites comparison with some of Thomas Hardy's characters. That he is modelled closely on certain aspects of the character of Jefferies' father is beyond doubt; James Luckett Jefferies acknowledged it himself, and said that some of the passages were drawn directly from his own life. A letter from Jefferies to the publishers, R. Bentley & Son, accompanied the manuscript of *Amaryllis* when he submitted it in May 1886, and in it he specifically and emphatically drew his publisher's attention to the character of Iden:

'I should like to call Mr Bentley's attention to the character of Iden, the farmer which he will see is real. Iden of Coombe Oaks is the Man of the Land in his strength and his weakness, his good and foolish qualities; I should particularly like Mr Bentley to take note of him.'

A month later Jefferies wrote again to Bentley. It was a longer letter, marked 'Private', and it had clearly been prompted by some reservations Bentley had expressed about the character of Farmer Iden, 'on the ground of the inconsistency of a rough farmer being at the same time a scholarly gentleman. I have been thinking how I could substantiate my character who is drawn from life and it has occurred to me that perhaps if I tell you I am myself the son of a farmer it may seem more credible to you. My father was a farmer working his own land (a small landowner too) and it was common enough to see him engaged in the work of the farm, his coat thick with fragments of adhering hay, his heavy boots wet from the water meadow and so on. But he was at the same time a scholar, a great reader with a considerable library of the best authors, and above all the keenest observation of nature and of natural phenomena... To him too I owe the manner of observing nature – if you could but get *him* to write you a book of natural history it would indeed be a book. But he has never written anything and never will. The other day (at the age of 70) he walked 20 miles (being still athletic) to see a herb which he had not previously seen growing. Now this is a man whom you might often have seen among his cattle or chopping down a tree.'

Coombe Oaks and the family life portrayed in *Amaryllis* are an idealised picture of Coate Farm and the author's family, but Jefferies was desperately anxious that his private life and family background should remain confidential. This was partly due to his intense personal shyness and a lifelong tendency to shrink from public attention. 'Six or seven compliers of biographical dictionaries have applied to me for such details which I have invariably refused – I have a great dislike of such private matters being published, at all events at present.' But he goes on in the same letter to hint, despite his declared pride, at some feeling of inadequacy about his family background. 'Not that I know anything to be ashamed of. I am only too proud to say I am the son of the soil and to add that my family have been farmers and landowners for nearly 300 years, a pedigree as good I think as many titled names can claim.' But the letter closes with Jefferies again urging Bentley to 'keep my bit of autobiography private for the present'. We can be forgiven for spotting a partly concealed but unmistakable chip on the shoulder.

His life was restless and the frequent moves he and his wife were later to make from one house to another were foreshadowed by a disrupted childhood. In 1852, at the age of four and in the year of the birth of his younger brother Henry, Richard Jefferies left Coate and for the next five years lived with Mrs Harrild, his mother's sister, at Sydenham. A month's holiday each year was the only contact he had with

Coate and its surroundings during that time, and it may have been significant for his later view of Coate and of rural life that his early days had been spent in suburbia, closer to the life of London than the society of rural Wiltshire. He learned to write and to read in the Harrild household before his irregular formal education began at a small preparatory school when he was seven. He was described as a sensitive, impulsive and nervous little boy, given to passionate loves and hates, quick to learn and with a good memory and a sharp eye for detail. He was also fond of reading and drawing.

In 1857, at the age of nine, he returned to his parents and three younger brothers at Coate and went to the National School in Newport Street, Old Swindon. In 1944 a former schoolboy acquaintance, then well into his nineties, remembered him as a boy apart from the others, wholly absorbed either in his books or his thoughts. 'Moony Dick' did not mix easily with his school-fellows, nor with others in later life. Jefferies knew this himself, and gives an overstated but unmistakable glimpse of how it may have appeared to him in his bleaker moments, in a short fragment entitled *Hyperion*, which remained unpublished until the centenary of his birth in 1948:

'There was once a youth in an obscure country village, quite lost in the rudest and most illiterate county of the West, who passed a great part of his time reading books and dreaming, so much so that he was useless upon the farm.'

That reads like many another writer's lament for a disadvantaged start in life, combined with a self-critical sense of his own isolation and uselessness for practical chores. Patrick Kavanagh felt the same as he grew up on the family small-holding in rural Ireland, 'before Dublin taught him to be wise', and later drew a wonderful self-portrait of his youth in the novel *Tarry Flynn*.

There are also some obvious parallels between the home backgrounds and early lives of Jefferies and D.H. Lawrence. Both were gifted, sensitive children, products of unhappy and unsettled family backgrounds in each of which there was nevertheless some glimmer of artistic and literary sensibility to attract and inspire. In *A Sin and a Shame* (1875) Jefferies wrote with a hint of anguish, 'How few of us are what we should have been had circumstances given our nature scope to expand itself! But most of us have been hemmed in and pressed down, and compelled to meet daily with dull and dispiriting circumstances, till at last these react upon our nature, and warp us from our original bias.' And the parallels with Lawrence might be pursued further by a comparative study of Jefferies' later sense of 'soul-life' and his affinity with and spiritual absorption into the natural world; and Lawrence's potent pantheism and love of the life of the earth as he wrote of it in, for example, *Women in Love*. But that lies outside the scope of this Introduction.

In November 1864, just after his sixteenth birthday, Jefferies and his slightly older cousin and neighbour Willie Cox ran away from home, on an impulse to visit the Continent and walk to Moscow. Why they chose that destination is not clear, but within a fortnight the two had returned from France, where the combined difficulties of a foreign language and a realisation of the size of the task they had undertaken made them turn back. They went straight to Liverpool but were arrested while trying to raise the fare for a cut-price passage to New York, and sent back to Swindon. It was a boyish adventure, prankish, brief and probably insignificant in itself, but that restlessness and the need to be on the move had come to the surface again. He did later visit the Continent, going in September 1870 to Brussels, which he liked despite seeing the grim spectacle of wounded soldiers returning in thousands from the battle of Sedan; and also to Paris, which he hated. His *The Plainest City in Europe* (1883) is a diatribe against the regimented soullessness of a city laid out in the grand manner. London's crowded informality was a joy to him in many unexpected ways. Paris was a sham.

London's metropolitan atmosphere excited and stimulated Jefferies. He was drawn to it partly by his need to work closely with the editors of the many London-based magazines and publishers for whom he wrote, partly by a need to be near libraries for background research, and also by the city's exuberant life. *The Lions in Trafalgar Square*, published posthumously, succeeds better than almost anything else he wrote in giving the lie to the commonly received perception of Jefferies as a bucolic writer. Calm amid the teeming, restless life of 'the four-million city', Landseer's vast statues guarding Nelson's column were altogether larger than life, and somehow more real and satisfying and alive to him. 'The immense lion here beside me expresses larger nature...massiveness exalts the mind. London is the only real place in the world. The cities turn towards London as young partridges run to their mother.' Parochial, a 'local writer', Jefferies' poetic imagination meant he could be bounded in a physical nutshell and still count himself a king of infinite space. And for that final image of affection he returns to his memories of the coveys among the stubble fields of Wiltshire.

From his teens Richard Jefferies evidently had a strong urge to write, almost a *cacoethes scribendi*, combined with a desire to succeed as a writer and to be seen as a successful, acknowledged author. That urge and ambition was fuelled by his early opportunities to write for the *North Wilts Herald* and the *Wilts and Gloucestershire Standard*, by a growing sense of his own abilities, and by that most compelling influence on every writer, the need to earn a living. Throughout his life his bread and butter was to be earned in the form of fees for magazine articles, mostly shortish pieces of two or three thousand words. But he wanted to be a novelist, and his first ventures in this genre were published largely at his own expense. Except for books of a very obscure or *recherché* nature, 'vanity publishing' has always been regarded as the last resort of the writer who has been rejected by commercial publishers but is still determined to see his work in print. As a jobbing journalist Jefferies was working among printers and publishers, and he was well placed to arrange to have his first novels published on that unsatisfactory basis. They are poor and disappointing things, weak and often derivative in plot and characterisation and over-blown in style. This was 'prentice work, best forgotten, but Jefferies was steadily learning his craft as a writer. Those juvenilia are far removed from the fluent assurance of his best journalism, his mature essays and the soul-baring complexities of some of his later writing.

Predictably, some of what Jefferies wrote has led to his being espoused by today's single-issue zealots in the cause of green consciousness and the banning of blood sports. In Jefferies it pleases them to see the reformed and contrite sportsman, an exemplar who moved towards a higher, more precious communion with the spirit of the natural world, and they try to recruit him to their cause. They quote, very selectively, from what he wrote. Yet Jefferies defies all attempts to invoke his writings in aid of any cause or dogma. In 1884, only a year after the publication of *The Story of My Heart*, he could still write a short but vivid piece for the *St. James' Magazine* which is full of the old, robust zest for 'the sense of woodcraft', a proud delight in deft gun handling and evidently eager memories of snap-shooting at woodcock, snipe and bolting rabbits with his favourite single-barrelled gun.

The Story of My Heart, Jefferies' 'autobiography of the mind' published in 1883, is a demanding and difficult book, and ultimately a flawed and unsatisfactory one. Many of the difficulties are of Jefferies' own making, in his choice of subject and his use of language. He struggles, sometimes with wonderfully illuminated and illuminating visionary glimpses but also with rambling, confused near-incoherence, to convey his inchoate sense of the numinous and the mystical in his view of the natural world. He stretches language to its limits in an eager, sometimes frenzied attempt to express what he felt. But he knew the limitations of language and the frustrations of his inarticulateness in tackling this intimate, metaphysical writing. Four years later, in *Nature and Books* (1887), he wrote of his longing for 'a great development in the power of *expressing* thoughts and feelings which are now thoughts and feelings only'. He knew his unresolved quest was to express 'thoughts yet dumb – chambers within the mind which require the key of new words to unlock'. *The Story of My Heart* is barely comprehensible, and then only in proportion to the reader's private and personal affinity with what Jefferies felt and tried to put into words.

It is tempting but probably unwise to attribute the mystical, metaphysical writing of Jefferies' last years to the morbid introspection said to be typical of the Romantic consumptive. His health, always delicate, had steadily worsened during his thirties and he seems to have suffered from a slow but progressive form of generalised tuberculosis, formally described as 'chronic fibroid phthisis', which was exacerbated by a tendency to hypochondria and a generally nervous disposition. The death of one of his children made him inconsolable and distraught to the extent that he could not leave his bed to attend the funeral. But his mind was restlessly inquiring and active and his need to write undiminished, and his wife took dictation when he was too weak to hold a pen. Longer periods of confinement to the house and to his bed might have led to more introspection, but much of his last work is imbued with a robust energy and vigour equal to anything he had written earlier. He had less opportunity now to exercise his unique ability to use his eyes, to see the countryside as only he knew how. But he was gifted with a clear and retentive memory and an ability to store images with photographic clarity. These were the reserves upon which he drew for his writing in those last months. He was a realist and knew he was dying, and that precious time was slipping past. His last years were astonishingly productive, with an important book on the red deer of the West Country in 1884, a succession of novels and collections of essays, introductions to others' books, and articles for magazines. New publications continued until the very last weeks of his life, and his widow collected and published in 1889 a number of important essays written just before his death. While he lay dying in Goring, in the last of a long succession of houses in Sussex and Surrey where he and his wife had lived, his very last dictated essay was a return to Swindon and Coate, entitled *My Old Village*.

Richard Jefferies died on 14th August 1887 and was buried in Broadwater Cemetery at Worthing, where his tombstone bears the inscription 'To the Prose Poet of England's Fields and Hedgerows'. Thirty-eight years later the naturalist and writer W.H. Hudson, a contemporary of Jefferies who was also to celebrate the landscape, the wild creatures and the country folk of Wiltshire in his own distinctive way, was buried just a few yards away. At his own request Hudson's tombstone was identical to Jefferies', a tall cross of white marble.

In the twenty years or so of his active writing career Jefferies' output was so prolific, and the range of his subjects and styles so extensive, that he is an author whose work tends to benefit from selection and editing. Taken as a whole, his writing is uneven in quality and often appears inconsistent in the views he takes and the standpoint from which he approaches his subjects. He sometimes tackled genres to which he was not suited, making repeated efforts to produce a good novel, but never achieving the necessary development and depth of plot and characterisation. Although *Amaryllis at the Fair* (1887), *Hodge and his Masters* (1880) and *After London* (1885) are important pieces of writing, their interest lies principally in the statements they make about Jefferies' perceptions of individual people, places and ideas. He is a master of the well-observed vignette, the tellingly drawn cameo, rather than of the richness, density and narrative development which the novel form demands. Jefferies' skills and talents were primarily as a journalist and observer essayist: he was more like William Cobbett than Thomas Hardy.

Much of his early writing shows unmistakable signs of inexperience, while his copious later essays were often written quickly to meet publishers' deadlines, and some bear the stamp of the hack journalist making a living by turning out competent but rather uninspired pieces at his editors' request. No journalist or columnist who submits copy to his editors almost daily can be expected to maintain a uniform standard of excellence. He is rather to be commended for whatever, generally high, quality he can achieve. And we should never lose sight of the fact that Jefferies was a professional writer, whose living depended on the fees his writing earned for him. Remembering what that greatest of Grub Street hacks, Samuel Johnson, said in his characteristically blunt dismissal of the concept of the writer as a Muse-inspired idealist – 'no man but a blockhead ever wrote, except for money' – we should bear in mind that the paid journalist usually writes what the public wants to read and what his editor wants to print and to pay him for. Edward Thomas, Jefferies' first and still his best biographer, saw that '...being a journalist, he had often to deal immediately, and in a transitory manner, with passing events, or to empty a page or two of his notebooks in response to an impulse assuredly no higher than habit or necessity'. This is not to imply any lack of beliefs and ideals or any cynical compromising of them; it is to recognise the realities of journalism and of journeyman writing. And we must add to this the important fact of Jefferies' youth. His cub-journalism began when he was barely seventeen years old and his writing throughout his twenties and thirties reflected the natural development of an adolescent growing into manhood and undergoing constant intellectual, emotional and moral development, continually seeking out and encountering new situations and ideas and philosophies. If Jefferies' work seems sometimes to be self-contradictory, shifting and inconsistent this is only because it mirrors the writer's personal quest for his own framework of beliefs and values. He is alert, receptive, impressionable, often passionate and sometimes confused.

In many of his essays, especially the economic and political writings, he can appear to shift his ground radically. One moment he appears to be an apologist for the squires and the landowning establishment, the next he inveighs against the iniquities of exploited labour, of demoralised communities and the shadow of the workhouse. This betrays his own genuine uncertainties. He was not possessed by any *idée fixe* nor entrenched in a dogmatic posture. His approach to his subjects is open-minded, eager to learn and susceptible to new ideas. The writings, and perhaps especially his more polemical pieces, show his humanity – by turns impassioned and quizzical, full of conviction and scepticism, and always attractively vulnerable.

In style, too, Richard Jefferies can be a difficult writer to assess adequately. The deceptively easy flow of his prose and the light touch of his writing draw the reader along in such a way to create an impression of effortless competence and thus perhaps of superficiality. But that stylistic ease is born of the art which conceals art. Jefferies admired the clarity and uncluttered simplicity of the prose writers of the early eighteenth century – old Iden in *Amaryllis at the Fair* has a favourite volume of Addison – and he would probably have agreed with Jonathan Swift that 'proper words in proper places makes the true definition of a style'.

'The page was a pale yellow, the type old fount, the edges rough, but where in a trim modern volume will you find language like his and ideas set forth with such transparent lucidity? How easy to write like that! – so simple, merely a letter to an intimate friend; but try!'

As time went by Jefferies wrote more and gained greater maturity as a writer and a clearer and more objective understanding of himself and his work, of how he approached his subject and of the principles which informed and guided his writing. But it was not until 1883, when he was thirty-five years old and within three years of his death, that he actually jotted down a brief *aide memoire* in one of his notebooks, spelling out for himself those principles:

'1. Simplicity – directness, 2. What I see, that only. 3. Eye memory. 4. Extreme delicacy of touch, outline. 5. Extreme delicacy of shade, graduation.'

The easy readability of Jefferies' writing can be traced not only to his felicitous choice of words and his ability to construct sentences which unfold naturally: it is also an effect of his style of punctuation, which is used sparingly and lightly. The pointing of most of his prose, and particularly his later work, is light even by today's standards, in marked contrast to the heavy and often contorted punctuation of a great deal of late Victorian writing.

The Story of Swindon (1875) (pp158-170) is a particularly rich example of Jefferies the journalist at his best, although there is a falseness of tone in the opening lines, which have the confident, breezy urbanity of the much-travelled man – 'we have all of us passed through Swindon Station, whether *en route* to Southern Wales, to warm Devon – the fern-land – to the Channel Islands, or to Ireland'. He passes quickly (but not without emphatic comment) over the discomforts and inadequacies of the old railway station for the fastidious traveller with his First Class ticket, and a century later we can be pardoned for a wry smile of recognition as he describes the food, an apparently perennial affliction for the rail traveller. But, for all that assumed worldly wisdom and thinly veiled *ennui*, Jefferies was actually much more parochial, in the strict sense of that word, and on a personal level this essay reveals a strong sense of the importance for him of his home area, and also his recognition of the ambiguous status of a community which he realised was at the same time profoundly agricultural and energetically industrial. The shepherds on the chalk downs continue their timeless husbandry within sight and sound of the great new rolling stock yards and the heavy engineering works of the Great Western Railway, the brainchild of Isambard Brunel and Daniel Gooch. Within, all is heat and massive power and Jefferies leads the reader with a deceptive simplicity into the mysteries of wheel construction and the engineers' skills. Here he shows the professional journalist's ability to grasp the technical complexities of heavy industry and to describe them in a form which is accurate, simple and readably alive for the layman, just as he describes the intricacies of the gunmaker's fine craftsmanship in 'The Boys' Gun' (from *Bevis*, 1882, and *Choosing a Gun*, 1879).

A further dimension is added to his remarkably multi-faceted piece of writing when he comes to a consideration, brief but telling, of the sociological and political implications of a small industrial powerhouse rising 'as Chicago rose, as if by magic' in a north Wiltshire town. There is an influx of Yorkshiremen, Irish and Scots from ' the shrewd North' and with them come new skills, new religious and intellectual diversity and stimuli, in the churches, chapels, the Mechanics' Institute reading room and the music hall. Not least, a new political power burgeons from the industrial initiatives of Brunel and Gooch: their work-force has a public voice and 'can return the man they choose to Parliament'. *The Story of Swindon* is powerful in content and effortless in style; it is writing which informs, stimulates and entertains the reader in a remarkable variety of ways in what is an essay of no more than average length.

Jefferies was conscious of the importance of a writer's style, both in his own work and in others'. In his Introduction to a new edition of Gilbert White's *The Natural*

History of Selborne he reflected that 'the simple character of the writings of Gilbert White have, perhaps, in these latter days somewhat deterred people from reading him. They seem so very simple, just as a boy might snatch a bloom of horse-chestnut and bring it home; so very easy to do that... The sense of repose is at first taken for lack of ability – the author is not one of the 'ablest' writers of the day; very inferior!' But this was a mistaken impression given by White's deceptively simple style, which was the product of mature reflection, of long familiarity with his subject matter and his notes, and of the experience which only time can bring. *The Natural History of Selborne* gave Jefferies the impression of a book which had been 'compiled in the evening...'

The reader of Jefferies might be forgiven for thinking the same of him. It certainly comes as a surprise to most of us to learn that some of his best work was written before he was thirty. There is often, though not always, a quality of mature repose in his writing which seems to indicate a much older man. In fact Jefferies' career as a published author began in his teens and ended with his death in his late thirties.

For all the clarity and simplicity of most of his writing, when we move away from the mainstream of Jefferies' middle period writings on wildlife and the rural scene and come to some of his later work, and especially to *The Story of My Heart: My Autobiography* (1883), we see a writer in evident difficulties, grappling with complex ideas and striving to express what matters to him most, to convey something of his personal vision in writing which, while it is never totally convoluted, still strains eagerly but impotently to express a spiritual state and a cosmic vision. Here is no ordinary rural essayist. Just as Jefferies himself looked deeply into the being and the essence of everything he saw, and then, reflexively and reflectively, into his own mind and spirit, his writings deserve from the reader a deeper and more intense scrutiny than his easy style seems to invite.

I have already mentioned White's *Natural History of Selborne* and it is interesting to see how readers of Richard Jefferies have repeatedly drawn comparisons between his work and that of Gilbert White, the late eighteenth century curate and natural historian of the parish of Selborne in Hampshire. The reviewer of *Wild Life in a Southern County*, writing in *Blackwood's Magazine* in April 1879, said that 'like our old friend, the incumbent of Selborne, nothing has escaped his notice. He has the eye of an artist for the beauties of nature... His quick observation catches each detail...' And if readers and critics have been quick to point to the similarities between these two close observers, each with his alert and searching eye, Jefferies himself was aware of an affinity with the Hampshire curate of the previous century. When a new edition of *The Natural History of Selborne* was published in the Scott Library series in 1887, Jefferies was asked to write an Introduction. In it he said Gilbert White 'had the quickest of eyes'. He admired White as a close and acute observer of the natural scene, but lamented that people were rarely mentioned and then almost incidentally. 'It must ever be regretted that he did not leave a natural history of the people of his day. We should then have had a picture of England just before the beginning of our present era, and a wonderful difference it would have shown.' Jefferies knew and loved the pages of White's *Selborne*, but they lacked that important ingredient, people living and working in a landscape. Without people, they lacked an important element of authenticity. For Jefferies, landscape and people were inextricably bound together in an intimate and precious relationship, one which was continually developing and changing. People, the land and their complex interplay were never static. Jefferies himself portrayed a countryside and rural society which had changed and was still changing, and which he knew would continue to evolve far into the future; and in considering White's parish of Selborne a century earlier he was conscious of how much that parish and its people, a microcosm of his beloved southern rural England, must have changed since their curate wrote his wonderful book. Change, in its twin guises of development and decay, is of the essence of Jefferies' vision of society, both rural and industrial. 'Rural Dynamite' and 'The Gentleman Farmer' (pp148-154; 130-133) are two good instances of this in the present selection.

The temptation to cast Jefferies in the role of a gifted visionary who portrayed in words a rural scene fixed forever in idyllic changelessness has caused many a reader to miss the mark. It profoundly misrepresents him. He firmly resists any temptation to indulge himself and his readers in a comfortable idyll of rural life. His occasional images of a pastoral Arcadia are rarely anything more than a cock-shy, evoked and set up only to be deflated and have its spuriousness exposed by Jefferies' constant return to uncompromising reality. Everywhere in his writing we find a firm underpinning of facts, a clearsighted perception of how things really are – the shepherd's hard, cold bed; the murky, tainted ale; the harshness of winter weather; the lurking shadow of penury and the work-house. This stemmed both from his journalistic training, with its disciplines of mastering facts quickly and objectively, and also from his own uncluttered clarity of perception. Animals and plants are seen and portrayed clearly with intimate understanding and affection – and a notable avoidance of sentimentality and anthropomorphism. When Jefferies 'stayed the shot' after stalking a rabbit, he did so not out of sentiment but out of curiosity and a desire to look longer and see more.

A recurrent theme in his writing is his celebration of the immutable and elemental beauty of land, water, sun and stars, but that permanency is balanced by continual evidence of new natural change and development. Jefferies' strong sense of the diversity and the riotous, seemingly untrammelled and unpremeditated richness of things grows stronger in much of his later work and is probably best expressed in *The Prodigality of Nature* (p192). In another piece from the same period, *Absence of Design in Nature* (p190), Jefferies expresses his joyful belief in the limitless possibilities in nature by his aggressive rejection of any cosmic or theological theory of a Grand Design. We cannot tell whether or not he had read William Paley's influential *Evidences of Christianity* (1974) which was still an important influence in cosmological and theological thought in Jefferies' day, but his essay is a vigorous rejection of any argument from design. Like Gerard Manley Hopkins a generation later, Jefferies saw natural things as 'all in a rush with richness', an almost Dionysian profligacy and profusion.

Jefferies has probably remained best known to modern readers through his frequently reprinted writings about wildlife, the countryside and field sports. The prominence given to some of these pieces in this selection is an attempt to reflect that fact. But in reading *The Gamekeeper at Home* (1878) and *The Amateur Poacher* (1879) we may be aware of an apparent irony, if not a downright contradiction, in the fact that Richard Jefferies was so wholly absorbed in the study of wildlife and the ways of wild creatures, but also so interested and skilled in shooting and so knowledgeable about game shooting and sporting guns. This is part of a larger and perennial question: how can the sportsman-naturalist reconcile a destructive pursuit of wildlife, whether it be with gun, rod or rifle, with a declared love of the quarry and an evident fascination with it? This apparent dilemma is easily resolved in the minds of most sporting naturalists, and the rationale by which that resolution is reached has perhaps been best expressed by Thoreau, who wrote: 'How much more game will he see who carries a gun, i.e., who goes to see it! Though you roam the woods all your days, you never will see by chance what he sees who goes on purpose to see it. One gets his living by shooting woodcock; most never see one in their lives.'

In fact, although Jefferies was a fine shot and an accomplished and knowledgeable sportsman, he soon moved beyond the enthusiasm for large bags of game which tend to be characteristic of youthful sportsmen, enjoying the freedom of the fields and the woods with guns in their hands and with the exuberant energy of the young. It is a common experience among even the keenest shots that, as they grow older, they become less and less concerned about the business of shooting. The pressing of the trigger and the counting of birds in the bag gives way to more general satisfaction which comes from the enjoyment of a day in the fields, in the fresh air, among a multitude of living things, alone or in the company of friends. Something of that can be seen in Jefferies' 'The Single-Barrel Gun' (pp54-56).

Although he often carried a gun, Jefferies used it less and less as time passed. But a walk over the Marlborough Downs with a gun – single-barrelled for preference – tucked under his arm remained a satisfying experience in various ways. To the local people of north Wiltshire a stroll with a gun was an acceptable way for a young man to spend his time: mere country walks 'nature study' would have seemed odd and pointless. Jefferies was tallish and lanky, with an easy loping stride, and despite delicate health and a weak constitution which were to lead to his early death, he was apparently a tireless walker. The gun under his arm and the pointer or the spaniel at his heels gave him an acceptable alibi for those long, solitary walks, and it kept an acute edge on his powers of observation. He explained this to his friend and mentor Oswald Crawfurd, editor of the *New Quarterly* and himself a considerable writer on wildlife and the countryside, in a letter dated December 1876: 'I studied natural history from Nature... I used to take a gun for nominal occupation, and sit in the hedge for hours, noting the ways and habits even of moles and snails.... The secret with all living creatures is – quiet. Be quiet, and you can form a connection, so to say, with everything, even with such a brute as the pike-fish.' Jefferies had learned to see and learn and recognise the minute particulars of leaf and twig, beetle and butterfly as he sat quietly in the hedgerows or stealthily stalked rabbits in the pastures around Coate. Silence and watchfulness counted for everything. The eye and the ear of the hunter are receptive and highly tuned; it matters little whether the trigger is pressed or not. 'Watching so often stayed the shot that at last it grew to be a habit: the mere simple pleasure of seeing birds and animals, when they were quite unconscious that they were observed, being too great to be stopped by the discharge. After carefully getting a wire over a jack (small pike); after waiting in a tree till a hare came along; after sitting in a mound till the partridges began to run together to roost; in the end the wire or gun remained unused... I have entered many woods just for the pleasure of creeping through the brake and the thickets. Destruction in itself was not the motive; it was an overpowering instinct for woods and fields.' In following his instinct Jefferies was teaching himself the skills of self-discipline, silence and still watchfulness which gave him such an all-seeing eye. That fine eye, which one minute is like a wide-angle lens taking in the whole sweep of a landscape and the next zooms into an intimate close-up of thorn and blossom, the hairs on a rabbit's coat or the markings on the individual feathers of a bird, was allied with a talent for expressing what had been seen. The combination made Richard Jefferies a considerable writer in his own short lifetime and has kept a long succession of re-issued editions and anthologies in print since his death a century ago.

Intimate understanding and close contact with birds and animals come, Jefferies believed, more easily to the man who carries a gun and practises the fieldcraft and the stalking skills of the solitary sportsman. He develops an awareness of individual species from far off, learns to recognise the 'jizz' of a creature long before he is close enough to see it really clearly. Jefferies singled out the partridge, the indigenous and endearing gamebird of English farmland, as an example of this. 'Anyone who has tried to get so near a partridge that he can see it as in a tinted plate before he recognises it will never know much about a partridge, because in so doing he is sure to disturb it long before. He must be able to recognise the bird afar in the furrows or to see it elsewhere while out of sight...'

Jefferies the naturalist knew how much he owed to his interest in shooting, for it had taught him to pass through the woods and meadows with quiet stealth, every sense alert. His is an extreme instance of what many sportsmen-naturalists have experienced. Nowadays it is fashionable to decry the activities of the Victorian naturalists and specimen hunters with their killing bottles, 'collecting guns' and their conviction that 'what's hit is history, what's missed is mystery'. Today's biologists have a host of technical aids to assist them in studying wildlife of all sorts. Many who have paused to analyse their motivation and the sense of satisfaction in what they do will acknowledge that their pursuit of wild things with telephoto lens, radio telemetry and 'twitcher's tick-list' is actually sublimated hunting. Their predecessors in earlier generations did what they could with rod and gun, net and trap, vascula, cabinet specimens and hand-lenses, and with voluminous notes recording their observations. Without their enthusiasm and dedication countless thousands of species of animals, birds, insects and plants would have remained unrecorded or little understood. Richard Jefferies belonged to that age and was part of that great tradition, to which we owe so much but which is so often misunderstood or condemned.

When a young writer or artist of genius dies, it is tempting but futile to speculate on what he might have achieved had he lived longer and had an opportunity to develop his skills in new ways. Richard Jefferies left a remarkable body of work, a rich diversity of subjects and styles produced in a comparatively short working life of barely twenty years. What was unpublished in his lifetime was patiently unearthed, researched and edited by later scholars, and the full range of his writing is now available, either in current anthologies or in the original editions of the many magazines for which he wrote.

An anthologist's task is always difficult and sometimes hazardous. To venture to select and edit from any writer's work is to risk incurring the criticism of others who also admire him. The selection which follows was not an easy one to make, nor does it purport to offer all of the best of Richard Jefferies. He was too prolific and too good a writer for that to be possible within one volume. But it is an attempt to sample some of the essays and extracts which seem to me to bring us closest to Jefferies, to give some impression of the range and diversity of his writing, and to take as a unifying theme Richard Jefferies' unique capacity for seeing things both as they appear and as they really are.

Colin Laurie McKelvie
Broad Chalke
Wiltshire
May 1987

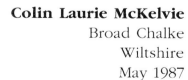

Chapter 1
Of Poachers and Keepers

Scarcely a keeper can be found who has not got one or more tales to tell of encounters with poachers, sometimes of a desperate character. There is a general similarity in most of the accounts, which exhibit a mixture of ferocity and cowardice on the side of the intruders. The following case, which occurred some years since, brings these contradictory features into relief.

There had been a great deal of poaching before the affray took place, and finally it grew to horse-stealing: one night two valuable horses were taken from the home park. This naturally roused the indignation of the owner of the estate, who resolved to put a stop to it. Orders were given that if shots were heard in the woods the news should be at once transmitted to head-quarters, no matter at what hour of the night.

One brilliant moonlight night, frosty and clear, the gang came again. A messenger went to the house, and, as previously arranged, two separate parties set out to intercept the rascals. The head keeper had one detachment, whose object it was to secure the main outlet from the wood towards the adjacent town - to cut off retreat. The young squire had charge of the other, which, with the under keeper as guide, was to work its way through the wood and drive the gang into the ambuscade. In the last party were six men and a mastiff dog; four of the men had guns, the gentleman only a stout cudgel.

They came upon the gang – or rather a part of it, for the poachers were somewhat scattered – in a 'drive' which ran between tall firs, and was deep in shadow. With a shout the four or five men in the 'drive,' or green lane, slipped back behind the trees, and two fired, killing the mastiff dog on the spot and 'stinging' one man in the legs. Quick as they were, the under keeper, to use his own words, 'got a squint of one fellow as I knowed and I lets drive both barrels in among the firs. But, bless you! it were all over in such a minute that I can't hardly tell 'ee how it were. Our squire ran straight at 'em; but our men hung back, though they had their guns and he had nothing but a stick. I just seen him, as the smoke rose, hitting at a fellow; and then, before I could step, I hears a crack, and the squire he was down on the sward. One of them beggars had come up behind, and swung his gun round, and fetched him a purler on the back of his head. I picked him up, but he was as good as dead, to look at;' and in the confusion the poachers escaped. They had probably been put up to the ambuscade by one of the underlings, as they did not pass that way, but seemed to separate and get off by various paths. The 'young squire' had to be carried home, and was ill for months, but ultimately recovered.

Not one of the gang was ever captured, notwithstanding that a member of it was recognised. Next day an examination of the spot resulted in the discovery of a trail of blood upon the grass and dead leaves, which proved that one of them had been wounded at the first discharge. It was traced for a short distance and then lost. Not till the excitement had subsided did the under keeper find that he had been hit; one pellet had scored his cheek under the eye, and left a groove still visible.

Some time afterwards a gun was picked up in the ferns, all rusty from exposure, which had doubtless been dropped in the flight. The barrel was very short – not more than eighteen inches in length – having been filed off for convenience of taking to pieces, so as to be carried in a pocket made on purpose in the lining of the coat. Now with a barrel so short as that, sport, in the proper sense of the term, would be impossible; the shot would scatter so quickly after leaving the muzzle that the sportsman would never be able to approach near enough. The use of this gun was clearly to shoot pheasants at roost.

The particular keeper in whose shed the man-trap still lies among the lumber thinks that the class of poachers who come in gangs are as desperate now as ever, and as ready with their weapons. Breech-loading guns have rendered such affrays extremely dangerous on account of the rapidity of fire. Increased severity of punishment may deter a man from entering a wood; but once he is there and compromised, the dread of a heavy sentence is likely to make him fight savagely.

The keeper himself is not altogether averse to a little fisticuffing, in a straightforward kind of way, putting powder and shot on one side. He rather relishes what he calls 'leathering' a poacher with a good tough ground-ash stick. He gets the opportunity now and then, coming unexpectedly on a couple of fellows rabbiting in a ditch, and he recounts the 'leathering' he has frequently administered with great gusto. He will even honestly admit that on one occasion – just one, not more – he got himself most thoroughly thrashed by a pair of hulking fellows.

'Some keepers,' he says, 'are always summoning people, but it don't do no good. What's the use of summoning a chap for sneaking about with a cur dog and a wire in his pocket? His mates in the village clubs together and pays his fine, and he laughs at you. Why, down in the town there them mechanic chaps have got a regular society to pay these here fines for trespass, and the bench they claps it on strong on purpose. But it ain't no good; they forks out the tin, and then goes and haves a spree at a public. Besides which, if I can help it, I don't much care to send a man to gaol – this, of course, is between you and me – unless he uses his gun. If he uses his gun there ain't nothing too bad for him. But these here prisons – every man as ever I knowed go to gaol always went twice, and kept on going. There ain't nothing in the world like a good ground-ash stick. When you gives a chap a sound dressing with that there article, he never shows his face in your wood no more. There's fields about here where them mechanics goes as regular as Saturday comes to try their dogs, as they calls it – and a precious lot of dogs they keeps among 'em. But they never does it on this estate: they knows my habits, you see. There's less summonses goes up from this property than any other for miles, and it's all owing to this here stick. A bit of ash is the best physic for poaching as I knows on.'

I suspect that he is a little mistaken in his belief that it is the dread of his personal prowess which keeps trespassers away – it is rather due to his known vigilance and watchfulness. His rather hasty notions of taking the law into his own hands are hardly in accord with the spirit of the times; but some allowance must be made for the circumstances of his life, and it is my object to picture the man as he is.

There are other dangers from guns beside these. A brown gaiter indistinctly seen moving some distance off in the tall dry grass or fern – the wearer hidden by the bushes – has not unfrequently been mistaken for game in the haste and excitement of shooting, and received a salute of leaden hail. This is a danger to which sportsman and keeper are both liable, especially when large parties are engaged in rapid firing; sometimes a particular corner gets very 'hot', being enfiladed for the moment by several guns. Yet, when the great number of men who shoot is considered, the percentage of serious accidents is small indeed; more fatal accidents probably happen through unskilled persons thoughtlessly playing with guns supposed not to be loaded, or pointing them in joke, then ever occur in the field. The ease with which the breech-loader can be unloaded or reloaded again prevents most persons from carrying it indoors charged; and this in itself is a gain on the side of safety, for perhaps half the fatal accidents take place within doors.

In farmsteads where the owner had the right of shooting, the muzzle-loader was – and still is, when not converted – kept loaded on the rack. The starlings, perhaps,

are making havoc of the thatch, tearing out straw by straw, and working the holes in which they form their nests right through, till in the upper story daylight is visible. When the whistling and calling of the birds tell him they are busy above, the owner slips quickly out with his gun, and brings down three or four at once as they perch in a row on the roof-tree. Or a labourer leaves a message that there is a hare up in the meadow or some wild ducks have settled in the brook. But men who have a gun always in their hands rarely meet with a mishap. The starlings, by-the-bye, soon learn the trick, and are cunning enough to notice which door their enemy generally comes out at, where he can get the best shot; and the moment the handle of that particular door is turned, off they go.

The village blacksmith will tell you of more than one narrow escape he has had with guns, and especially muzzle-loaders, brought to him to repair. Perhaps a charge could not be ignited through the foulness of the nipple, and the breech had to be unscrewed in the vice; now and then the breech-piece was so tightly jammed that it could not be turned. Once, being positively assured that there was nothing but some dirt in the barrel and no powder, he was induced to place it in the forge fire; when – bang! a charge of shot smashed the window, and the burning coals flew about in a fiery shower. In one instance a blacksmith essayed to clear out a barrel which had become choked with a long iron rod made red-hot: the explosion which followed drove the rod through his hand and into the wooden wall of the shed. Smiths seem to have a particular fondness for meddling with guns, and generally have one stowed away somewhere.

It was not wonderful that accidents happened with the muzzle-loaders, considering the manner in which they were handled by ignorant persons. The keeper declares that many of the cottagers, who have an old single-barrel, ostensibly to frighten the birds from their gardens, do not think it properly loaded until the ramrod jumps out of the barrel. They ram the charge, and especially the powder, with such force that the rebound sends the rod right out, and he has seen those who were not cottagers follow the same practice. A close-fitting wad, too tight for the barrel, will sometimes cause the rod to spring high above the muzzle: as it is pushed quickly down it compresses the air in the tube, which expands with a sharp report and drives the rod out.

Loading with paper, again, has often resulted in mischief: sometimes a smouldering fragment remains in the barrel after the discharge, and on pouring in powder from the flask it catches and runs like a train up to the flask, which may burst in the hand. For this reason to this day some of the old farmers, clinging to ancient custom, always load with a clay tobacco pipe-bowl, snapped off from the stem for the purpose. It is supposed to hold just the proper charge, and as it is detached from the horn or flask there is no danger of fire being communicated to the magazine; so that an explosion, if it happened, would do no serious injury, being confined to the loose powder of the charge itself. Paper used as wads will sometimes continue burning for a short time after being blown out of the gun, and may set fire to straw, or even dry grass.

The old folk, therefore, when it was necessary to shoot the starlings on the thatch, or the sparrows and chaffinches which congregate in the rickyards in such extraordinary numbers – in short, to fire off a gun anywhere near inflammable materials – made it a rule to load with green leaves, which would not burn and could do no harm. The ivy leaf was a special favourite for the purpose – the broad-leaved ivy which grows against houses and in gardens – because it is stout, about the right size to double up and fold into a wad, and is available in winter, being an evergreen, when most other leaves are gone. I have seen guns loaded with ivy leaves many times. When a gun gets foul the ramrod is apt to stick tight if paper is used after pushing it home, and unless a vice be handy no power will draw it out. In this dilemma the old plan used to be to fire it into a hayrick, standing at a short distance; the hay, yielding slightly, prevented the rod from breaking to pieces when it struck.

Most men who have had much to do with guns have burst one or more. The keeper in the course of years has several accidents of the kind; but none since the breech-loader has come into general use, the reason of course being that two charges cannot be inadvertently inserted one above the other, as frequently occurred in the old guns.

I had a muzzle-loading gun burst in my hands some time since: the breech-piece split, and the nipple, hammer, and part of the barrel there blew out. Fortunately no injury was done; and I should not note it except for the curious effect upon the tympanum of the ear. The first sense was that of a stunning blow on the head; on recovering from which the distinction between one sound and another seemed quite lost. The ear could not separate or define them, and whether it was a person speaking, a whistle, the slamming of a door, or the neigh of a horse, it was all the same. Tone, pitch, variation there was none. Though perfectly, and in fact painfully, audible, all sounds were converted into a miserable jangling noise, exactly like that made when a wire in a piano has come loose and jingles. This annoying state of things lasted three days, after which it gradually went off, and in a week had entirely disappeared. Probably the sound of the explosion had been much increased by the cheek slightly touching the stock in the moment of firing, the jar of the wood adding to the vibration. This gun belonged to another person, and was caught up, already loaded, to take advantage of a favourable chance; it is noticeable that half the accidents happen with a strange gun.

Shot plays curious freaks sometimes: I know a case in which a gun was accidentally discharged in a dairy paved as most dairies are with stone flags. The muzzle was pointed downwards at the time – the shot struck the smooth stone floor, glanced off and up, and hit another person standing almost at right angles, causing a painful wound. It is a marvel that more birdkeepers do not get injured by the bursting of the worn-out firelocks used to frighten birds from the seed. Some of these are not only rusty, but so thin at the muzzle as almost to cut the hand if it accidentally comes into contact with any force.

A collection of curious old guns might be made in the villages; the flint-locks are nearly all gone, but there are plenty of single-barrels in existence and use which were converted from that ancient system. In the farmhouses here and there may be found such a weapon, half a century old or more, with a barrel not quite equal in length to the punt-gun, but so long that, when carried under the arm of a tall man, the muzzle touches the ground where it is irregular in level. It is slung up to the beam across the ceiling with leathern thongs – one loop for the barrel and the other for the stock. It is still serviceable, having been kept dry; and the owner will tell you that he has brought down pigeons with it at seventy yards.

Every man believes that his particular gun is the best in the locality to kill. The owner of this cumbrous weapon, if you exhibit an interest in its history, will take you into the fields and point out a spot where forty years ago he or his immediate ancestor shot four of five wild geese at once, resting the barrel on the branch of a tree in the hedge and sending a quarter of a pound of lead whistling among the flock. The spot the wild geese used to visit in the winter is still remembered, though they come there no more; drains and cultivation having driven them away from that southern district. In the course of the winter, perhaps, a small flock may be seen at a great height passing over, but they do not alight, and in some years are not observed at all.

There is a trick sometimes practised by poachers which enables them to make rabbits bolt from their holes without the assistance of a ferret. It is a chemical substance emitting a peculiar odour, and, if placed in the burrows drives the rabbits out. Chemical science, indeed, has been called to the aid of poaching in more ways than one: fish, for instance, are sometimes poisoned, or killed by an explosion of dynamite. These latter practices have, however, not yet come into general use, being principally employed by those only who have had some experience of mining or quarrying.

There is a saying that an old poacher makes the best gamekeeper, on the principle of setting a thief to catch a thief: a maxim however, of doubtful value, since no other person could so thoroughly appreciate the tempting opportunities which must arise day after day. That keepers themselves are sometimes the worst of depredators must be admitted. Hitherto I have chiefly described the course of action followed by honest and conscientious men, truly anxious for their employers' interests, and taking a personal pride in a successful shooting season. But there exists a class of keepers of a very different order, who have done much to bring sport itself into unmerited odium.

The blackleg keeper is often a man of some natural ability – a plausible, obsequious rascal, quick in detecting the weak points of his employer's character, and in practising upon and distorting what were orginally generous impulses. His game mainly depends upon gaining the entire confidence of his master; and, not being embarrassed by considerations of self-esteem, he is not choice in the use of means to that end. He knows that if he can thoroughly worm himself into his employer's good opinion, the unfavourable reports which may be set afloat against him will be regarded as the mere tittle-tattle of envy; for it is often an amiable weakness on the part of masters who are really attached to their servants to maintain a kind of partisanship on behalf of those whom they have once trusted.

Such a servant finds plentiful occasions for dexterously gratifying the love of admiration innate in us all. The manliest athlete and frankest amateur – who would blush at the praise of social equals – finds it hard to resist the apparently bluff outspoken applause of his inferiors bestowed on his prowess in field sports, whether rowing or riding, with rod or gun. Of course it frequently happens that the sportsman really does excel as a shot; but that in no degree lessens the insidious effect of the praise which seems extorted in the excitement of the moment, and to come forth with unpremeditated energy.

The next step is to establish a common ground of indignation; for it is to be observed that those who unite in abuse of a third person have a stronger bond of sympathy than those who mutually admire another. If by accident some unfortunate *contretemps* should cause a passing irritation between his master and the owner of a neighbouring estate, the keeper loses no opportunity of heaping coals upon the fire. He brings daily reports of trepass. Now the other party's keepers have been beating a field beyond their boundaries; now they have ferreted a bank to which they have no right. Another time they have prevented straying pheasants from returning to the covers by intercepting their retreat; and a score of similar tricks. Or perhaps it is the master of a pack of hounds against whom insinuations are directed: 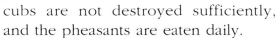 cubs are not destroyed sufficiently, and the pheasants are eaten daily.

Sometimes it is a tenant-farmer with a long lease, who cannot be quickly ejected, who has to bear the brunt of these attacks. He is accused of trapping hares and rabbits: he sets the traps so close to the preserves that the pheasants are frequently caught and mortally injured; he is suspected of laying poisoned grain about. Not content with this he carries his malice so far as to cause the grass or other crops in which outlying nests or young broods are sheltered to be cut before it is ripe, with the object of destroying or driving them away; and he presents the mowers whose scythes mutilate game with a quart of beer as reward, or furnishes his shepherds with lurchers for poaching. He encourages the gipsies to encamp in the neighbourhood and carry on nightly expeditions by allowing them the use of a field in which to put their vans and horses. With such accounts as these, supported by what looks like evidence, the blackleg keeper gradually works his employer into a state of intense irritation, meantime reaping the reward of the incorruptible guardian and shrewd upright servitor.

At the same time, in the haze of suspicion he has created, the rascal finds a cloak for his own misdeeds. These poachers, trespassers, gipsies, foxes, and refractory tenants afford a useful excuse to account for the comparative scarcity of game. 'What on earth has become of the birds, and where the dickens are the hares?' asks the angry proprietor. In the spring he recollects being shown by the keeper, with modest pride, some hundreds of young pheasants, flourishing exceedingly. Now he finds the broods have strangely dwindled, and he is informed that these enemies against whom all along he has been warned have made short work of them. If this explanation seems scarcely sufficient, there is always some inexplicable disease to bear the blame: the birds had been going on famously when suddenly they were seized by a mysterious epidemic which decimated their numbers.

All this is doubly annoying, because, in addition to the loss of anticipated sport, there has been an exorbitant expenditure. The larger the number of young broods of pheasants early in the year the better for the dishonest keeper, who has more chances of increasing his own profit, both directly and indirectly. In the first place, there is the little business of buying eggs, not without commissions. More profit is found in the supply of food for the birds: extras and petty disbursements afford further room for pickings.

Then, when the game has been spirited away, the keeper's object is to induce his employer to purchase full-grown pheasants - another chance of secret gratuities - and to turn them out for the battue. That institution is much approved of by keepers of this character, for, the pheasants being confined to a small area, there is less personal exertion than is involved in walking over several thousand acres to look after hares and partridges.

By poisoning his master's mind against someone he not only covers these proceedings but secures himself from the explanation which, if listened to, might set matters right. The accused, attempting to explain, finds a strong prejudice against him, and turns away in dudgeon. Such underhand tricks sometimes cause mischief in a whole district. An unscrupulous keeper may set people of all ranks at discord with each other.

In these malpractices, and in the disposal of game which is bulky, he is occasionally assisted by other keepers of congenial character engaged upon adjacent estates. Gentlemen on intimate terms naturally imagine that their keepers mutually assist each other in the detection of poaching – meeting by appointment, for instance, at night, as the police do, to confer upon their beats. When two or three are thus in league it is not difficult for them to dispose of booty; they quickly get into communication with professional receivers; and instances have been known in which petticoats have formed a cover for a steady if small illegal transport of dead game over the frontier.

For his own profit a keeper of this kind may indeed be trusted to prevent poaching on the part of other persons, whose gains would be his loss, since there would remain less for him to smuggle. Very probably it may come to be acknowledged on all sides that he is watchful and always about: an admission that naturally tends to raise him in the esteem of his employer.

Those who could tell tales – his subordinate assistants – are all more or less implicated, as in return for their silence they are permitted to get pickings: a dozen rabbits now and then, good pay for little work, and plenty of beer. If one of them lets out strange facts in his cups, it signifies nothing: no one takes any heed of a labourer's beerhouse talk. The steward or bailiff has strong suspicions, perhaps, but his motions are known, and his prying eyes defeated. As for the tenants, they groan and bear it.

It is to be regretted that now and then the rural policeman becomes an accomplice in these nefarious practices. His position of necessity brings him much into contact with the keepers of the district within his charge. If they are a 'shady' lot what with plenty of drink, good fellowship, presents of game, and insidious suggestions of profit, it is not surprising that a man whose pay is not the most liberal should gradually fall away from the path of duty. The keeper can place a great temptation in his way – i.e. occasional participation in shooting when certain persons are absent: there are few indeed who can resist the opportunity of enjoying sport. The rural constable often has a beat of very wide area, thinly populated: it is difficult to tell where he may be; he has a reasonable pretext for being about at all hours, and it is impossible that he should be under much supervision. Perhaps he may have a taste for dogs, and breed them for sale, if not openly, on the sly. Now the keeper can try these animals or even break them in a friendly way; and when once he has committed himself, and winked at what is going on, the constable feels that he may as well join and share altogether. At outlying wayside 'publics' the keeper and the constable may carouse to the top of their bent: the landlord is only too glad to be on good terms with them; his own little deviations pass unnoticed, and if by accident they are discovered he has a friend at court to give him a good character.

The worthy pair have an engine of oppression in their hands which effectually overawes the cottagers: they can accuse them of poaching; and if not proceeding to the ultimatum of a summons, which might not suit their convenience, can lay them under suspicion, which may result in notice to quit their cottages, or to give up their allotment gardens; and a garden is almost as important to a cottager as his weekly wages. In this way a landlord whose real disposition may be most generous may be made to appear a perfect tyrant, and be disliked by the whole locality. It is to the interest of the keeper and the constable to obtain a conviction now and then; it gives them the character of vigilance.

Sometimes a blackleg keeper, not satisfied with the plunder of the estate under his guardianship must needs encroach on the lands of neighbouring farmers occupying under small owners; and so further ill-will is caused. In the end and exposure takes place, and the employer finds to his extreme mortification how deeply he has been deceived; but the discovery may not be made for years. Of course all keepers of this character are not systematically vicious: many are only guilty occasionally, when a peculiarly favourable opportunity offers.

Another class of keeper is rather passively than actively bad. This is the idle man, whose pipe is ever in his mouth and whose hands are always in his pockets. He is often what is called a good-natured fellow – soft spoken, respectful, and willing; liked by everybody; a capital comrade in his own class, and, in fact, with too many friends of a certain set.

Gamekeeping is an occupation peculiarly favourable to loafing if a man is inclined that way. He can sit on the rails and gates, lounge about the preserves, go to sleep on the sward in the shade; call at the roadside inn, and, leaning his gun against the tree from which the sign hangs, quaff his quart in indolent dignity. By degrees he easily falls into bad habits, takes too much liquor, finds his hands unsteady, becomes too lazy to repress poaching (which is a weed that must be constantly pulled up, or it will grow with amazing rapidity), and finally is corrupted, and shares the proceeds of bolder rascals. His assistants do as they please. He has no control over them: they know too much about him.

It is a curious fact that there are poaching villages and non-poaching villages. Out of a dozen or more parishes forming a petty sessional district one or two will become notorious for this propensity. The bench never meet without a case from them, either for actual poaching or some cognate offence. The drinking, fighting, dishonesty, low gambling, seem ceaseless - like breeding like – till the place becomes a nest of rascality. Men hang about the public houses all day, betting on horses, loitering; a blight seems to fall upon them, and a bad repute clings to the spot for years after the evil itself has been eradicated.

If a weak keeper gets among such a set as this he succumbs; and the same cause hastens the moral decay of the constable. The latter has a most difficult part to maintain. If he is disposed to carry out the strict letter of his instructions, that does not do – there is a prejudice against too much severity. English feeling is anti-Draconian; and even the respectable inhabitants would rather endure some little rowdyism than witness an over interference with liberty. If the constable is good natured, and loth to take strong measures, he either becomes a semi-accomplice or sinks to a nonenity. It is difficult to find a man capable of controlling such a class; it requires tact, and something of the gift of governing men.

By contact with bad characters a weak keeper may be contaminated without volition of his own at first: for we know the truthful saying about touching on pitch.

The misfortune is that the guilty when at last exposed become notorious; and their infamy spreads abroad, smirching the whole class to which they belong. The honest conscientious men remain in obscurity and get no public credit, though they may far outnumber the evil-disposed.

To make a good keeper it requires not only honesty and skill, but a considerable amount of 'backbone' in the character to resist temptation and to control subordinates. The keeper who has gone to the bad becomes one of the most mischievous members of the community: the faithful and upright keeper is not only a valuable servant but a protection to all kinds of property.

from *The Gamekeeper At Home*.

Chapter 2

Lurcher-Land

The time of the apple-bloom is the most delicious season in Sarsen village. It is scarcely possible to obtain a view of the place, although it is built on the last slope of the Downs, because just where the ground drops and the eye expects an open space plantations of fir and the tops of tall poplars and elms intercept the glance. In ascending from the level meadows of the vale thick double mounds, heavily timbered with elm, hide the houses until you are actually in their midst.

Those only know a country who are acquainted with its footpaths. By the roads, indeed, the outside may be seen; but the footpaths go through the heart of the land. There are routes by which mile after mile may be travelled without leaving the sward. So you may pass from village to village; now crossing green meads, now cornfields, over brooks, past woods, through farmyard and rick ' barken.' But such tracks are not mapped, and a stranger misses them altogether unless under the guidance of an old inhabitant.

At Sarsen the dusty road enters the more modern part of the village at once, where the broad signs hang from the taverns at the crossways and where the loafers steadily gaze at the new comer. The Lower Path, after stile and hedge and elm, and grass that glows with golden buttercups, quietly leaves the side of the double mounds and goes straight through the orchards. There are fewer flowers under the trees, and the grass grows so long and rank that it has already fallen aslant of its own weight. It is choked, too, by masses of clogweed, that springs up profusely over the site of old foundations; so that here ancient masonry may be hidden under the earth. Indeed, these orchards are a survival from the days when the monks laboured in vineyard and garden, and mayhap even of earlier times. When once a locality has got into the habit of growing a certain crop it continues to produce it for century after century; and thus there are villages famous for apple or pear or cherry, while the district at large is not at all given to such culture.

The trunks of the trees succeed each other in endless ranks, like columns that support the most beautiful roof of pink and white. Here the bloom is rosy, there white prevails: the young green is hidden under the petals that are far more numerous than leaves, or even than eaves will be. Though the path really is in shadow as the branches shut out the sun, yet it seems brighter here than in the open, as if the place were illuminated by a million tiny lamps shedding the softest lustre. The light is reflected and apparently increased by the countless flowers overhead.

The forest of bloom extends acre after acre, and only ceases where hedges divide, to commence again beyond the boundary. A wicket gate, all green with a film of vegetation over the decaying wood, opens under the very eaves of a cottage, and the path goes by the door – across a narrow meadow where deep and broad trenches, green now, show where ancient stews or fishponds existed, and then through a farmyard onto a lane. Tall poplars rise on either hand, but there seem to be no houses; they stand in fact a field's breadth back from the lane, and are approached by footpaths that every few yards necessitate a stile in the hedge.

When a low thatched farmhouse does abut upon the way, the blank white wall of the rear part faces the road, and the front door opens on precisely the other side. Hard by is a row of beehives. Though the modern hives are at once more economical and humane, they have not the old associations that cling about the straw domes topped with broken earthenware to shoot off the heavy downfall of a thunder-storm.

Everywhere the apple-bloom; the hum of bees; children sitting on the green beside the road, their laps full of flowers; the song of finches; and the low murmur of water that glides over flint and stone so shadowed by plants and grasses that the sunbeams cannot reach and glisten on it. Thus the straggling flower-strewn village stretches along beneath the hill and rises up the slope, and the swallows wheel and twitter over the gables where are their hereditary nesting-places. The lane ends on a broad dusty road, and, opposite, a quiet thatched house of the larger sort stands, endways to the street, with an open pitching before the windows. There, too, the swallows' nests are crowded under the eaves, flowers are trained against the wall, and in the garden stand the same beautiful apple trees. But within, the lower part of the windows - that have recess seats – are guarded by horizontal rods of iron, polished by the backs of many men. It is an inn, and the rods are to save the panes from the impact of an excited toper's arm.

The talk today, as the brown brandy, which the paler cognac has not yet superseded, is consumed and the fumes of coarse tobacco and the smell of spilt beer and the faint sickly odour of evaporating spirits overpower the flowers, is of horses. The stable lads from the training stables far up on the Downs drop in or call at the door without dismounting. Once or twice in the day a tout calls and takes his 'grub', and scribbles a report in the little back parlour. Sporting papers, beer-stained and thumb-marked, lie on the tables; framed portraits of racers hang on the walls. Burly men, who certainly cannot ride a race, but who have horse in every feature, puff cigars and chat in jerky monosyllables that to an outsider are perfectly incomprehensible. But the glib way in which heavy sums of money are spoken of conveys the impression that they dabble in enormous wealth.

There are dogs under the tables and chairs; dogs in the window-seat; dogs panting on the stone flags of the passage, after a sharp trot behind a trap, choosing the coolest spot to loll their red tongues out; dogs outside in the road; dogs standing on hind legs, and painfully lapping the water in the horse-trough; and there is a yapping of puppies in the distance. The cushions of the sofa are strewn with dogs' hairs, and once now and then a dog leisurely hops up the staircase.

Customers are served by the landlady, a decent body enough in her way: her son, the man of the house, is up in the 'orchut' at the rear, feeding his dogs. Where the 'orchut' ends in a paddock stands a small shed: in places the thatch on the roof has fallen through in the course of years and revealed the bare rafters. The bottom part of the door has decayed, and the long nose of a greyhound is thrust out sniffing through a hole. Dickon, the said son, is delighted to undo the padlock for a visitor who is 'square'. In an instant the long hounds leap up, half a dozen at a time, and I stagger backwards, forced by the sheer vigour of their caresses against the doorpost. Dickon cannot quell the uproarious pack: he kicks the door open, and away they scamper round and round the paddock at headlong speed.

What joy it is to them to stretch their limbs! I forget the squalor of the kennel in watching their happy gambols. I cannot drink more than one tumbler of brown brandy and water; but Dickon overlooks that weakness, feeling that I admire his greyhounds. It is arranged that I am to see them work in the autumn.

The months pass, and in his trap with the famous trotter in the shafts we roll up the village street. Apple-bloom and golden fruit too are gone, and the houses show more now among the bare trees; but as the rim of the ruddy November sun comes forth from the edge of a cloud there appears a buff tint everywhere in the background. When elm and ash are bare the oaks retain their leaves, and these are illumined by the autumn beams. Overtopped by tall elms and hidden by the orchards, the oaks were hardly seen in summer; now they are found to be numerous and give the prevailing hue to the place.

Dickon taps the dashboard as the mare at last tops the hill, and away she speeds along the level plateau for the Downs. Two greyhounds are with us; two more have gone on under charge of a boy. Skirting the hills a mile or two, we presently leave the road and drive over the turf: there is no track, but Dickon knows his way. The rendezvous is a small fir plantation, the young trees in which are but shoulder-high. Below is a plain entirely surrounded by the hills, and partly green with root crops: more than one flock of sheep is down there, and two teams ploughing the stubble. Neither the ploughmen nor the shepherds take the least heed of us, except to watch for the sport. The spare couple are fastened in the trap; the boy jumps up and takes the reins. Dickon puts the slip on the couple that are to run first, and we begin to range.

Just at the foot of the hill the grass is tall and grey; there, too, are the dead dry stalks of many plants that cultivation has driven from the ploughed fields and that find a refuge at the edge. A hare starts from the very verge and makes up the Downs. Dickon slips the hounds, and a faint halloo comes from the shepherds and the ploughmen. It is a beautiful sight to see the hounds bound over the sward; the sinewy back bends like a bow, but a bow that, instead of an arrow, shoots itself; the deep chests drink the air. Is there any moment so joyful in life as the second when the chase begins? As we gaze, before we even step forward, the hare is over the ridge and out of sight. Then we race and tear up the slope; then the boy in the trap

flaps the reins and away goes the mare out of sight too.

Dickon is long and rawboned, a powerful fellow, strong of limb, and twice my build; but he sips too often at the brown brandy, and after the first burst I can head him. But he knows the hills and the route the hare will take, so that I have but to keep pace. In five minutes as we cross a ridge we see the game again; the hare is circling back – she passes under us not fifty yards away, as we stand panting on the hill. The youngest hound gains, and runs right over her; she doubles, the older hound picks up the running. By a furze-bush she doubles again; but the young one turns her – the next moment she is in the jaws of the old dog.

Again and again the hounds are slipped, now one couple, now the other: we pant, and can scarcely speak with running, but the wild excitement of the hour and the sweet pure air of the Downs supply fresh strength. The little lad brings the mare anywhere: through the furze, among the flint-pits, jolting over the ruts, she rattles along with sure alacrity. There are five hares in the sack under the straw when at last we get up and slowly drive down to the highway, reaching it some two miles from where we left it. Dickon sends the dogs home by the boy on foot; we drive round and return to the village by a different route, entering it from the opposite direction.

The reason of these things is that Sarsen has no great landlord. There are fifty small proprietors, and not a single resident magistrate. Besides the small farmers, there are scores of cottage owners, every one of whom is perfectly independent. Nobody cares for anybody. It is republic without even the semblance of a Government.

from: *The Amateur Poacher.*

Chapter 3

Shooting a Rabbit

Towards half-past five or six o'clock on a summer afternoon the shadow of a summer-rick will be found to have lengthened sufficiently to shelter anyone who sits behind it from the heat of the sun. For this purpose a margin of shadow is necessary, as just within the edge, though the glare ceases, the heat is but little diminished. The light is cut off with a sharp line; the heat, as if refracted, beds in, so that earlier in the afternoon, when the shade would but just include your feet as you sat on the sward, there would not be the anticipated relief from the oppressive warmth. Ladies sometimes go into the garden to read under a favourite tree and are surprised that it is not cool there; but the sun, nearly vertical at the time, scarcely casts a shade beyond the boughs. There must be a shadow into which you can retire several yards from the verge, as into a darkened cave, before the desired effect can be enjoyed. About six the sun perceptibly declines, and can be seen at once without throwing the head back to look up; and then the summer-rick has a conical shadow of some extent. It is, too, the time when the rabbits in the burrows along the adjacent mound begin to think of coming out for their evening feed. A summer-rick of course stands in aftermath, which is short, and allows of everything being seen in it at a glance. This rick is about twenty yards from the hedge, and the burrow, or the prinicipal part of it, as you sit with your back leaning against the hay, is on the left-hand side. Place the double-barrel on the sward close to the rick, with the muzzle towards the burrow. If the gun were stood up against the rick it would not improbably be considered a suspicious object by the first old rabbit that came out, nor could it be got to the shoulder without several movements. But it can be lifted up from the grass, where it lies quite concealed, sidling it up slowly, brushing the rick, without any great change of attitude, and in the gradual imperceptible manner which is essential to success. Sometimes when the rabbit is in full view, right out in the field, the gun must be raised with the deliberate standstill motion of the hour hand on a clock, which if watched does not apparently move, but looked at again presently has gone on. The least jerk – a sudden motion of the arm – is sure to arouse the rabbit's attention. The effect is as with us when reading intently – if anything passes quickly across the corner of the eye we look up involuntarily. Had it passed gradually it would not have been observed. If possible, therefore, in choosing the spot for an ambush the burrow should be on the left hand, whether you sit behind a rick, a tree, or in a dry ditch. Otherwise this slow clockwork motion is very difficult; for to shoot to the right is never convenient, and in a constrained position sometimes nearly impossible.

When expecting a rabbit in front or to the left it has occasionally happened that one has approached me almost from behind and on the right, where without turning the body it would be actually impossible to bring the gun to bear. Such a movement must alarm not only the particular rabbit, but any that might be about to come out in front; so that the only course is to let the creature remain and resolutely refuse the temptation to try and take aim. This difficulty of shooting to the right is why gamekeepers and others who do much potting learn to fire from the left shoulder, when they can command both sides. The barrel should be placed near the rick and lifted almost brushing it, so that it may be hidden as much as possible till the moment of pressing the trigger. Rabbits and all animals and birds dislike anything pointed at them. They have too good memories, and it is quite within probability that an old rabbit may be out who, though not then hit, or stung only in the skin, may recollect the flash and the thunderous roar which issued from similar threatening orifices. I used to try when waiting on a mound to get a 'gicks', or cow-parsnip, or a frond of fern or some brome grass, to partly overhang the barrel, so that its presence might not be suspected till the sight was taken. Now, having placed the gun ready and arranged yourself comfortably, next determine to forget the burrow entirely, and occupy the mind with anything rather than rabbits. They will never come out while watched for, and every impatient peep round the side of the rick simply prolongs the time. Nor is a novel of any use: whether it is the faint rustle of the leaves or the unconcious changes of position while reading, but no rabbit will venture near, no wood-pigeon will pass over while there is a book on the knee. Look at anything – look, at the grass. At the tip much of it is not pointed but blunt and brown as if burned; these are the blades recently severed by the scythe. They have pushed up higher but bear the scar of the wound. Bare spots by the furrows are where the mower swept his scythe through ant hills, leaving the earth exposed to the hot sun. Fond as the partridges are of ants' eggs, the largest coveys cannot make much impression upon the immense quantity of these insects. The partridges too frequently are diminished in numbers, but not from lack of particular food. A solitary humble-bee goes by to the ditch; he does not linger over the aftermath. Before it was cut the mowing grass was populous with insects: the aftermath has not nearly so many, though the grasshoppers are more visible, as they can be seen after they alight, which is not the case when the grass is tall. A chaffinch or greenfinch may come out from the hedge and perch on the sloping roof of the summer-rick, probably after the seeds in the plants among the hay. The kestrel hawk occasionally swoops down on to a summer-rick, stays for a second, and glides away again.

If you should chance to be waiting like this near a cattle-shed, perhaps you may see the keen muzzle of a weasel peep out from a sparrow's hole in the thatch of the roof. Yonder across the field is a gateway in the hedge, without either gate or rail, through which every now and then passes a blackbird or a thrush, and lesser birds, scarce distinguishable in the distance, flit across. The note of the grasshopper lark, not unlike a very small and non-sonorous bell continually agitated, sounds somewhere; it rings for several minutes, then stops, and rings again with short intervals. For a while it is difficult to tell whence it comes; the swift iteration of exactly the same note gives no indication of locality. But presently the eye seems guided by some unconscious sympathy with the ear to a low hawthorn bush which grows isolated a little way from the ditch a hundred yards down. The bird is there. Under an elm in the hedge on the right hand a gap was mended very early in the spring by driving in a stake and bending down some bushes. The top of the stake is the perch of a flycatcher; he leaves it every few seconds to catch insects floating past, now one side and now the other of the hedge, but immediately returns. His feeble and rather irritating call is repeated at intervals. From the same hedge comes, too, the almost incessant cry of young birds, able to fly, but not yet to find their own food. The dry scent of hay emanates from the summer-rick; the brown stalks of plants, some hollow hedge-parsley mown by the shore of the ditch, project from the side. Now the shadow of a tree which has been silently approaching from behind has reached the rick, and even extends beyond. Something suddenly appears in the gate-way across the field: a rabbit hops with much deliberation through the opening and stays to nibble among the clover, which always grows where the ground has been trodden but not worn bare by cattle. It would seem as if the wild rabbit and the tame did not feed on the same kind of food: the succulent plants carried home in such quantities for the tame animals often grow thickly near large burrows and to all appearance untouched. When shot in the act of grazing in meadows the wild rabbit has seldom anything but grass in his teeth. No doubt he does vary it, yet the sow-thistle flourishes by his bury. The gateway is far beyond the range of small shot, but if the rabbits are coming out there so they may be here. Very gently, with no jerk or rapid motion, take off your hat, and looking rather at the outline of the rick than at the hedge, slowly peer round so that at first sight of anything you may stay at once and not expose yourself. There is something brown on the grass, not fifteen yards distant; but it is too low, it does not stand above the short aftermath; it is a rabbit, but too young. Another inch of cautious craning round and there is a rabbit on the shore of the ditch, partly hidden by some hawthorn. He is large enough, but it is chance if he can be got: even if severely hit he has but to tumble and kick in a few feet to the bury. Retire as slowly as you advanced and wait again.

A rabbit is out now close to the bush where the grass-hopper lark still sings; and another comes forth there shortly afterwards. The first runs twenty or thirty yards into the meadow; the rabbit across at the distant gateway becomes aware that there is company near, and goes to meet it. Further still, on the right hand, there are two or three brown specks in the grass, which stay a long time in one spot, and then move. Something catches the eye on the mound near at hand: it is a rabbit hopping along the ridge of the bank, now visible and now hidden by the bushes. Lower down, a very young one nibbles at the grass which grows at the edge of the sand thrown out from the bury. The rabbit moving along the top of the mound is well within shot, but he, too, if hit will certainly escape, and it is uncertain if he can be hit hard, for although visible to the eye, there are many twigs and branches interposing which would lessen the force of the charge, or even avert it. He has now disappeared; he has gone out into the field on the other side. There seem rabbits everywhere except where wished: what a pity you did not sit behind the isolated hawthorn yonder or near the distant gateway through which a second rabbit comes. The long-drawn discordant call of a heron sounds; glancing up he floats over with outstretched wings. They are so broad that he does not seem far, yet he is very likely 200 yards high. He loves to see the shadows lengthening beneath him as he sails, till they reach the hedges on the eastern side of the fields, so that he may find the shallow corner of the pool already dusky when he reaches it. The strained glance drops to the grass again – Ah! there is a rabbit on the left side now, scarce five-and-twenty, certainly less than thirty yards away, and almost on a level with the rick, well out therefore from the ditch and the burrows. The left hand steals to the barrels, the right begins to lift the broad stock, first to the knee, then gradually – with slow clockwork motion – to the waistcoat. Stay, he moves to choose a fresh grazing place – but only two yards. The gun rises, the barrels still droop but the stock is more than halfway up. Stay again – the rabbit moves, but only turns his back completely, and immediately the gun comes to the shoulder. Stay again – is he full or nearly full grown, or is he too small? Is it a buck, or a doe? If the latter, she should be spared at that season. If full-grown though a buck, he will be very little good at this time of the year. You must judge by the height of the ears, the width across the flanks, and the general outline, by calling to mind previous experience. On comparison with others that you have shot you think this rabbit is little more than half-grown, not quite three quarters – that is, tender and white, and the best for the summer season. But looking along the barrels the hump of the buck intervenes; if hit there he will be cut all to pieces. Shut the lips and cry gently, 'Tcheck!' Instantly the rabbit rises to his haunches with ears up straight. As instantaneously a quick sight is taken at the poll and the trigger pressed. The second barrel is ready, but do not move or rise, or you will most likely miss with that barrel, disconcerted by jumping up. It is not needed; the rabbit is down kicking on his side, but it is merely a convulsive kick which jerks the already lifeless and limp body without progress. As you stoop to pick him up the kick ceases. There is a tremor in the flanks, a little blood oozes up the hollow of the ear, and it is over. Had he crept as far as the threshold of his bury the full dark eyeball would have been dimmed by the sand thrown on it by his last effort.

If you have the patience to resume your seat and wait, you may very likely obtain another shot presently from the same ambush. The young rabbits, which are the sort you want, have not yet had much experience of danger, and may venture forth again, or at all events another may be got in other parts of the same field. I remember firing eight successive times in the same meadow during one evening, by changing about from summer-rick to summer-rick. Once I crept on hands and knees some sixty or eighty yards, keeping a rick all the time between me and the rabbit and so shot him. In long grass by lying down at full length and dragging my limbs behind me – progressing rather by the arms only than with aid of the knees – I have approached rabbits straight across the open meadow without the least shelter, crawling towards them right, as it were, before their faces. At the least perking-up of ears or sign of alarm I stopped. The top of my head was never above the bennets and sorrel, so that the least lowering of my neck was sufficient to hide me altogether. The very fact of approaching in front was favourable, as rabbits do not seem able to see so well straight before them as in any other direction. Hares are notoriously deficient of vision in that way, and rabbits in some degree share the defect. But such approach, whether with gun or rifle, can only be accomplished by the exercise of extreme patience and unwavering attention upon the animals, so that the faintest suspicion may be allayed by stillness. After such an amount of trouble you naturally wish to make quite sure of your game, and would rather wait some time till the rabbit turns and offers a sure mark, than see him presently scramble wounded into a burrow. The shoulder is the safest spot; a rabbit will often run with shot in the head, but pellets near the heart are usually deadly; besides which, if the shoulder is disabled, it does not matter how much he kicks, he cannot guide himself, and so cannot escape. But as the shoulder is the very best part for eating – like the wing of the fowl – it is desirable when shooting a young rabbit not to injure the flesh there or cause it to be bloodstained. You must, then, wait till near enough to put plenty of shot in the head, enough to stun at once. When you can see the eyeball distinctly you are sure of killing, and it is the deadliest spot if you can draw a bead on it. For in this kind of shooting the one object should be to kill out-right, merely to wound is both cruel and bad economy. Summer-ricks are not general now, the hay being carted to the yard, and sheltered by the rick-cloth, but large hay-cocks occasionally remain some time in the fields; or you may hide behind a tree, a hawthorn, or projecting bush. A chance shot may be obtained sometimes by walking very quietly up to a hedge and peering through, but many rabbits are lost when shooting at them through a hedge. If there is one out in the grass on the other side, with a little manoeuvring you may manage to get an aim clear of boughs. But if the rabbit be not killed on the instant he is nearly sure to escape, since it is always slow work and sometimes impossible to force one's way through a thick hedge. By the time you have a run round to the gate the rabbit is dying four feet deep in the mound. With a dog it might be different, but dogs cannot well be taken for ambush-shooting; even a dog often fails when a rabbit has so long a start as thirty yards. The most difficult running shot at a rabbit is perhaps when he crosses a gateway on the other side; the spars, though horizontal, somehow deceive the eye, and generally receive most of the shot. Nor is it easy to shoot over a gate if at a short distance from it. The easiest place to procure a rabbit is where there is a hollow or a disused quarry. Such hollows may be seen in meadows at the foot of wooded slopes. If a hedge bounds or crosses the hollow, if there is a burrow in it, you have only to walk in the evening gently up to the verge, and taking care your head is not visible too soon, are sure to get a shot, as the rabbits do not for some time scent or see any one above them. Where they feed in the bottom of an old quarry the same thing may be done. Burrows in such places should not be

31

ferreted too much, nor the rabbits too much disturbed. The owner will then be able to shoot a rabbit almost whenever he wishes; a thing he certainly cannot do elsewhere; for although there may be a hundred in a mound, they may not be out just when he wants them. Some people used to take pleasure in having 'blue' rabbits about their grounds. These were the descendants of black tame animals turned out long previously; their colour toned down by interbreeding with the wild. Some thought that they could distinguish between the wood rabbit and the rabbit of the hill or the field warrens, and would pronounce where you had shot your game; the one having a deeper brown than the other, at least in that locality. But of recent years the pleasant minutiae of sport, not alone concerning rabbits, have rather fallen into disuse and oblivion.

from *Chronicles of The Hedges.*

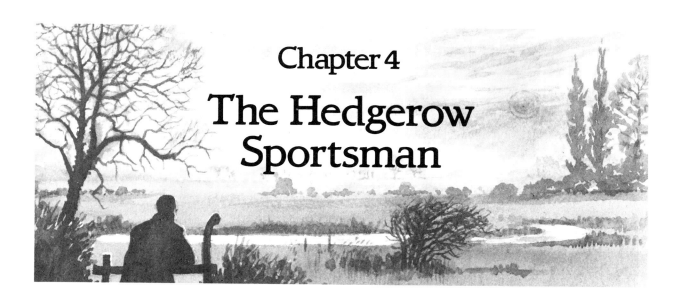

Chapter 4
The Hedgerow Sportsman

With the advent of winter comes round the favourite shooting season for a large and increasing class of gunners. These are the hedgerow sportsmen, who in numbers, in activity, and in the amusement they enjoy for their money have already far outstripped those bloated aristocrats the preservers of game.

The last five-and-twenty years, which have revolutionized the art of construction fire-arms, have brought about no less notable changes in the ownership of shot-guns. Thirty years ago the owner of a double-barrelled gun was a man of some means and even a single gun that could be trusted not to burst was hardly to be procured without the expenditure of gold coin. At the present day a very serviceable fowling-piece can be had for a song; and the idlest workman can by a moderate exercise of self-denial save enough to afford himself a double gun which to our grandfathers would have seemed a marvellous work of art. It may be said that to use these guns is a more costly matter, inasmuch as a yearly licence to do so is required; but we shall see that to elude the law imposing this necessity is not difficult, at least in the neighbourhood of large towns, whilst even in other places where the tax is more likely to be exacted the amount is not large enough to deter many persons from a favourite diversion.

Accordingly, as soon as the first frosts have begun to shorten the supply of food for wild birds, and urged them to seek it in more public and exposed places, you may see the hedgerow sportsman sallying forth for his day's sport. On a Sunday morning you may hear the country for miles round London and other populous towns resounding with an almost constant fusillade from the hedgerow brigade. On ordinary occasions the bag consists of quite small birds; but when the ground is covered with snow or hardened by a black frost, then the chase assumes a new character, and offers irresistible attractions. Then not only may blackbirds and thrushes be shot at twenty yards' range without the necessity of stalking them or lying in wait, but such more wary quarry as missel-thrushes, jays and wood-pigeons, may often be secured; and a crafty gunner with a good knowledge of his country need not despair of even bringing home such honourable trophies as fieldfares or redwings. In a severe and prolonged frost, such as that of last year, the bird tribe, from wrens and robins up to magpies, lapwings, and even wild ducks, are more or less at the mercy of the hedge-popper. He never knows, when he starts at daybreak, whether he may not with a little good luck bring back quite a pocketful of such large game.

The hedgerow sportsman who is an adept at his art will choose his ground in accordance with the weather and the season. On a fine and sunny morning he will take his walk across the neighbouring common or heath, or along some road of which the broad grassy sides are overgrown with furze. Here the linnets and bramble-finches will present a pretty easy mark as they sit piping on the tips of the gorse and blackberry bushes. In duller weather a likely place will be the banks of some river or pond, where the reed-warblers and marsh-tits flit about from bush to bush and the lively little water-wagtails trot along in wanton play unsuspectful of their fate. Here, too, there is the chance of an occasional water-rat, and perhaps a moorhen or coot. The cleverest and best-equipped of these water-side sportsmen are attended by a retriever, in the shape of some hideous cur, who has been painfully taught to fish out of the water the trophies of his owner's prowess. Any Sunday during the winter months the slimy and frowsy banks of the Thames between Chelsea and Isleworth may be seen at low water patrolled by ill-looking men, prowling about the tangled undergrowth which lines the bank, and at prolonged intervals startling the passing boatman by a dull report which signalizes the death of a small bird. When it is absolutely wet the high road is the best place for this species of gunner. The sparrows and other little birds are fond of taking their hurried bath in the puddles made by the showers, and the thick hedges which usually line a highway afford a good shelter from wind and rain. Here, therefore, a nice miscellaneous bag may be made, especially if there are orchards within easy range; for here the various kinds of tits may, with a little patience, be observed playing round the tree trunks and branches, and may be brought down by the careful sportsman as he leans over the field-gate. Sometimes an unoffending hedgehog will be found by the trusty cur, who betrays his discovery by a series of semi-frantic yelps and leaps. But this creature is seldom treated to a charge of shot, for the very good reason that by being saved alive in a bag he may before he dies afford excellent sport to a whole circle of stay-at-home sportsmen and their dogs.

These birds and beasts constitute the usual quarry of the hedgerow sportsman. Rather a poor show, it may be thought, for the expenditure of much time and energy, and several pennyworths of ammunition. But, in fact, it is all a question of taste and fashion and opportunity. The Parisian angler is well satisfied if in a long summer evening he can hook six or eight ounces of gudgeon; and there is no reason in nature why the Cockney gunner should not be equally proud of his half-pound of game in the shape of chaffinches and tom-tits. Or let us look at the matter in another way. You yourself are probably quite as pleased at killing a snipe as a partridge, and still more delighted at bagging a woodcock than the handsomest cock-pheasant. Is not, therefore, the hedgerow sportsman entitled to reason in a similar way? May he not be as proud of his larks and buntings, and rats and squirrels, as you of your hares and pheasants? It is true that song-birds are thought by some sentimental persons to add a charm to the country: but the five-shilling householder does not care for sentiment; his epithet for sentiment is not of a flattering or even mentionable kind. You may perhaps suppose that the sportsmen who troop forth, either in parties or one by one, to wage war against finches and tits do not enjoy their day as much as you do a bout at cover-shooting. But you are as much mistaken in this as in the former supposition. You, with all your expense and trouble in rearing and preserving game, and after being denounced as a tyrant at the neighbouring town-hall, will still find yourself, as you shoulder your breechloader, hampered and thwarted in a hundred ways. In the first place you have your boundary-fences, which you cannot overpass. You are afraid for your life to shoot a fox; and you have most likely a more or less fixed limit to the liberty of shooting at hen-pheasants. Then you have an absurd but firmly-rooted objection to firing at a sitting hare or rabbit, or even a running pheasant. You are not thought much of if you fire 'into the brown' of a covey of partridges or if you cut down the bird which rose before your neighbour before he had time to shoot. From all these vexatious restrictions the hedgerow sportsman is free. He walks where he pleases, subject only to the precaution of looking out as he goes that no keeper is in sight. Is he accosted by one of these hated minons of a selfish and purse-proud class, he is nowise abashed: he is not in 'pursuit of game', and cannot be punished in any way that he cares for. Should he get a pot-shot at a hare or partridge, no doubt he will not be such a 'soft' as to refuse it; and it will be hard if the dead body cannot be hid somewhere in a hedge and smuggled home at a convenient season. But as for the law of trespass, our hero snaps his fingers at it. He would be insulted if you only hinted that he could not pay the paltry fine. Still, he does not like paying; and therefore he for the most part avoids being caught. One man can run nearly as fast as another; and if the keeper should give chase, the trespasser will generally be able to get to the road or common before the chase has been witnessed by any third party who will give evidence about it. Then our friend has no squeamish scruples as to how he makes his bag – whether by a pot-shot or a flying or running shot, whether at a distance of five or fifty yards. Provided he can kill or capture, he has done all that he desires. All is fish that comes to his net; and in his love of destructive warfare all is fair, and no blow is foul. A charming equality is recognized by him among all wild feathered creatures; and being at liberty to blaze at them without distinction of size or species, he metes out with complaisant impartiality to them all that which he considers their due.

There is another great and conspicuous merit in hedgerow sport. It is an admirable school to fit a man for the exciting and profitable occupation of a poacher. Many men who have not hesitated to fire upon a keeper, and who have stocked half a shop with pheasants in their day, have begun by being nothing more than hedgerow sportsmen. The knowledge of wild life which lies open to the hedge-popper, and the dexterity in shooting and hiding which he often acquires, are invaluable qualities in the man who desires to graduate in the art of covert-robbing; and oftentimes a taste for pillage of this sort is gained in preliminary raids upon the haunts of skylarks and waterfowl. The spirit of adventure grows quickly with indulgence; and from the devastation of a hedgerow and an appearance before the 'beak' for trepass it is not so long a step as some people suppose to the depopulation of a pheasant covert and an indictment for killing and slaying a night watcher. Let us exemplify this statement – as facts are more convincing than words – by quoting from a letter written recently to one of the morning papers. The writer is a farmer at Shepherd's-bush, a district which is just now much affected by the class of sportsmen we are describing. After mentioning that the shooting nuisance exists all the week, but is worst on Sunday, when it begins at daybreak and goes on till dusk, he says: 'I give my men instructions to stop any person shooting on my fields; and on more than one occasion they have been threatened with a charge of shot for thus interfering with the sport. I have been deliberately shot at and wounded in the face when chasing these trespassers.' Who does not see that in these suburban sportsmen there exist all the makings of a poacher of the most advanced type?

What is the object which the hedgerow sportsman has in view when he organizes his battues or his solitary campaigns against the small creatures of the air? Occasionally the bag is worth handing over to the wife of his bosom, to be made into a pudding. But there is profit also in the pursuit for those who are minded to recoup themselves for their expenses, or to lay by a little hoard against the contingency of a magisterial fine. The dyers who purvey cheap humming-birds for hats and bonnets are ready to purchase at a very remunerative price the skins or dead bodies of any small bird. A few dabs of colour skilfully bestowed, and the addition of a sham beak or tuft, soon transform the wren or robin into a gorgeous native of South America; and the cheap milliners' shops do a great business in the sale of these articles of finery. Perhaps, however, the sportsman will dispose of his booty in a more romantic way by himself presenting it to the village Cressid or to some Lais of the East-end, who will wear it as a bird of paradise, and only to her most intimate acquaintances divulge the fact that it was slain by the skilful and devoted hand of 'Bill'.

Is there any remedy for this destruction of small birds, by which our lanes and fields are rapidly being cleared of their chief ornaments, and the destroyers of pernicious grubs and insects? It is much to be feared that there is none what-ever. We commented upon the imperfection of the late Wild Birds Protection Act when it was before Parliament, and pointed out how inadequate it would prove even in the season called 'close'. But the Act does not even touch the legion of winter gunners, who do by far the most extensive mischief. The law of trespass is set at naught; and as for the law respecting licences and the utility of the police in this matter, it may be sufficient to quote one more extract from the letter written by the farmer at Shepherd's-bush. He has, as he says, made many applications to the police, but they have never given him the name of a single person who thus trespasses on his farm; while often the ownership of a gun is a partnership affair, and one licence does duty for all the partners. What goes on at Shepherd's-bush and Wormwood Scrubs may be witnessed at hundreds of places every Sunday and as the abundance and cheapness of guns increases, so in proportion do the numbers of our song-birds, as well as of our rarer ornithological visitors, diminish.

from *Chronicles of the Hedges.*

Chapter 5

Unofficial Fishing

The streams are no more sacred from marauders than the woods and preserves. The brooks and upper waters are not so full of fish as formerly, the canal into which they fall being netted so much; and another cause of the diminution is the prevalence of fish-poaching, especially for jack, during the spawning season and afterwards. Though the keepers can check this within their own boundaries, it is not of much use.

Fish-poaching is simple and yet clever in its way. In the spawning time jack fish, which at other periods are apparently of a solitary disposition, go in pairs, and sometimes in trios, and are more tame than usual. A long slender ash stick is selected, slender enough to lie light in the hand and strong enough to bear a sudden weight. A loop and running noose are formed of a piece of thin copper wire, the other end of which is twisted round and firmly attached to the smaller end of the stick. The loop is adjusted to the size of the fish – it should not be very much larger, else it will not draw up quick enough, nor too small, else it may touch and disturb the jack. It does not take much practice to hit the happy medium. Approaching the bank of the brook quietly, so as not to shake the ground, to the vibrations of which fish are peculiarly sensitive, the poacher tries if possible to avoid letting his shadow fall across the water.

Some persons' eyes seem to have an extraordinary power of seeing through water, and of distinguishing at a glance a fish from a long swaying strip of dead brown flag, or the rotting pieces of wood which lie at the bottom. The ripple of the breeze, the eddy at the curve, or the sparkle of the sunshine cannot deceive them; while others, and by far the greater number, are dazzled and see nothing. It is astonishing how few persons seem to have the gift of sight when in the field.

The poacher, having marked his prey in the shallow yonder, gently extends his rod slowly across the water three or four yards higher up the stream, and lets the wire noose sink without noise till it almost or quite touches the bottom. It is easier to guide the noose to its destination when it occasionally touches the mud, for refraction distorts the true position of objects in water, and accuracy is important. Gradually the wire swims down with the current, just as if it were any ordinary twig or root carried along, such as the jack is accustomed to see, and he therefore feels no alarm. By degrees the loop comes closer to the fish, till with steady hand the poacher slips it over the head, past the long vicious jaw and gills, past the first fins, and pauses when it has reached a place corresponding to about one-third of the length of the fish, reckoning from the head. That end of the jack is heavier than the other, and the 'lines' of the body are there nearly straight. Thus the poacher gets a firm hold – for a fish, of course, is slippery – and a good balance. If the operation is performed gently the jack will remain quite still, though the wire rubs against his side: silence and stillness have such a power over all living creatures. The poacher now clears his arm and, with a sudden jerk, lifts the fish right out of the stream and lands him on the sward.

So sharp is the grasp of the wire that it frequently cuts its way through the scales, leaving a mark plainly visible when the jack is offered for sale. The suddenness and violence of the compression seem to disperse the muscular forces, and the fish appears dead for the moment. Very often, indeed, it really is killed by the jerk. This happens when the loop either has not passed far enough along the body or has slipped and seized the creature just at the gills. It then garottes the fish. If, on the other hand, the wire has been passed too far towards the tail, it slips off that way, the jack falling back into the water with a broad white band where the wire has scraped the scales. Fish thus marked may not unfrequently be seen in the stream. The jack, from its shape, is specially liable to capture in this manner; long and well balanced, the wire has every chance of holding it. This poaching is always going on; the implement is so easily obtained and concealed. The wire can be carried in the pocket, and the stick may be cut from an adjacent copse.

The poachers observe that after a fish has once escaped from an attempt of the kind it is ever after far more difficult of capture. The first time the jack was still and took no notice of the insidious approach of the wire gliding along towards it; but the next – unless a long interval elapses before a second trial – the moment it comes near he is away. At each succeeding attempt, whether hurt or not, he grows more and more suspicious, till at last to merely stand still or stop while walking on the bank is sufficient for him; he is off with a swish of the tail to the deeper water, leaving behind him a cloud, so to say, of mud swept up from the bottom to conceal the direction of his flight. For it would almost seem as if the jack throws up this mud on purpose; if much disturbed he will quite discolour the brook. The wire does a good deal to depopulate the stream, and is altogether a deadly implement.

But a clever fish-poacher can land a jack even without a wire, and with no better instrument than a willow stick cut from the nearest osier-bed. The willow, or withy as it is usually called, is remarkably pliant, and can be twisted into any shape. Selecting a long slender wand, the poacher strips it of leaves, gives the smaller end a couple of twists, making a noose and running knot of the stick itself. The mode of using it is precisely similar to that followed with a wire, but it requires a little more dexterity, because, of course, the wood, flexible as it is, does not draw up so quickly or so closely as the metal, neither does it take so firm a grip. A fish once caught by a wire can be slung about almost anyhow, it holds so tightly. The withy noose must be jerked up the instant it passes under that part of the jack where the weight of the fish is balanced – the centre of gravity; if there is an error in this respect it should be towards the head, rather than towards the tail. Directly the jack is thrown out upon the sward he must be seized, or he will slip from the noose, and possibly find his way back again into the water. With a wire there is little risk of that; but then the withy does not cut its way into the fish.

This trick is often accomplished with the common withy – not that which grows on pollard trees, but in osier-beds; that on the trees is brittle. But a special kind is sought for the purpose, and for any other requiring extreme flexibility. It is, I think, locally called the stone osier, and it does not grow so tall as the common sorts. It will tie like string. Being so short, for poaching fish it has to be fastened to a thicker and longer stick, which is easily done; and some prefer it to wire because it looks more natural in the water and does not alarm the fish, while, should the keeper be about, it is easily cut up in several pieces and thrown away. I have heard of rabbits, and even hares, being caught with a noose of this kind of withy, which is as 'tough as wire'; and yet it seems hardly possible, as it is so much thicker and would be seen. Still, both hares and rabbits, when playing and scampering about at night, are sometimes curiously heedless, and foolish enough to run their necks into anything.

With such a rude implement as this some fish-poachers will speedily land a good basket of pike. During the spawning season, as was observed previously, jack go in pairs, and now and then in trios, and of this the poacher avails himself to take more than one at a haul. The fish lie so close together - side by side just at that time – that it is quite practicable, with care and judgement, to slip a wire over two at once. When near the bank two may even be captured with a good withy noose: with a wire a clever hand will make a certainty of it. The keeper says that on one occasion he watched a man operating just without his jurisdiction, who actually succeeded in wiring three jacks at once and safely landed them on the grass. They were small fish, about a pound to a pound and a half each, and the man was but a few minutes in accomplishing the feat. It sometimes happens that after a heavy flood, when the brook has been thick with suspended mud for several days, so soon as it has gone down fish are more than usually plentiful, as if the flood had brought them up-stream: poachers are then particularly busy.

Fresh fish – that is, those who are new to that particular part of the brook – are, the poachers say, much more easily captured than those who have made it their home for some time. They are, in fact, more easily discovered; they have not yet found out all the nooks and corners, the projecting roots and the hollows under the banks, the dark places where a black shadow falls from overhanging trees and is with difficulty pierced even by a practised eye. They expose themselves in open places, and meet an untimely fate.

Besides pike, tench are occasionally wired, and now and then even a large roach; the tench, though a bottom fish, in the shallow brooks may be sometimes detected by the eye, and is not a difficult fish to capture. Every one has heard of tickling trout: the tench is almost equally amenable to titillation. Lying at full length on the sward, with his hat off lest it should fall into the water, the poacher peers down into the hole where he has reason to think tench may be found. This fish is so dark in colour when viewed from above that for a minute or two, till the sight adapts itself to the dull light of the water, the poacher cannot distinguish what he is searching for. Presently, having made out the position of the tench, he slips his bared arm in slowly, and without splash, and finds little or no trouble as a rule in getting his hand close to the fish without alarming it: tench, indeed, seem rather sluggish. He then passes his fingers under the belly and gently rubs it. Now it would appear that he has the fish in his power, and has only to grasp it. But grasping is not so easy; or rather it is not so easy to pull a fish up through two feet of superincumbent water which opposes the quick passage of the arm. The gentle rubbing in the first place seems to soothe the fish, so that it becomes perfectly quiescent, except that it slowly rises up in the water, and thus enables the hand to get into proper position for the final seizure. When it has risen up towards the surface sufficiently far – the tench must not be driven too near the surface, for it does not like light and will glide away – the poacher suddenly snaps as it were; his thumb and fingers, if he possibly can manage it, closing on the gills. The body is so slimy and slippery that there alone a firm hold can be got, though the poacher will often flick the fish out of water in an instant so soon as it is near the surface. Poachers evidently feel as much pleasure in practising these tricks as the most enthusiastic angler using the implements of legitimate sport.

No advantage is thought too unfair to be taken of fish; nothing too brutally unsportsmanlike. I have seen a pike killed with a prong as he lay basking in the sun at the top of the water. A labourer stealthily approached, and suddenly speared him with one of the sharp points of the prong or hayfork he carried: the pike was a good-sized one too.

The stream, where not strictly preserved, is frequently netted without the slightest regard to season. The net is stretched from bank to bank. and watched by one man, while the other walks up the brook thirty or forty yards, and drives the fish down the current into the bag. With a long pole he thrashes the water, making a good deal of splash, and rousing up the mud, which fish dislike and avoid. The pole is thrust into every hiding-place, and pokes everything out. The watcher by the net knows by the bobbing under of the corks when a shoal of roach and perch, or a heavy pike, has darted into it, and instantly draws the string and makes his haul. In this way, by sections at a time, the brook, perhaps for half a mile, is quite cleared out. Jack, however, sometimes escape; they seem remarkably shrewd and quick to learn. If the string is not immediately drawn when they touch the net, they are out of it without a moment's delay: they will double back up stream through all the splashing and mud, and some will even slide as it were between the net and the bank if it does not quite touch in any place, and so get away.

In its downward course the brook irrigates many water meadows, and to drive the stream out upon them there are great wooden hatches. Sometimes a gang of men, discovering that there is a quantity of fish thereabouts, will force down a hatch, which at once shuts off or greatly diminishes the volume of water flowing down the brook, and then rapidly construct a dam across the current below it with the mud of the

'... proud of his half-pound of game in the shape of chaffinches...'
(*The Hedgerow Sportsman*)

'... such more wary quarry as missel-thrushes... may often be secured.'
(*The Hedgerow Sportsman*)

'The poacher extends his rod'
(*Unofficial Fishing*)

shore. Above this dam they thrash the water with poles and drive all the fish towards it, and then make a second dam above the first so as to enclose them in a short space. In the making of these dams speed is an object, or the water will accumulate and flow over the hatch; so hurdles are used, as they afford a support to the mud hastily thrown up. Then with buckets, bowls, and 'scoops', they bale out the water between the two dams, and quickly reduce their prey to wriggling helplessness. In this way whole baskets full of fish have been taken, together with eels; and nothing so enclosed can escape.

The mere or lake by the wood is protected by sharp stakes set at the bottom, which would tear poachers' nets; and the keeper does not think any attempt to sweep it has been made of late years, it is too well watched. But he believes that night lines are frequently laid: a footpath runs along one shore for some distance, and gives easy access, and such lines may be overlooked. He is certain the eels are taken in that way despite his vigilance.

Trespassing for crayfish, too, causes much annoyance. I have known men to get bodily up to the waist into the great ponds, a few of which yet remain, after carp. These fish have a curious habit of huddling up in hollows under the banks; and those who know where these hollows and holes are situated can take them by hand if they can come suddenly upon them. It is said that now and then fish are raked out of the ponds with a common rake (such as is used in haymaking) when lying on the mud in winter.

from *The Gamekeeper at Home.*

Chapter 6
Modern Sporting Guns

In no field of enterprise has modern mechanical industry made a more rapid advance or displayed more remarkable ingenuity than in the improvement and perfection of sporting arms. Indeed, when we compare the appliances within the reach of the sportsman of to-day with those accessible to his grandfather, it will be evident that he is separated by almost as wide a gulf from that time as the modern rifleman is from the bowman who fought at Cressy and Agincourt. At the beginning of the century sporting arms were so comparatively rude and imperfect that the balance of vantage must have lain decidedly with the quarry. Two of the most essential conditions of success in shooting – namely, a rapid and certain ignition of the charge – were then denied to the sportsman, on account of no better means of discharging his weapon being available to him than the primitive flint and steel. We have heard from the mouths of men whose shooting recollections went back to the beginning of this century that nothing more depressing can be conceived than a damp day's sport with a flintlock. The sportsman covered his bird, allowing a margin undreamt of in these days for the wildest grouse, and had the satisfaction of hearing a long, slow fizzing in the pan before the gun would go off (if haply it went off at all), while the bird flew away perfectly happy. What snipe or woodcock could have had to fear in those days is problematical; though it is mentioned as a wonderful feat, in the biography of a late consul-general in Turkey who was a noted snap-shot in his day, that he killed seventy-two woodcocks in six hours with only a flintlock to depend upon. The introduction of percussion caps was an immense step in advance, inasmuch as it provided a certain and rapid means of ignition and discharge – always supposing the nipples were carefully tended – thereby bringing the bird so much nearer the gun. Here, however, until the introduction of breech-loaders, all improvement ceased. The tedious process of loading had still to be gone through; to clean the gun in the field was impossible; and if in this necessary operation the greatest care was not exercised in wiping out the barrels, the least bit of two left in was sufficient, when kindled by the first discharge, to blow off the loader's hand as he poured in the second charge. From all this the introduction of breech-loaders some twenty years since delivered sportsmen. At first, it is true, they were looked somewhat shyly upon because of their showing an inferior pattern and penetration as compared with the orthodox muzzle-loaders; and it is remarkable that many competent judges despaired at that time of their ever showing shooting equal to a well-made muzzle-loader. This defect, which was no doubt owing to waste of power caused by leakage, has since been remedied by the practically air-tight systems of breech action which have been devised by the ingenuity of gun-smiths and mechanicians. No doubt in time friction must deteriorate any system of breech action, however well conceived or well executed; but no sportsman would grudge the slight additional outlay this might involve in comparison with the enormous compensatory advantages offered. The sole real advantage belonging to muzzle-loaders – that of enabling the sportsman to vary his charge without encumbering himself with additional cartridges, is not one which can be of much moment in this country, where the atmosphere and wind never vary very much in the course of a single day's sport, and where shooting is a pastime of the comparatively wealthy, who can afford the luxury of loaders.

It is curious to note, after muzzle-loaders had been finally driven from the field, how long the rival merits of pin-fire and central-fire were debated, and how slow sportsmen and gunmakers were to recognize the fact that with the pin-fire system a perfectly air-tight breech is unattainable, and that therefore a greater or less waste of power is unavoidable. It is but a very short time since gunmakers ceased to advertise pin-fire guns, and even now there must be many sportsmen using them up. On the Continent generally, and in Belguim and Germany in particular, pin-fire for a long time resolutely held its ground against its rival, and for aught we know may do so still; and this may be said in favour of the system, that it has the advantage of letting you know when the gun is loaded. In Germany a short time ago, central-fire cartridges were quite unobtainable, as many English sportsmen must have found to their cost. In France, where for a long time central fire was practically unknown, it has at last asserted its supremacy, and the best French gunmakers now turn out hardly anything but central-fire guns, at, it may be noted, generally speaking very moderate prices. From central fire to hammerless guns would appear to be a logical step. Once grant that the best way of igniting a cartridge is the shock of a small piston, and it seems to us that there is no longer any *raison d'etre* for fingering hammers. No doubt many conservatives object to hammerless guns on the score that such a weapon is not like a gun, or rather not like the object which they have been accustomed to associate in their minds with the idea of a gun. In that sense it might be urged with truth that a Snider-Enfield is much more like a gun than a Martini-Henry, and yet the latter is by far the more efficient weapon. Of course the sensation of having no hammers to finger must be somewhat perplexing at first to one who may have been accustomed for a quarter of a century or more to the old system; but when any sportsman has once 'got into the way of it', as the saying goes, we can hardly imagine his preferring to retain hammers, considering the much more rapid discharge which is attainable by the use of a hammerless gun. Another great advantage offered by these guns is the freedom from clogging in damp weather of the strikers, which in a hammerless gun are under cover. It is true that it has been alleged against some kinds that water is liable to get into the locks through the connection between the pistons which raise the tumblers to full cock and the outside. But this defect has been removed, if we mistake not, by more than one gunmaker. Bearing these advantages in mind, we cannot be surprised at the rapid favour into which these guns have grown since their introduction into the market, on the other side of the Channel as well as this, and which would seem to augur that, as far at least as locks are concerned, the hammerless lock is 'the lock of the future'.

On the other hand, that modification in the old system of boring known as 'choking', by which the muzzle of the gun is constricted, and which has so wonderfully improved the pattern and penetration of shot-guns, seems to us likely to affect a much narrower class of sportsmen. To the great majority of these in Great Britain shooting means only a few days' or at most a week's relaxation with the partridges from the care and worry of business; and such men have not the opportunity, unless they happen to possess a much more than ordinary aptitude for the use of the fowling-piece, of becoming such proficients with the gun as to make choke-bores of much practical use to them. We think it would be pretty safe to conclude that the limits within which much execution can be done by the average sportsman may be laid down at from forty to fifty yards, and he no doubt would do best by contenting himself with a cylinder bore for the first barrel and modified choke for the second. The question assumes, of course, quite a different complexion when we consider the case of those who are fortunate enough to be able to indulge in pheasant preserves and grouse moors, and who can afford to devote enough time to sport to become really good shots. To this class, no doubt, choke-bored guns have proved a great boon. But to employ such guns with any effect a man must be a first-rate shot, and the number of really good shots is hardly likely to increase to any great extent. Important, therefore, and valuable as the introduction of choke-boring has proved to many sportsmen, we can hardly look forward to its exercising much influence upon the larger proportion of the lovers of the trigger.

from *Chronicles of the Hedges.*

Chapter 7

Choosing a Gun

The first thought of the amateur sportsman naturally refers to his gun, and the questions arise: What sort of a gun do I want? Where can I get it? What price shall I pay? In appearance there can be no great difficulty in settling these matters, but in practice it is really by no means easy. Some time since, being on a visit to the Metropolis, I was requested by a friend to get him a gun, and accepted the commission, as M. Emile Ollivier went to war, with a light heart, little dreaming of the troubles that would start up in the attempt to conscientiously carry it out. He wanted a good gun, and was not very scrupulous as to maker or price, provided that the latter was not absolutely extravagant. With such *carte blanche* as this it seemed plain-sailing, and, indeed, I never gave a second thought to the business till I opened the door of the first respectable gunmaker's shop I came across, which happened to be no great distance from Pall Mall. A very polite gentleman immediately came forward, rubbing his hands as if he were washing them (which is an odd habit with many), and asked if there was anything he could do for me, Well, yes, I wanted a gun. Just so – they had one of the largest stocks in London, and would be most happy to show me specimens of all kinds. But was there any special sort of gun required, as then they could suit me in an instant.

'Hum! Ah! Well, I – I' – feeling rather vague – 'perhaps you would let me see your catalogue – '

'Certainly.' And a handsomely got-up pamphlet, illustrated with woodcuts, was placed in my hands, and I began to study the pages. But this did not suit him; doubtless, with the practice of his profession, he saw at once the uncertain manner of the customer who was feeling his way, and thought to bring it to a point.

'You want a good, useful gun, sir, I presume?'

'That is just it' – shutting the catalogue; quite a relief to have the thing put into shape for one!

'Then you can't do better than take our new patent double-action so-and-so. Here it is' – handing me a decent-looking weapon in thorough polish, which I begin to weigh in my hands, poise it to ascertain the balance, and to try how it comes to the present, and whether I can catch the rib quick enough, when he goes on: 'We can let you have that gun, sir, for ten guineas.'

'Oh indeed! But that's very cheap, isn't it?' I thoughtlessly observe, putting the gun down.

My friend D. had mentioned a much higher amount as his ultimatum. The next instant I saw in what light my remark would be taken. It would be interpreted in this way: Here we have either a rich amateur, who doesn't care what he gives, or else a fool who knows nothing about it.

'Well, sir, of course it's our very plainest gun' – the weapon is tossed carelessly into the background – 'in fact, we sometimes call it our gamekeeper gun. Now, here is a really fine thing – neatly finished, engraved plates, first choice stock, the very best walnut, price – ' He names a sum very close to D.'s outside.

I handle the weapon in the same manner, and for the life of me cannot meet his eye, for I know that he is reading me, or thinks he is, like a book. With the exception that the gun is a trifle more elaborately got up, I cannot see or feel the slightest difference, and begin secretly to suspect that the price of guns is regulated according to the inexperience of the purchaser – a sort of sliding scale, gauged to ignorance, and rising or falling with its density! He expatiates on the gun and points out all its beauties.

'Shooting carefully registered, sir. Can see it tried, or try it yourself, sir. Our range is barely three-quarters of an hour's ride. If the stock doesn't quite fit your shoulder, you can have another – the same price. You won't find a better gun in all London.'

I can see that it really is a very fair article, but do not detect the extraordinary excellencies so glibly described. I recollect an old proverb about the fool and the money he is said to part with hastily. I resolve to see more variety before making the final plunge; and what the eloquent shopkeeper thinks is my growing admiration for the gun which I continue to handle is really my embarassment, for as yet I am not hardened, and dislike the idea of leaving the shop without making a purchase after actually touching the goods. But D.'s money – I must lay it out to the best advantage. Desperately I fling the gun into his hands, snatch up the catalogue, mutter incoherently, 'Will look it through – like the look of the thing – call again,' and find myself walking aimlessly along the pavement outside.

An unpleasant sense of having played a rather small part lingered for some time, and ultimately resolved itself into a determination to make up my mind as to exactly what D. wanted, and on entering the next shop, to ask to see that, and that only. So, turning to the address of another gunmaker, I walked towards it slowly, revolving in my mind the sort of shooting D. usually enjoyed. Visions of green fields, woods just beginning to turn colour, puffs of smoke hanging over the ground, rose up, and blotted out the bustling London scene. The shops glittering with their brightest goods placed in front, the throng of vehicles, the crowds of people, faded away, the pace increased and the stride lengthened as if stepping over the elastic turf, and the roar of the traffic sounded low, like a distant waterfall. From this reverie the rude apostrophes of a hansom-cabman awoke me – I had walked right into the stream of the street, and instead of the awning boughs of the wood found a whip upheld, threatening chastisement for getting in the way. This brought me up from imagination to logic with a jerk, and I began to check off the uses D. could put his gun to on the fingers. (1) I knew he had a friend in Yorkshire, and shot over his moor every August. His gun, then, must be suited to grouse-shooting, and must be light, because of the heat which often prevails at that time, and renders dragging a heavy gun many miles over the heather – before they pack – a serious drawback to the pleasure of the sport. (2) He had some partridge-shooting of his own, and was peculiarly fond of it. (3) He was always invited to at least two battues. (4) A part of his own shooting was on the hills, where the hares were very wild, where there was no cover, and they had to be knocked over at long distances, and took a hard blow. That would require (a) a choke-bore, which was not suitable either, because in covers the pheasants at short ranges would not unlikely get 'blown,' which would annoy the host; or (b) a heavy, strong gun, which would take a stiff charge without too much recoil. But that, again, clashed with the light gun for shooting in August. (5) He had latterly taken a fancy to wild-fowl shooting by the coast, for which a very hard-hitting, long-range gun was needed. It would never do if D. could not bring down a duck. (6) He was notorious as a dead shot on snipe – this told rather in favour of a light gun, old system of boring; for where would a snipe or a woodcock be if it chanced to get 200 pellets into it at twenty yards? You might find the claws and fragments of the bill if you looked with a microscope. (7) No delicate piece of workmanship would do, because he was careless of his gun, knocked it about anyhow, and occasionally dropped it in a brook. And here was the shop-door; imagine the state of confusion my mind was in when I entered!

This was a very 'big' place: the gentleman who approached had a way of waving his hand – very white and jewelled – and a grand, lofty idea of what a gun should cost. 'Twenty, thirty, forty pounds – some of the £30 were second-hand, of course – we have a few, a very few, second-hand guns' – such was the sweeping answer to my first mild inquiry about prices. Then, seeing at once my vacillating manner, he, too, took me in hand, only in a terribly earnest, ponderous way from which there was no escape. 'You wanted a good general gun – yes; a thoroughly good, well-finished, *plain* gun (great emphasis on the 'plain'). Of course, you can't get anything new for *that* money, finished in style. Still, the plain gun will shoot just as well (as if the shooting part was scarcely worth consideration). We make the very best plain-finished article for five-and-twenty guineas in London. By-the-by, where is your shooting, sir?' Thrust home like this, not over-gratified by a manner which seemed to say, 'Listen to an authority,' and desiring to keep an incog., I mutter something about 'abroad.' 'Ah – well, then, this article is precisely the thing, because it will carry ball, an immense advantage in any country where you may come across large game.'

'How far will it throw a ball?' I ask, rather curious on that subject, for I was under the impression that a smooth-bore of the usual build is not much to be relied on in that way – far less, indeed, than the matchlocks made by semi-civilized nations. But it seems I was mistaken.

'Why – a hundred yards point-blank, and ten times better to shoot with than a rifle.'

'Indeed!'

'Of course, I mean in cover, as you're pretty sure to be. Say a wild boar is suddenly started: well, you pull out your No.4 shot-cartridge, and push in a ball; you shoot as well again – snap-shooting with a smooth-bore in jungle or bush. There's not a better gun turned out in town than that. It's not the slightest use your looking for anything cheaper – rebounding locks, best stocks, steel damascene barrels; fit for anything from snipe to deer, from dust to buck-shot – '

'But I think – ' Another torrent overwhelms me.

'Here's an order for twenty of these guns for Texas, to shoot from horseback at buffalo – ride in among them, you know.'

I look at my watch, find it's much later than I imagine, remark that it is really a difficult thing to pick out a gun, and seize the door-handle.

'When gentlemen don't exactly know what they're looking for it *is* a hard job to choose a gun' – he smiles sarcastically, and shuts me out politely.

The observation seems hard, after thinking over guns so intently; yet it must be aggravating to attempt to serve a man who does not know what he wants – yet (one's mood changes quickly) it was his own fault for trying to force, to positively force, that twenty-five-guinea thing on me instead of giving me a chance to choose. I had seen rows on rows of guns stacked round the shop, rank upon rank; in the background a door partly open permitted a glimpse of a second room, also perfectly coated with guns, if such an expression is permissible. Now, I look on ranges of guns like this much the same as on a library. Is there anything so delicious as the first exploration of a great library – alone – unwatched? You shut the heavy door behind you slowly, reverently, lest a noise should jar on the sleepers of the shelves. For as the Seven Sleepers of Ephesus were dead and yet alive, so are the souls of the authors in the care of their ancient leathern binding. You walk gently round the walls pausing here to read a title, there to draw out a tome and support it for a passing glance – half in your arms, half against the shelf. The passing glance lengthens till the weight becomes too great, and with a sigh you replace it, and move again, peering up at those titles which are foreshortened from the elevation of the shelf, and so roam from folio to octavo, from octavo to quarto, till at last, finding a little work whose value, were it in the mart, would be more than its weight in gold, you bear it to the low leather-covered arm-chair and enjoy it at your ease. But to sip the full pleasure of a library you must be alone, and you must take the books yourself from the shelves. A man to read must read alone. He may make extracts, he may *work* at books in company; but to read, to absorb, he must be solitary. Something in the same way – except in the necessity for solitude, which does not exist in this case – I like to go through a battery of guns, picking up this one, or that, glancing up one, trying the locks of another, examining the thickness of the breech. Why did not the fellow say, 'There are our guns; walk round, take down what you please, do as you like, and don't hurry. I will go on with some work while you examine them. Call me if you want any explanation. Spend the day there if you like, and come again to-morrow.' It would have been a hundred chances to one that I had found a gun to suit D., for the shop was a famous one, the guns really good, the workmanship unimpeachable, and the stock to select from immense. But let a thing be never so good, one does not care to have it positively thrust on one.

By this time my temper was up, and I determined to go through with the business, and get the precise article likely to please D., if I went to every maker in the Metropolis. I went to very nearly every prominent man – I spent several days at it. I called at shops whose names are household words wherever an English sportsman can be found. Some of them, though bright to look at from the pavement, within were mean, and even lacked cleanliness. The attendants were often incapable of comprehending that a customer *may* be as good a judge of what he wants as themselves; they have got into a narrow routine of offering the same thing to everybody. No two shops were of the same opinion: at one you were told that the choke was the greatest success in the world; at another, that they only shot well for one season, quickly wearing out; at a third, that such and such a 'grip' or breech-action was perfect; at a fifth, that hammerless guns were the guns of the future, and elsewhere, that people detested hammerless guns because it seemed like learning to shoot over again. Finally, I visited several of the second-hand shops. They had some remarkably good guns – for the leading second-hand shops do not care to buy a gun unless by a crack maker – but the cheapness was a delusion. A new gun might be got for the same money, or very little more. Their system was like this. Suppose they had a really good gun, but, for aught you could tell, twenty or thirty years old (the breech-action might have been altered), for this they would ask, say £25. The original price of the gun may have been £50, and if viewed *only* with regard to the original price, of course that would be a great reduction. But for the £25 a new gun could be got from a maker whose goods, if not so famous, were thoroughly reliable, and who guaranteed the shooting. In the one case you bought a gun about whose previous history you knew absolutely nothing beyond the mere fact of the barrels having come at first-hand from a leading maker. But they may have been battered about – rebored; they may be scored inside by someone loading with flints; twenty things that are quite unascertainable may have combined to injure its original perfection. The cheapness will not stand the test of a moment's thought – that is, if you are in search of excellence. You buy a name and trust to chance. After several days of such work as this, becoming less and less satisfied at every fresh attempt, and physically more fatigued than if I had walked a hundred miles, I gave it up for awhile, and wrote to D. for more precise instructions.

When I came to quietly reflect on these experiences, I found that the effect of carefully studying the subject had been to plunge me into utter confusion. It seemed as difficult to choose a gun as to choose a horse, which is saying a good deal. Most of us take our shooting as we take other things – from our fathers – very likely use their guns, get into their style of shooting; or if we buy guns, buy them because a friend wants to sell, and so get hold of the gun that suits us by a kind of happy chance. But to begin *de novo*, to select a gun from the thousand and one exhibited in London, to go conscientiously into the merits and demerits of the endless varieties of locks and breeches, and to come to an impartial decision, is a task the magnitude of which is not easily described. How many others who have been placed in somewhat similar positions must have felt the same ultimate confusion of mind, and perhaps at last, in sheer despair, plunged, and bought the first that came to hand, regretting for years afterwards that they had not bought this or that weapon, which had taken their fancy, but which some gunsmith interested in a patent had declared obsolete!

D. settled the question, so far as he was concerned, by ordering two guns: one bored in the old style for ordinary shooting, and a choked gun of larger bore for the ducks. But all this trouble and investigation gave rise to several not altogether satisfactory reflections. For one thing, there seems a too great desire on the part of gunmakers to achieve a colossal reputation by means of some new patent, which is thrust on the notice of the sportsman and of the public generally at every step and turn. The patent very likely is an admirable thing, and quite fulfils the promise so far as the actual object in view is concerned. But it is immediately declared to supersede everything – no gun is of any use without it: you are compelled to purchase it whether or no, or you are given to understand that you are quite behind the age. The leading idea of the gunmaker nowadays is to turn out a hundred thousand guns of one particular pattern, like so many bales of cloth; everybody is to shoot with this, their speciality,and everything that has been previously done is totally ignored. The workman in the true sense of the word – the artist in guns – is either extinct, or hidden in an obscure corner. There is no individuality about modern guns. One is exactly like another. That is very well, and necessary for military arms, because an army must be supplied with a single pattern cartridge in order to simplify the difficulty of providing ammunition. They fail even in the matter of ornament. The design – if it can be called design – on one lock-plate is repeated on a thousand others, so with the hammers. There is no originality about a modern gun; as you handle it you are conscious that it is well put together, that the mechanism is perfect, the barrels true, but somehow it feels *hard*; it conveys the impression of being machine-made. You cannot feel the *hand* of the maker anywhere, and the failure, the flatness, the formality of the supposed ornament, is depressing. The ancient harquebuss makers far surpassed the very best manufacturers of the present day. Their guns are really artistic – works of true art. The stocks of some of the German wheel-lock guns of the sixteenth and seventeeth centuries are really beautiful specimens of carving and design. Their powder-horns are gems of workmanship –

hunting-scenes cut out in ivory, the minutest detail rendered with life-like accuracy. They graved their stags and boars from Nature, not from conventional designs; the result is that we admire them now because Nature is constant, and her fashions endure. The conventional 'designs' on our lock-plates, etc., will in a few years be despised; they have no intrinsic beauty. The Arab of the desert, wild, untrammelled, ornaments his matchlock with turquoise. Our machine-made guns, double-barrel, breech-loading, double-grip, rebounding locks, first-choice stocks, laminated steel, or damascus barrels, choke-bore, and so forth, will, it is true, mow down the pheasants at the battue as the scythe cuts down the grass. There is slaughter in every line of them. But is slaughter everything? In my idea it is not, but very far from it. Were I offered the choice of participation in the bloodiest battue ever arranged – such as are reserved for princes – the very best position, and the best-finished and swiftest breech-loader invented, or the freedom of an English forest, to go forth at any time and shoot whatever I chose, untrammelled by any attendants, on condition that I only carried a wheel-lock, I should unhesitatingly select the second alternative. There would be an abiding pleasure in the very fact of using so beautiful a weapon – just in the very handling of it, to pass the fingers over the intricate and exquisite carving. There would be pleasure in winding up the lock with the spanner; in adjusting the pyrites to strike fire from the notches of the wheel; in priming from a delicate flask graven with stag and hounds. There would be delight in stealing from tree to tree, in creeping from bush to bush, through the bracken, keeping the wind carefully, noiselessly gliding forward – so silently that the woodpecker should not cease tapping in the beech, or the pigeon her hoarse call in the oak, till at last within range of the buck. And then! First, if the ball did not hit the vital spot, if it did not pass through the neck, or break the shoulder, inevitably he would be lost, for the round bullet would not break up like a shell, and smash the creature's flesh and bones into a ghastly jelly, as do the missiles from our nineteenth century express rifles. Secondly, if the wheel did not knock a spark out quickly, if the priming had not been kept dry, and did not ignite instantly, the aim might waver, and all the previous labour be lost. Something like skill would be necessary here. There would be art in the weapon itself, skill in the very loading, skill in the approach, nerve in holding the gun steady while the slow powder caught from the priming and expelled the ball. That would be sport. An imperfect weapon – well, yes; but the imperfect weapon would somehow harmonize with the forest, with the huge old hollow oaks, the beeches full of knot-holes, the mysterious thickets, the tall fern, the silence and solitude. It would make the forest seem a forest – such as existed hundreds of years ago; it would make the chase a real chase, not a foregone conclusion. It would equalize the chances, and give the buck 'law'. In short, it would be real shooting. Or with smaller game – I fancy I could hit a pheasant with a wheel-lock if I went alone, and *flushed the bird myself.* In that lies all the difference. If your birds are flushed by beaters, you may be on the watch, but that very watching unnerves by straining the nerves, and then the sudden rush and noise flusters you, and even with the best gun of modern construction you often miss. If you spring the bird yourself the noise may startle you, and yet somehow you settle down to your aim and drop him. With a wheel-lock, if I could get a tolerably clear view, I think I could bring him down. If only a brace rewarded a day's roaming under oak and beech, through fern and past thicket, I should be amply satisfied. With the antique weapon the spirit of the wood would enter into one. The chances of failure add zest to the pursuit. For slaughter, however, our modern guns are unsurpassed.

Another point which occurs to one after such an overhauling of guns as I went through is the price charged for them. There does seem something very arbitrary in the charges demanded, and one cannot help a feeling that they bear no proportion to the real value or cost of production. It may, of course, be said that the wages of workmen are very high – although workmen as a mass have long been complaining that such is not really the case. The rent of premises in fashionable localities is also high, no doubt. For my part, I would quite as soon buy a gun in a village as in a crowded thoroughfare of the Metropolis; indeed rather sooner, since there would probably be a range attached where it could be tried. To be offered a range, as is often the case in London, half an hour out – which, with getting to the station and from the station at the other end, to the place and back, may practically mean half a day – is of little use. If you could pick up the gun in the shop, stroll outside and try it at once, it would be ten times more pleasant and satisfactory. A good gun is like the good wine of the proverb – if it were made in a village, to that village men would go or send for it. The materials for gunmaking are, surely, not very expensive – processes for cheapening steel and metal generally are now carried to such an extent, and the market for metals has fallen to an extraordinary extent. Machinery and steam-power to drive it is, no doubt, a very heavy item; but are we so anxious for machinery and machine-made guns? Are you and I anxious that ten thousand other persons should shoot with guns exactly, precisely like ours in every single particular? That is the meaning of machinery. It destroys the individuality of sport. We are all like so many soldiers in an army corps firing Government Martini-Henries. In the sporting ranks one does not want to be a private. I wonder some clever workman does not go and set himself up in some village where rent and premises are low, and where a range could be got close to his door, and deliberately set down to make a name for really first-rate guns, at a moderate price, and with some pretensions to individuality and beauty. There is water-power, which is cheaper than steam, running to waste all over the country now. The old grist-mills, which may be found three or four in a single parish sometimes, are half of them falling into decay, because we eat American wheat now, which is ground in the city steam-mills, and a good deal imported ready ground as flour. Here and there one would think sufficient water-power might be obtained in this way. But even if we admit that great manufactories are extremely expensive to maintain, wages high, rent dear, premises in fashionable streets fabulously costly, yet even then there is something in the price of guns not quite the thing. You buy a gun and pay a long price for it: but if you attempt to sell it again you find it is the same as with jewellery, you can get hardly a third of its original cost. The intrinsic value of the gun then is less than half its advertised first cost-price. The second-hand gun offered to you for £20 has probably cost the dealer about £6, or £10 at the most. So that, manage it 'how you will', you pay a sum quite out of proportion to the intrinsic value. It is all very well to talk about the market, custom of trade, supply and demand, and so forth, though some of the cries of the political economist (notably the Free Trade cry) are now beginning to be questioned. The value of a thing is what it will fetch, no doubt, and yet that is a doctrine which metes out half-justice only. It is justice to the seller, but, argue as sophistically as you like, it is not justice to the purchaser.

I should recommend any gentleman who is going to equip himself as a sportsman to ask himself before he starts the question that occurred to me too late in D's case: What kind of shooting am I likely to enjoy? Then, if not wishing to go to more expense than absolutely necessary, let him purchase a gun precisely suited to the game he will meet. As briefly observed before, if the sportsman takes his sport early in the year, and practically in the summer – August is certainly a summer month – he will like a light gun; and as the grouse at that time have not packed, and are not difficult of access, a light gun will answer quite as well as a heavy arm, whose powerful charges are not required, and which simply adds to the fatigue. Much lighter guns are used now than formerly; they do not last so long, but few of us now look forward forty years. A gun of $6^1/_2$ pounds' weight will be better than anything else for summer work. All sportsmen say it is a toy and so it is, but a very deadly one. The same weapon will equally well do for the first of September (unless the weather has been very bad), and for a few weeks of partridge-shooting. But if the sport comes later in the autumn, a heavier gun with a stronger charge (alluding to guns of the old style of boring) will be found useful. For shooting when the leaves are off a heavier gun has, perhaps, some advantages.

Battue-shooting puts a great strain upon a gun, from the rapid and continuous firing, and a pheasant often requires a hard knock to grass him successfully. You never know, either, at what range you are likely to meet with him. It may be ten yards, it may be sixty; so that a strong charge, a long range, and considerable power of penetration are desirable, if it is wished to make a good performance. I recommend a powerful gun for pheasant-shooting, because probably in no other sport is a miss so annoying. The bird is large and in popular estimation, therefore ought not to get away. There is generally a party at the house at the time, and shots are sure to be talked about, good or bad, but especially the latter, which some men have a knack of noticing, though they may be apparently out of sight, and bring up against you in the pleasantest way possible: 'I say, you were rather in a fluster, weren't you, this morning? Nerves out of order – eh?' Now, is there anything so aggravating as to be asked about your nerves? It is, perhaps, from the operation of competition that pheasants, as a rule, get very little law allowed them. If you want to shine at this kind of sport, knock the bird over, no matter when you see him – if his tail brushes the muzzle of your gun: every head counts. The fact is, if a pheasant is allowed law, and really treated as game, he is not by any means so easy a bird to kill as may be supposed.

If money is no particular object, of course the sportsman can allow himself a gun for every different kind of sport, although luxury in that respect is apt to bring with it its punishment, by making him but an indifferent shot with either of his weapons. But if anyone wishes to be a really good shot, to be equipped for almost every contingency, and yet not to go to great expense, the very best course to follow is to buy two good guns, one of the old style of boring, and the other nearly or quite choked. The first should be neither heavy nor light – a moderately weighted weapon, upon which thorough reliance may be placed up to fifty yards, and that under favourable circumstances may kill much farther. Choose it with care, pay a fair price for it, and adhere to it. This gun, with a little variation in the charge, will suit almost every kind of shooting, from snipe to pheasant. The choke-bore is the reserve gun, in case of specially long range and great penetration being required. It should, perhaps, be a size larger in the bore than the other. Twelve-bore for the ordinary gun, and ten for the second, will cover most contingencies. With a ten-bore choke, hares running wild on hills without cover, partridge coveys getting up at fifty or sixty yards in the same kind of country, grouse wild as hawks, ducks, plovers, and wild-fowl generally, are pretty well accessible. If not likely to meet with duck, a twelve-bore choke will do equally well. Thus armed, if opportunity offers, you may shoot anywhere in Europe. The cylinder-bore will carry an occasional ball for a boar, a wolf, or fallow-deer, though large shot out of the choke will, perhaps, be more effective – so far, at least, as small deer are concerned. If you can afford it, a spare gun (old-style boring) is a great comfort, in case of an accident to the mechanism.

from *The Hills and the Vale*.

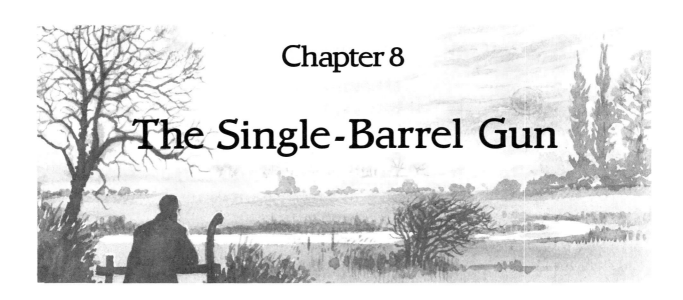

Chapter 8

The Single-Barrel Gun

The single-barrel gun has passed out of modern sport; but I remember mine with regret, and think I shall some day buy another. I still find that the best double-barrel seems top-heavy in comparison; in poising it the barrels have a tendency to droop. Guns, of course, are built to balance and lie level in the hand, so as to almost aim themselves as they come to the shoulder; and those who have always shot with a double-barrel are probably quite satisfied with the gun on that score. To me there seems too much weight in the left hand and towards the end of the gun. Quickness of firing keeps the double-barrel to the front; but suppose a repeater were to be invented, some day, capable of discharging two cartridges in immediate succession? And if two cartridges, why not three? An easy thought, but a very difficult one to realise. Something in the power of the double-barrel – the over-whelming odds it affords the sportsman over bird and animal – pleases. A man feels master of the copse with a double-barrel; and such a sense of power, though only over feeble creatures, is fascinating. Besides, there is the delight of effect; for a clever right and left is sure of applause, and makes the gunner feel 'good' in himself. Doubtless, if three barrels could be managed, three barrels would be more saleable than doubles. One gun-maker has a four-barrel gun, quite a light weight too, which would be a tremendous success if the creatures would obligingly run and fly a little slower, so that all four cartridges could be got in. But that they will not do. For the present, the double-barrel is the gun of the time.

Still I mean some day to buy a single-barrel, and wander with it as of old along the hedges, aware that if I am not skilful enough to bring down with the first shot I shall lose my game. It is surprising how confident of that one shot you may get after a while. On the one hand, it is necessary to be extremely keen; on the other, to be sure of your own self-control, not to fire uselessly. The bramble-bushes on the shore of the ditch ahead might cover a hare. Through the dank and dark-green aftermath a rabbit might suddenly come bounding, disturbed from the furrow where he had been feeding. On the sandy paths which the rabbits have made aslant up the mound, and on their terraces, where they sit and look out from under the boughs, acorns have dropped ripe from the tree. Where there are acorns there may be pheasants; they may crouch in the fern and dry grey grass of the hedge thinking you do not see them or else rush through and take wing on the opposite side. The only chance of a shot is as the bird passes a gap – visible while flying a yard – just time to pull the trigger. But I would rather have that chance than have to fire between the bars of a gate; for the horizontal lines cause an optical illusion, making the object appear in a different position from what it really is in, and half the pellets are sure to be buried in the rails. Wood-pigeons, when eagerly stuffing their crops with acorns, sometimes forget their usual caution; and, walking slowly, I have often got right underneath one – as unconscious of his presence as he was of mine, till a sudden dashing of wings against boughs and leaves announced his departure. This he always makes on the opposite side of the oak, so as to have the screen of the thick branches between himself and the gunner. The wood-pigeon, starting like this from a tree, usually descends in the first part of his flight, a gentle downward curve followed by an upward rise, and thus comes into view at the lower part of the curve. He still seems within shot, and to afford a good mark; and yet experience has taught me that it is generally in vain to fire. His stout quills protect him at the full range of the gun. Besides, a wasted shot alarms everything within several hundred yards; and in stalking with a single-barrel it needs as much knowledge to choose when not to fire as when you may.

The most exciting work with the single-barrel was woodcock shooting; woodcock being by virtue of rarity a sort of royal game, and a miss at a woodcock a terrible disappointment. They have a trick of skimming along the very summit of a hedge, and looking so easy to kill: but as they fly, the tops of tall briers here, willow-rods next, or an ash-pole often intervene, and the result is apt to be a bough cut off and nothing more. Snipes, on the contrary, I felt sure of with the single-barrel, and never could hit them so well with a double. Either at starting, before the snipe got into his twist, or waiting till he had finished that uncertain movement, the single-barrel seemed to drop the shot with certainty. This was probably because of its perfect natural balance, so that it moved as if on a pivot. With the single I had nothing to manage but my own arms; with the other I was conscious that I had a gun also. With the single I could kill farther, no matter what it was. The single was quicker at short shots – snap-shots, as at rabbits darting across a narrow lane; and surer at long shots, as at a hare put out a good way ahead by the dog.

For everything but the multiplication of slaughter I liked the single best; I had more of the sense of woodcraft with it. When we consider how helpless a partridge is, for instance, before the fierce blow of shot, it does seem fairer that the gunner should have but one chance at the bird. Partridges at least might be kept for single-barrels: great bags of partridges never seemed to me quite right. Somehow it seems to me that to take so much advantage as the double-barrel confers is not altogether in the spirit of sport. The double-barrel gives no 'law'. At least to those who love the fields, the streams, and woods for their own sake, the single-barrel will fill the bag sufficiently, and will permit them to enjoy something of the zest men knew before the invention of weapons not only of precision but of repetition: inventions that rendered them too absolute masters of the situation. A single-barrel will soon make a sportsman the keenest of shots. The gun itself can be built to an exquisite perfection – lightness, handiness, workmanship, and performance of the very best. It is said that you can change from a single-barrel shot-gun to a sporting rifle and shoot with the rifle almost at once; while many who have been used to the slap-dash double cannot do anything for some time with a rifle. More than one African explorer has found his single-barrel smooth-bore the most useful of all the pieces in his battery; though, of course, of much larger calibre than required in our fields.

from *The Open Air*

'Woodcock skimming along the hedge'
(*The Single-Barrel Gun*)

'A Kestrel hawk occasionally swoops down on a summer rick'
(*Shooting a Rabbit*)

'the cheap milliners' shops do a great business in the sale of these articles of finery'
(*The Hedgerow Sportsman*)

Chapter 9

The Boys' Guns

'Here's the place,' said Mark. 'This is where the cave ought to be,' pointing at a spot where the sandy cliff rose nearly perpendicular; 'and then we ought to have a hut over it.'

'Poles stuck in and leaning down and thatched.'

'Yes, and a palisade of thick stakes stuck in in front of the door.'

'So that no one could take us by surprise at night.'

'And far enough off for us to have our fire inside.'

'Twist bushes in between the stakes.'

'Quite impassable to naked savages.'

'How high?'

'Seven feet.'

'Or very nearly.'

'We could make a bed, and sleep all night.'

'Wouldn't it be splendid to stop here altogether?'

'First-rate; no stupid sillinesses.'

'No bother.'

'Have your dinner when you like.'

'Nobody to bother where you've been to.'

'Let's live here.'

'All right. Only we must have a gun to shoot birds and things to eat,' said Bevis. 'It's no use unless we have a gun; it's not proper, nor anything.'

'No more it is,' said Mark; 'we must have a gun. Go and stare at Frances.'

'But it takes such a time, and then you know how slow Jack is. It would take him three months to make up his mind to lend us the rifle.'

'So it would,' said Mark; "Jack's awful slow, like his old mill-wheel up there.'

'Round and round,' said Bevis. 'Boom and splash and rumble' – swinging his arm – 'round and round, and never get any farther.'

'Not an inch,' said Mark. 'Stop; there's Tom's gun.' He meant the birdkeeper's.

'Pooh!' said Bevis; 'that's rotten old rusty rubbish. Isn't there anybody we could borrow one of?'

'Nobody,' said Mark; 'they're all so stupid and afraid.'

'Donks.'

'Awful donks! Let's sell our watches and buy one,' said Mark. 'Only they would ask what we had done with our watches.'

'I know,' said Bevis, suddenly kicking up his heels, then standing on one foot and spinning round – 'I know!'

'What is it? Quick! Tell me!'

'Make one,' said Bevis.

'Make one?'

'A matchlock,' said Bevis. 'Make a matchlock. And a matchlock is quite proper, and just what they used to have – '

'But the barrel?'

'Buy an iron tube,' said Bevis 'They have lots at Latten, at the ironmonger's; buy an iron pipe, and stop one end – '

'I see,' said Mark. 'Hurrah!' and up went his heels, and there was a wild capering for half a minute.

'The bother is to make the breech,' said Bevis. 'It ought to screw, but we can't do that.'

'Ask the blacksmith,' said Mark; 'we need not let him know what it's for.'

'If he doesn't know we'll find out somehow,' said Bevis.

'Come on, let's do it directly. Why didn't we think of it before?'

They returned towards the boat.

'Just won't it be splendid,' said Mark. 'First, we'll get everything ready, and then get shipwrecked proper, and be as jolly as anything.'

"Matchlocks are capital guns,' said Bevis, 'they're slow to shoot with, you know, but they kill better than rifles. They have long barrels, and you put them on a rest to take steady aim, and we'll have an iron ramrod too, so as not to have the bother of making a place to put the rod in the stock, and to ram down bullets to shoot the tigers or savages.'

'Jolly!'

'The stock must be curved,' said Bevis; 'not like the guns, broad and flat, but just curved, and there must be a thing to hold the match; and just remind me to buy a spring to keep the hammer up, so that it shall not fall till we pull the trigger – it's just opposite to other guns, don't you see? The spring is to keep the match up, and you pull against the spring. And there's a pan and a cover to it – a bit of tin would do capital – and you push it open with your thumb. I've seen lots of matchlocks in glass cases, all inlaid gold and silver.'

'We don't want that.'

'No, all we want is the shooting. The match is the bother – '

'Would tar-cord do?'

'We'll try; first let's make the breech. Take up the anchor.'

Mark picked up the anchor, and put it on board. They launched the Pinta, and set sail homewards, Mark steering. As they were running right before the wind, the ship went at a great pace.

'That's the Mozambique,' said Bevis, as they passed through the strait where they had had to make so many tacks before.

'Land ho!' said Mark, as they approached the harbour.

'We've had a capital sail.'

'First-rate,' said Bevis. 'But let's make the matchlock.'

Now that he had succeeded in tacking he was eager to go on to the next thing, especially the matchlock gun. The hope of shooting made him three times as ready to carry out Mark's plan of the cave on the island. After furling the sails, and leaving everything shipshape, they ran home and changed their jackets, which were soaked.

Talking upstairs about the barrel of the gun, they began to think it would be an awkward thing to bring home; people would look at them walking through the town with an iron pipe, and when they had got it home, other people might ask what it was for. Presently Mark remembered that John Young went to Latten that day with the horse and cart to fetch things; now if they bought the tube, Young could call for it, and bring it in the cart and leave it at his cottage. Downstairs they ran, and up to the stables, and as they came near, heard the stamp of a cart-horse, as it came over. Mark began to whistle the tune –

> John Young went to town
> On a little pony,
> Stuck a feather in his hat,
> And called him Macaroni.

'Macaroni!' said he, as they looked in at the stable-door. 'Macaroni' did not answer; the leather of the harness creaked as he moved it.

'Macaroni!' shouted Mark. He did not choose to reply to such a nickname.

'John!' said Bevis.

'Eez – eez,' replied the man, looking under the horse's neck, and meaning 'Yes, yes.'

'Fetch something for us,' said Mark.

'Pint?' said John laconically.

'Two' said Bevis.

'Ar-right,' (all right) said John, his little brown eyes twinkling 'Ar-right you.' For a quart of ale there were few things he would not have done: for a gallon his soul would not have a moment's consideration, if it had stood in the way.

> Bell, book and candle shall not drive me back
> When pewter tankard beckons to come on!

They explained to him what they wanted him to do.

'Have you got a grate in your house?' said Bevis.

'A yarth,' said John, meaning an open hearth. 'Burns wood.'

'Can you make a hot fire – very hot – on it?'

'Rayther. Bellers.' By using the bellows.

'What could we have for an anvil?'

'Be you going a-blacksmithing?'

'Yes; what will do for an anvil?'

'Iron quarter,' said John. 'There's an ould iron in the shed. Shall I take he whoam?' An iron quarter is a square iron weight, weighing twenty-eight pounds: it would make a useful anvil. It was agreed that he should do so, and they saw him put the old iron weight, rusty and long disused, up in the cart.

'If you wants anybody to blow the bellers,' said he, 'there's our Loo – she'll blow for yer. Be you going to ride?'

'No,' said Bevis; 'we'll go across the fields.'

Away they went by the meadow footpath, a shorter route to the little town, and reached it before John and his cart. At the ironmonger's they examined a number of pipes, iron and brass tubes. The brass looked best, and tempted them, but on turning it round they fancied the join showed, and was not perfect; and of course that would not do. Nor did it look so strong as the iron; so they chose the iron, and bought five feet of stout tube – the best in the shop – with a bore of five-eights; and afterwards a brass rod, which was to form the ramrod. Brass would not cause a spark in the barrel.

John called for these in due course, and left them at his cottage. The old rogue had his quart, and the promise of a shilling, if the hearth answered for the blacksmithing. In the evening, Mark, well primed as to what he was to ask, casually looked in at the blacksmith's down the hamlet. The blacksmith was not in the least surprised; they were both old frequenters; he was only surprised one or both had not been before.

Mark pulled some of the tools about, lifted the sledge, which stood upright, and had left its mark on the iron 'scale' which lay on the ground an inch deep. Scale consists of minute particles which fly off red-hot iron when it is hammered – the sparks, in fact, which, when they go out, fall, and are found to be metal; like the meteors in the sky, the scale shooting from Vulcan's anvil, which go out and drop on the earth. Mark lifted the sledge, put it down, twisted up the vice, and untwisted it, while Jonas, the smith, stood blowing the bellows with his left hand, and patting the fire on the forge with his little spud of a shovel.

'Find anything you want,' he said presently.

'I'll take this,' said Mark. 'There's sixpence.' He had chosen a bit of iron rod, short, and thicker than their ramrod. Bevis had told him what to look for.

'All right, sir – anything else?'

'Well,' said Mark, moving towards the door, 'I don't know' – then stopping with an admirable assumption of indifference. 'Suppose you had to stop up one end of a pipe, how should you do it?'

'Make it white-hot,' said the smith. 'Bring it to me.'

'Will white-hot shut tight?'

'Quite tight – it runs together when hit. Bring it to me. I say, where's the punt?' grinning. His white teeth gleamed between his open lips – a row of ivory set in a grimy face.

'The punt's at the bottom,' said Mark, with a louring countenance.

'Nice boys,' said the smith. 'You're very nice boys. If you was mine – ' He took up a slender ash plant that was lying on the bench, and made it ply and whistle in the air.

Mark tossed his chin, kicked the door open, and walked off. 'I say! – I say!' shouted the smith. 'Bring it to me.'

'Keep yourself to yourself,' said Mark loftily. Boys indeed! The smith swore, and it sounded in his broad, deep chest like the noise of the draught up the furnace. He was angry with himself – he thought he had lost half a crown, at least, by just swishing the stick up and down. If you want half a crown, you must control your feelings.

Mark told Bevis what the smith had said, and they went to work, and the same evening filed off the end of the rod Mark had bought. Bevis's plan was to file this till it almost fitted the tube, but not quite. Then he meant to make the tube red-hot – almost white – and insert the little block. He knew that heat would cause the tube to slightly enlarge, so that the block being cold could be driven in; then as the tube cooled it would shrink in and hold it tight, so that none of the gas of the powder could escape.

The block was to be driven in nearly half an inch below the rim; the rim was to be next made quite white-hot, and in that state hammered over till it met in the centre, and overlapped a little. Again made white-hot, the overlapping (like the paper of a paper tube doubled in) was to be hammered and solidly welded together. The breech would then be firmly closed, and there would not be the slightest chance of its blowing out. This was his own idea, and he explained it to Mark.

They had now to decide how long the barrel should be. They had bought rather more tube than they wanted. Five, or even four, feet would be so long, the gun would be inconvenient to handle, though with a rest, and very heavy. In a barrel properly built up, the thickness gradually decreases from the breech to the muzzle, so that as the greatest weight is nearest the shoulder the gun balances. But this iron tube was the same thickness from one end to the other, and in consequence, when held up horizontally, it seemed very heavy at the farther extremity.

Yet they wanted a long barrel, else it would not be like a proper matchlock. Finally, they fixed on forty inches, which would be long, but not too long; with a barrel of three feet four inches they ought, they considered, to be able to kill at a great distance. Adding the stock, say fifteen inches, the total length would be four feet seven.

Next morning, taking their tools and a portable vice in a flag-basket, as they often did to the boat, they made a detour and went to John Young's cottage. On the doorstep there sat a little girl without shoes or stockings; her ragged frock was open at the neck. At first, she looked about twelve years old, as the original impression of age is derived from height and size. In a minute or two she grew older, and was not less than fourteen. The rest of the family were in the fields at work, Loo had been left to wait upon them. Already she had a huge fire burning on the hearth, which was of brick; the floor too was brick. With the door wide open they could hardly stand the heat till the flames had fallen. Bevis did not want so much flame; embers are best to make iron-hot. Taking off their jackets they set to work, put the tube in the fire, arranged the anvil, screwed the vice to the deal table, which, though quite clean, was varnished with grease that had sunk into the wood, selected the hammer which they thought would suit, and told Loo to fetch them her father's hedging-gloves.

These are made of thick leather, and Mark thought he could hold the tube better with them, as it would be warm from one end to the other. The little block of iron, to form the breech, was filed smooth, so as to just not fit the tube. When the tube was nearly white-hot, Mark put on the leather gloves, seized and placed the colder end on the anvil, standing the tube with glowing end upwards.

Bevis took the iron block, or breech-piece, with his pincers, inserted it in the white-hot tube, and drove it down with a smart tap. Some scale fell off and dropped on Mark's shirt sleeve, burning little holes through to his skin. he drew his breath between his teeth, so sudden and keen was the pain of the sparks, but did not flinch. Bevis hastily threw his jacket over Mark's arms, and then gave the block three more taps, till it was flush with the top of the tube.

By now the tube was cooling, the whiteness superseded by a red, which gradually became dull. Mark put the tube again in the fire, and Loo was sent to find a piece of sacking to protect his arm from the sparks. His face was not safe, but he had sloped his hat over it, and held his head down. There were specks on his hat where the scale or sparks had burnt it. Loo returned with a sack, when Bevis, who had been thinking, discovered a way by which Mark might escape the sparks.

He pulled the table along till the vice fixed to it projected over the anvil. Next time Mark was to stand the tube upright just the same, but to put it in the vice, and tighten the vice quickly, so that he need not hold it. Bevis had a short punch to drive the block or breech-piece deeper into the tube. Loo, blowing at the embers, with her scorched face close to the fire, declared that the tube was ready. Mark drew it out, and in two seconds it was fixed in the vice, but with the colder end in contact with the anvil underneath. Bevis put his punch on the block and tapped it sharply till he had forced it half an inch beneath the rim.

He now adjusted it for the next heating himself, for he did not wish all the end of the tube to be so hot; he wanted the end itself almost white-hot, but not the rest. While it was heating they went out of doors to cool themselves, leaving Loo to blow steadily at the embers. She watched their every motion as intent as a cat a mouse; she ran with her naked brown feet to fetch and carry; she smiled when Mark put on the leather gloves, for she would have held it with her hands, though it had been much hotter.

She would have put her arm on the anvil to receive a blow from the hammer; she would have gone down the well in the bucket if they had asked her. Her mind was full of this wonderful work – what could they be making? But her heart and soul were filled with these great big boys with their beautiful sparkling eyes and white arms, white as milk, and their wilful, imperious ways. How many times she had watched them from afar! To have them so near was almost too great a joy; she was like a slave under their feet; they regarded her less than the bellows in her hands.

Directly the tube was white-hot at the extremity, she called them. Mark set the tube up; Bevis carefully hammered the rim over, folding it down on the breech-block. Another heating, and he hammered the yielding metal still closer together, welding the folds. A third heating, and he finished it, deftly levelling the projections. The breech was complete, and it was much better done than they had hoped. As it cooled the tube shrank on the block; the closed end of the tube shrank too, and the breech-piece was incorporated into the tube itself. Their barrel was indeed far safer at the breech than scores of the brittle guns turned out cheap in these days.

Loo, seeing them begin to put their tools in the flag-basket, asked, with tears in her eyes, if they were not going to do any more? They had been there nearly three hours, for each heating took some time, but it had not seemed ten minutes to her. Bevis handed the barrel to her, and told her to take great care of it; they would come for it at night. It was necessary to smuggle it up into the armoury at home, and that could not be done by day. She took it. Had he given it in charge of a file of soldiers it could not have been safer; she would watch it as a bird does her nest.

Just then John came in, partly for his luncheon, partly out of curiosity to see how they were getting on. 'Picters you be!' said John.

Pictures they were – black and grimy, not so much from the iron as the sticks and logs, half-burnt, which they had handled; they were, in fact, streaked and smudged with charcoal. Loo instantly ran for a bowl of water for them to wash, and held the towel ready. She watched them down the hill, and wished they had kicked her or pulled her hair. Other boys did; why did not they touch her? They might have done so. Next time she thought she would put her naked foot so that they would step on it; then if she cried out perhaps they would stroke her.

In the afternoon they took two spades up to the boat. The wind had fallen as usual, but they rowed to New Formosa. The Pinta, being deep in the water and heavy with ballast, moved slowly, and it was a long row. Mark cut two sticks, and these were driven into the face of the sand cliff, to show the outline of the proposed cave. It was to be five feet square, and as deep as they could dig it.

They cleared away the loose sand and earth at the foot in a few minutes, and began the excavation. The sand at the outside was soft and crumbled, but an inch deep it became harder, and the work was not anything like so easy as they had supposed. After pecking with the spades for a whole hour, each had only cut out a shallow hole.

'This is no good,' said Mark; 'we shall never do it like this.'

'Pickaxes,' said Bevis.

'Yes; and hatchets,' said Mark. "We could chop this sand best.'

'So we could,' said Bevis. "There are some old hatchets in the shed; we'll sharpen them; they'll do.'

They worked on another half-hour, and then desisted; and cutting some more sticks stuck them in the ground in a semi-circle before the cliff, to mark where the palisade was to be fixed. The New Sea was still calm, and they had to row through the Mozambique all the way to the harbour.

In the evening they ground two old hatchets, which being much worn and chipped, had been thrown aside, and then searched among the quantites of stored and seasoned wood and poles for a piece to make the stock of the matchlock. There were beech, oak, elm, ash, fir – all sorts of wood lying about in the shed and workshop. Finally, they selected a curved piece of ash, hard and well seasoned. The curve was nearly what was wanted, and being natural it would be much stronger. This was carried up into the armoury to be shaved and planed into shape.

At night they went for the barrel. Loo brought it and Bevis, as he thought, accidentally stepped on her naked foot, crushing it between his heel and the stones at the door. Loo cried out.

'Oh dear!' said he, 'I am so sorry. Here – here's sixpence, and I'll send you some pears.'

She put the sixpence in her mouth and bit it, and said nothing. She indented the silver with her teeth, disappointed because he had not stroked her, while she stood and watched them away.

They smuggled the barrel up into the armoury, which was now kept more carefully locked than ever, and they even put it where no one could see it through the keyhole. In the morning, as there was a breeze from the westward, they put the hatchets on board the Pinta, and sailed away for New Formosa. The wind was partly favourable, and they reached the island in three tacks. The hatchets answered much better, cutting out the sand well, so that there soon began to be two holes in the cliff.

They worked a little way apart, each drilling a hole straight in, and intending to cut away the intervening wall afterwards, else they could not both work at once. By dinner-time there was a heap of excavated sand and two large holes. The afternoon and evening they spent at work on the gun. Mark shaved at the stock; Bevis filed a touch-hole to the barrel; he would have liked to have drilled the touch-hole, but that he could not do without borrowing the blacksmith's tools, and they did not want him to know what they were about.

For four days they worked with their digging at the cave in the morning, and making the matchlock all the rest of the day. The stock was now ready. It was simply curved and smoothed with sand-paper; they intended afterwards to rub it with oil till it took a little polish like the handles of axes. The stock was almost as long as the barrel, which fitted into a groove in it, and was to be fastened in with copper wire when all was ready.

Bevis at first thought to cut a mortise in the handle of the stock to insert the lock, but on consideration he feared it would weaken the stock, so he chiselled a place on the right side where the lock could be counter-sunk. The right side of the stock had been purposely left somewhat thicker for the pan. The pan was a shallow piece of tin screwed on the stock and sunk in the wood, one end closed, the other to be in contact with the barrel under the touch-hole. In this pan the priming was to be placed. Another piece of tin working on a pivot formed of a wire nail (these nails are round) was to cover the pan like a slide or lid, and keep the priming from dropping out or being blown off by the wind.

Before firing, the lid would have to be pushed aside by the thumb, and the outer corner of it was curled over like a knob for the thumb-nail to press against. The lock was most trouble, and they had to make many trials before they succeeded. In the end it was formed of a piece of thick iron wire. This was twisted round itself in the centre, so that it would work on an axle or pivot.

It was then heated red-hot, and beaten flat or nearly so. This blacksmith's work they could do at home, for no one could have guessed what it was for. One end was bent, so that though fixed at the side of the stock, it would come underneath for the trigger, for in a matchlock trigger and hammer are in a single piece. The other end curved over to hold the match, and this caused Bevis some more thought, for he could not split it like the matcholders of the Indian matchlocks he had seen in cases.

Bevis drew several sketches to try and get at it, and at last twisted the end into a spiral of two turns. The match, which is a piece of cord prepared to burn slowly, was to be inserted in the spiral, the burning end slightly projecting, and as at the spiral the iron had been beaten thin, if necessary it could be squeezed with thumb and finger to hold the cord tighter, but Bevis did not think it would be necessary to do that.

Next the spring was fixed behind, and just above the trigger end in such a way as to hold the hammer end up. Pulling the trigger you pulled against the spring, and the moment the finger was removed the hammer sprang up; this was to keep the lighted match away from the priming till the moment of firing. The completed lock was covered with a plate of brass screwed on, and polished till it shone brightly. Bevis was delighted after so much difficulty to find that it worked perfectly. The brass ramrod had been heated at one end, and enlarged there by striking it while red-hot, which caused the metal to bulge, and they now proceeded to prove the barrel before fastening it in the stock.

Powder was easily got from Latten; they bought a pound of loose powder at three-halfpence the ounce. This is like black dust, and far from pure, for if a little be flashed off on paper or white wood it leaves a broad smudge, but it answered their purpose very well. While Bevis was fretting and fuming over the lock, for he got white-hot with impatience, though he would and did do it, Mark had made a powder-horn by sawing off the pointed end of a cow's horn, and fitting a plug of wood into the mouth. For their shot they used a bag, and bought a mould for bullets.

The charger to measure the powder was a brass-drawn cartridge-case, two of which Mark had chanced to put in his pocket while they were at Jack's. It held more than a charge, so they scratched a line inside to show how far it was to be filled. At night the barrel was got out of the house, and taken up the meadows, three fields away, to a mound they had chosen as the best place. Mark brought a lantern, which they did not light till they arrived, and then put it behind the bushes, so the light should not show at a distance.

The barrel was now charged with three measures of powder and two of shot rammed down firm, and then placed on the ground in front of a tree. From the touch-hole a train of powder was laid along the dry ground round the tree, so that the gun could be fired while the gunner was completely protected in case the breech blew out.

A piece of tar-cord was inserted in a long stick split at the end. Mark wished to fire the train, and having lit the tar-cord, which burned well, he stood back as far as he could and dropped the match on the powder. Puff – Bang! They ran forward, and found the barrel was all right. The shot had scored a groove along the mound and lost itself in the earth; the barrel had kicked back to the tree, but it had not burst or bulged, so that they felt it would be safe to shoot with. Such a thickness of metal, indeed, would have withstood a much greater strain, and their barrel, rude as it was, was far safer than many flimsy guns.

The last thing to be made was the rest. For the staff they found a straight oak rod up in the lumber-room, which had once been used as a curtain-rod to an old-fashioned four-poster. Black with age, it was hard and rigid, and still strong; the very thing for their rest. The fork for the barrel to lie in was a difficulty, till Bevis hit on the plan of forming it of two pieces of thick iron wire. These were beaten flat at one end, a hole was bored in the top of the staff, and the two pieces of wire driven in side by side, when their flatness prevented them from moving. The wires were then drawn apart and hammered and bent into a half-circle on which the stock would rest.

The staff was high enough for them to shoot standing, but afterwards it was shortened, as they found it best to aim kneeling on one knee. When the barrel was fastened in the stock by twisting copper wire round, it really looked like a gun, and they jumped and danced about the bench-room till the floor shook. After handling it for some time they took it to pieces, and hid it till the cave should be ready, for so long a weapon could not be got out of the house very easily, except in sections. Not such a great while previously they had felt that they must not on any account touch gunpowder, yet now they handled it and prepared to shoot without the least hesitation. The idea had grown up gradually. Had it come all at once it would have been rejected; but it had grown so imperceptibly that they had become accustomed to it, and never questioned themselves as to what they were doing.

Absorbed in the details and the labour of constructing the matchlock, the thinking and the patience, the many trials, the constant effort had worn away every other consideration but that of success. The labour made the object legitimate. They gloried in their gun; and in fact, though so heavy, it was a real weapon capable of shooting, and many a battle in the olden times was won with no better. Bevis was still making experiments, soaking cord in various compositions of saltpetre, to discover the best slow match.

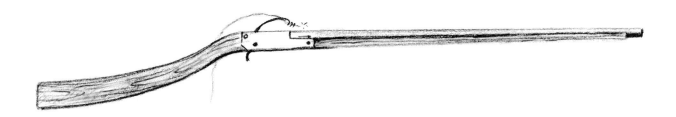

By now the cave began to look like a cave, for every morning, sailing or rowing to New Formosa, they chopped for two or three hours at the hard sand. This cave was Mark's idea; but once started at work Bevis became as eager as he, and they toiled like miners. After the two headings had been driven in about five feet, they cut away the intervening wall, and there was a cavern five feet square, large enough for both to sit down in.

They had intended to dig in much deeper, but the work was hard, and, worse than that, slow, and now the matchlock was ready they were anxious to get on the island.

'Yellow-hammers,' said Bevis, turning to his journal again; 'what are yellow-hammers?'

'Unknown birds,' said Mark. 'We don't know half the birds – nobody has ever put any name to them, nobody has ever seen them: call them, let's see – gold-dust birds -'

'And greenfinches?'

'Ky-wee – Ky-wee,' said Mark, imitating the greenfinches' call.

'That will do capital – Ky-wees,' said Bevis.

'There's a horse-matcher here,' said Mark. The horse-matcher is the bold hedge-hawk or butcher bird. 'The one that sticks the humble bees on the thorns.'

'Bee-stickers – no, bee-killers: that's down,' said Bevis. Besides which he wrote down nettle-creepers (whitethroats), goldfinch, magpie, chaffinch, tree-climber, kestrel-hawk, linnets, starlings, parrots, and parrakeets. 'I shall get up early tomorrow morning,' he said. 'I'll load the matchlock to-night, I want to shoot a heron.'

He loaded the matchlock with ball, and soon afterwards they let the curtain down at the door, and went to bed, Bevis repeating 'Three o'clock, three o'clock, three o'clock,' at first aloud and then to himself, so as to set the clock of his mind to wake him at that hour. Not long after they were asleep, Pan as usual went out for his ramble.

Bevis's clock duly woke him about three, and lifting his head he could see the light through the chinks of the curtain, but he was half inclined to go to sleep again, and stayed another quarter of an hour. Then he resolutely bent himself to conquer sleep, slipped off the bed, and put on his boots quietly, not to wake Mark. Taking the matchlock, he went out and found that it was light, the light of the moon mingling with the dawn, but it was misty. A dry vapour, which left no dew, filled the wood so that at a short distance the path seemed to go into and lose itself in the mist.

Bevis went all round the island, following the path they had made. On the Serendib side he neither saw nor heard anything, but as he came back up the other shore, a lark began to sing far away on the mainland, and afterwards he heard the querulous cry of a peewit. He walked very cautiously, for this was the most likely side to find a heron, but whether they heard his approach or saw him – for they can see almost as far as a man when standing, by lifting their long necks – he did not find any. When he reached the spot where the 'blaze' began that led to Kangaroo Hill, he fancied he saw something move in the water a long way off through the mist.

He stopped behind a bush and watched, and in a minute he was sure it was something, perhaps a duck. He set up the rest, blew the match, opened the lid of the pan, knelt down and looked along the barrel till he had got it in a line with the object. If the gun had been loaded with shot he would have fired at once, for though indistinct through the vapour he thought it was within range, but as he had ball, he wanted to see if it would come nearer, as he knew he could not depend on a bullet over thirty yards. Intent on the object, which seemed to be swimming, he began to be curious to know what it was, for it had now come a little closer, and he could see it was not a duck, for it had no neck; it was too big for a rat: it must be the creature that visited the island and took their food – the idea of shooting this animal and surprising Mark with it delighted him.

He aimed along the barrel, and got the sight exactly on the creature, then he thought he would let it get a few yards closer, then he depressed the muzzle just a trifle, remembering that it was coming towards him, and if he did not aim somewhat in front the ball would go over.

Now it was near enough he was sure – he aimed steadily, and his finger began to draw the match down when he caught sight of the creature's eye. It was Pan.

'Pan!' said Bevis. He got up, and the spaniel swam steadily towards him.

'Where have you been, sir?' he said sternly. Pan crouched at his feet, not even shaking himself first. 'You rascal – where have you been?'

Bevis was inclined to thrash him, he was so angry at the mistake he had almost made, angry with the dog because he had almost shot him. But Pan crouched so close to the ground under his very feet that he did not strike him.

'It was you who frightened the herons,' he said. Pan instantly recognised the change in the tone of his voice, and sprang up, jumped round, barked, then shook the water from his shaggy coat. It was no use evidently now to think of shooting a heron; the spaniel had alarmed them, and Bevis returned to the hut. He woke Mark, and told him.

'That's why he's so lazy in the morning,' said Mark. 'Don't you recollect? He sleeps all the morning.'

'And won't eat anything.'

'I believe he's been home,' said Mark. 'Very likely Polly throws the bones out still by his house.'

'That's it: you old glutton!' said Bevis.

Pan jumped on the bed, licked Mark, then jumped on Bevis's knees, leaving the marks of his wet paws, to which the sand had adhered; then he barked and wagged his tail as much as to say,

'Am I not clever?'

'Oh yes,' said Mark, 'you're very knowing, but you won't do that again.'

'No, that you won't sir,' said Bevis. 'You'll be tied up to-night.'

'Tight as tight,' said Mark.

'Just think,' said Bevis. 'He must have swum all down the channel we came up on the catamaran. Why, it's a hundred and fifty yards –'

'Or two hundred – only some of it is shallow. Perhaps he could bottom some part –'

'But not very far – and then run all the way home, and then all the way back, and then swim off again.'

'A regular voyage – and every night too.'

'You false old greedy Pan!'

'To leave us when we thought you were watching us while we slept.'

'To desert your post, you faithless sentinel.'

Pan looked from one to the other, as if he understood every word; he rolled up the whites of his eyes and looked so pious, they burst into fits of laughter. Pan wagged his tail and barked doubtfully; he had a shrewd suspicion they were laughing at him, and he did not like it. In fact, it was not only the fleshpots that had attracted Pan from his post and led him to traverse the sea and land, and undergo such immense exertion, it was to speak to a friend of his.

They thought it of no use to go to sleep again now, so they lit the fire and prepared the breakfast. By the time it was ready the mist had begun to clear; the sky became blue overhead, and while they were sitting at table under the awning, the first beams shot along over Serendib to their knees. Bevis said after breakfast he should practise with the matchlock, till he could hit something with the bullets. Mark wanted to explore the unknown river, and this they agreed to do; but the difficulty, as usual, was the dinner. There was nothing in their larder but bacon for rashers, and that was almost gone. Rashers become wearisome, ten times more wearisome when you have to cook them too.

Bevis said he must write his letter home – he was afraid he might have delayed too long – and take it to Loo to post that night; then he would write out a list of things, and Loo could buy them in the town, potted meats, and tongues, and soups, that would save cooking, only it was not quite proper. But Mark got over that difficulty by supposing that they fetched them from the wreck before it went to pieces.

So having had their swim, Bevis set up his target – a small piece of paper with a black spot, an inch in diameter, inked in the centre – on the teak, and fired his first shot at forty yards. The ball missed the teak tree altogether, they heard it crash into a bramble bush some way beyond. Bevis went five yards nearer next time, and the bullet hit the tree low down, two feet beneath the bull's-eye. Then he tried at thirty yards, and as before, when he practised, the ball hit the tree five or six inches lower than the mark. He tried four times at this distance, and every time the bullet struck beneath, so that it seemed as if the gun threw the ball low.

Some guns throw shot high, and some low, and he supposed the matchlock threw low. So he aimed the fifth time above the centre, and the ball grazed the bark of the tree on the right-hand side very much as Mark's had done. Bevis stepped five yards nearer, if he could not hit it at twenty-five yards, he did not think it would be his fault. He aimed direct at the piece of paper, which was about five inches square, but the bullet struck three inches beneath, though nearly in a line; that is, a line drawn down through the middle of the paper would have passed a little to the left of the bullet-hole.

This was better, so now he tried five yards closer, as it appeared to improve at every advance, and the ball now hit the paper at its lower right-hand edge. Examining the bullet-holes in the bark of the tree, and noticing they were all low and all on the right-hand side, Bevis tried to think how that could be. He was quite certain that he had aimed perfectly straight, and as he was now so accustomed to the puff from the priming, that did not disconcert him. He kept his gaze steadily along the barrel till the actual explosion occurred, and the smoke from the muzzle obscured the view. It must be something in the gun itself.

Bevis put it on the rest unloaded, aimed along, and pulled the trigger, just as he would have done had he been really about to shoot. Nothing seemed wrong. As the heavy barrel was supported by the rest, and the stock pressed firm to his shoulder, pulling the trigger did not depress the muzzle as it often does with rifles.

He aimed again, and all at once he saw that the top sight must be the cause. The twisted wire was elevated about an eighth of an inch, and when he aimed he got the top of the sight to bear on the paper, so that, instead of his glance passing level along the barrel; it rose slightly, from the breech to the top of the sight. The barrel was more than a yard long, so that when the top of the sight was in a line with the object, the muzzle was depressed exactly an eighth of an inch. An eighth of an inch at one yard, was a quarter at two yards, three eights at three yards, at four half an inch, at eight it was an inch, at sixteen two inches, and at twenty-four three inches. This was very nearly enough of itself to account for the continual misses. In a gun properly made, the breech is thicker than the muzzle, and this greater thickness, like a slight elevation, corrects the sight; the gun, too, is adjusted. But the matchlock was the same thickness from end to end, and till now, had not been tried to determine the accuracy of the shooting.

Bevis got a file and filed down the sight, till it was only a sixteenth of an inch high, and then loading again, he aimed in such a way that the sight should cover the spot he wished to strike. He could see both sides of the sight, but the exact spot he wanted to hit was hidden by it. He fired, and the ball struck the paper about an inch below and two inches to the right of the centre. Next time the bullet hit very nearly on a level with the centre, but still on the right side.

This deflection he could not account for; the sight was in the proper position, and he was certain he aimed correctly. But at last he was compelled to acknowledge that there was a deflection, and persuaded himself to allow for it. He aimed the least degree to the left of the bull's-eye – just the apparent width of the sight – and so that he could see the bull's-eye on its right, the sight well up. He covered the bull's-eye first with the sight, then slightly moved the barrel till the bull's-eye appeared on the right side, just visible. The ball struck within half an inch of the bull's-eye. Bevis was delighted.

He fired again, and the ball almost hit the very centre. Next time the bullet hit the preceding bullet, and was flattened on it. Then Mark tried, and the ball again went within a mere trifle of the bull's-eye. Bevis had found out the individual ways of his gun. He did not like allowing for the deflection, but it was of no use, it had to be done, and he soon became reconciled to the concession. The matchlock had to be coaxed like the sailing-boat and our ironclads, like fortune and Frances.

Bevis was so delighted with the discovery, that he fired bullet after bullet, Mark trying every now and then, till the paper was riddled with bullet-holes, and the teak tree coated with lead. He thought he would try at a longer range, and so went back to thirty-five yards; but though he allowed a little more, and tried several ways, it was of no use, the bullet could not be relied on. At twenty yards they could hit the bull's-eye, so that a sparrow or even a wren, would not be safe; beyond that, errors crept in which Bevis could not correct.

These were probably caused by irregularities in the rough bore of the barrel, which was only an iron tube. When the powder exploded, the power of the explosion drove the ball, by sheer force, almost perfectly straight – point-blank – for twenty or twenty-five yards. Then the twist given by the inequalities of the bore, and gained by the ball by rubbing against them, began to tell; sometimes one way, sometimes another, and the ball became deflected, and hardly twice the same way.

Bevis was obliged to be content with accuracy up to twenty, or at most twenty-five yards. At twenty he could hit an object the size of a sparrow; at twenty-five of a blackbird, after twenty-five he might miss his straw hat. Still, it was a great triumph to have found out the secret, and to be certain of hitting even at that short range.

'Why, that's how it was with Jack's rifle!' he said. 'It's only a dodge you have to find out.'

'Of course it is; if he would lend it to us, we should soon master it,' said Mark. 'And now let's go to the unknown river.'

from *Bevis*

Chapter 10

Learning to Shoot

The Governor having been rowed to the island, examined the fortifications, read the journal, and looked at the iron-pipe gun; and afterwards, reflecting upon these things, came to the conclusion that it would be safer and better in every way to let Bevis have the use of a good breech-loader. He evidently must shoot; and if so he had better shoot with a proper gun. When this decision was known, Mark's Governor could do nothing less, and so they both had good guns put into their hands.

In truth, the prohibition had long been rather hollow, more traditional than effectual. Bevis had accompanied his Governor several autumns in the field, and shot occasionally, and he had been frequently allowed to try his skill at the starlings flying to and fro the chimney. Besides which, they shot with Jack and knew all about it perfectly well. They were fortunate in living in the era of the breech-loader, which is so much safer than the old muzzle-loading gun. There was hardly a part of the muzzle-loader which in some way or other did not now and then contribute to accidents. With the breech-loader you can in a moment remove the very possibility of accident by pulling out the cartridges and putting them in your pocket.

Bevis and Mark knew very well how to shoot, both from actual, if occasional, practice, and from watching those who did shoot. The Governor, however, desirous that they should excel, gave them a good drilling in this way.

Bevis had to study his position at the moment when he stopped and lifted the gun. His left foot was to be set a little in front of the other, and he was to turn very slightly aside, the left shoulder forwards. He was never to stand square to the game. He was to stand upright, perfectly upright like a bolt. The back must not stoop nor the shoulders be humped and set up till the collar of the coat was as high as the poll. Humping the shoulders at the same time contracts the chest, and causes the coat in front to crease, and these creases are apt to catch the butt of the gun as it comes to the shoulder and divert it from its proper place.

There is no time to correct this in the act of shooting, so that the habit of a good position should be acquired that it may be avoided. He had, too, to hold his head nearly upright, and not to crane his neck forward till the cheek rested on the stock, while the head was aside in the manner of the magpie peering into a letter. He was to stand upright, with his chest open and his shoulders thrown back, like Robin Hood with his six foot yew drawing the arrow to his ear.

Bevis was made to take his double-barrel upstairs, into the best bedroom - this is the advantage of the breech-loader, take the cartridges out and it is as harmless as a fire-iron – where there was a modern cheval-glass. The mirrors downstairs were old and small, and the glass not perfectly homogeneous, so that unless the reflection of the face fell just in the centre a round chin became elongated. Before the cheval-glass he was ordered to stand sideways and throw up the gun quickly to the 'present'; then, holding it there, to glance at himself.

He saw his frame arched forward, his back bent, his shoulders drawn together, the collar of his coat up to his poll behind, the entire position cramped and awkward. Now he understood how unsightly it looked, and how difficult it is to shoot well in that way. Many good sportsmen by dint of twenty years' cramping educate their awkwardness to a successful pitch. It needs many years to do it; but you can stand upright at once.

He altered his posture in a moment, looked, and saw himself standing easily, upright but easily, and found that his heart beat without vibrating the barrel, as it will if the chest be contracted, and that breathing did not throw the gun out of level. Instead of compressing himself to the gun, the gun fitted to him. The gun had been his master and controlled him, now he was master of the gun.

Next he had to practise the bringing of the gun to the shoulder – the act of lifting it – and to choose the position from which he would usually lift it. He had his free choice, but was informed that when once he had selected it he must adhere to it. Some generally carry the gun on the hollow of the left arm with the muzzle nearly horizontal to the left. Some under the right arm with the left hand already on the stock. Some with the muzzle upwards aslant with both hands also. Now and then one waits with the butt on his hip; one swings his gun anyhow in one hand like an umbrella; a third tosses it over his shoulder with the hammers down and the trigger-guard up, and jerks the muzzle over when the game rises. Except in snap-shooting, when the gun must of necessity be held already half-way to the shoulder, it matters very little which the sportsman does, nor from what position he raises his gun.

But the Governor insisted that it did matter everything that the position should be habitual. That in order to shoot with success, the gun must not be thrown up now one way and now another, but must almost invariably, certainly as a rule, be lifted from one recognised position. Else so may trifling circumstances interfere with the precision without which nothing can be done – a crease of the coat, a button, the sleeve, or you might, forgetting yourself, knock the barrel against a bough.

To avoid these you must take your mind from the game to guide your gun to the shoulder. If you took your mind from the game the continuity of the glance was broken, and the aim snapped in two, not to be united. Therefore, he insisted on Bevis choosing a position in which he would habitually carry his gun when in the presence of game.

Bevis at once selected that with the gun in the hollow of his left arm the muzzle somewhat upwards; this was simply imitation, because the Governer held it in that way. It is, however, a good position, easy for walking or waiting for ground game or for game that flies, for hare or snipe, for everything except thick cover or brushwood, or moving in a double mound, when you must perforce hold the gun almost perpendicular before you to escape the branches. This being settled, and the Governor having promised him faithfully that if he saw him carry any other way he would lock the gun up for a week each time, they proceeded to practise the bringing of the gun up to the shoulder, that is to the present.

The left hand should always grasp the stock at the spot where the gun balances, where it can be poised on the palm like the beam of weights and scales. Instead of now taking it just in front of the trigger-guard, now on the trigger-guard, now six or seven inches in front, carelessly seizing it in different places as it happens, the left hand should always come to the same spot. It will do so undeviatingly with a very little practice and without thought or effort, as your right hand meets your friend's to shake hands.

If it comes away to the same spot the left hand does not require shifting after the butt touches the shoulder. The necessary movements are reduced to a minimum. Grasping it then at the balance, lift it gently to the shoulder, neither hastily nor slowly, but with quiet ease. Bevis was particularly taught not to throw the butt against his shoulder with a jerk; he was to bring it up with a deliberate motion of 'hefting.' 'Hefting' is weighing in the hands – you are asked to 'heft' a thing – to take it and feel, by raising it, what you think it weighs.

With this considerate ease Bevis was to 'heft' his gun to the shoulder, and only to press it there sufficiently to feel that the butt touched him. He was not to hold it loosely, nor to pull it against his shoulder as if he were going to mortise it there. He was just to feel it. If you press the gun with a hard iron stiffness against the shoulder you cannot move it to follow the flying bird: you pull against and resist yourself. On the other hand, if loosely held the gun is apt to shift.

The butt must touch his shoulder at the same place every time. Those who have not had this pointed out to them frequently have the thick or upper part of the butt high above the shoulder, and really put nothing but the narrow and angular lower part against the body. At another time, throwing it too low, they have to bend and stoop over the gun to get an aim. Or it is pitched up the chest, and not to the shoulder at all – to the edge of the chest, or again to the outside of the shoulder on the arm. They never bring it twice to the same place, and must consequently change the inclination of the head at every shot. A fresh effort has, therefore, to be gone through each time to get the body and the gun to fit.

Bevis was compelled to bring the butt of his gun up every time to the same spot well on his shoulder, between his chest and his arm, with the hollow of the butt fitting like a ball in its socket. One of the great objects of this mechanical training was that he should not have to pay the least attention to the breech of the gun in aiming. All that he had to do with was the sight. His gun, when he had thus practised, came up exactly level at once.

It required no shifting, no moving of the left hand farther up or lower down the stock; no pushing of the butt higher up the shoulder, or to this side or that. His gun touched his shoulder at a perfect level, as straight as if he had thrust out his hand and pointed with the index finger at the bird. Not the least conscious effort was needed, there was nothing to correct; above all there was not a second's interruption of the continuity of glance – the look at the game. The breech was level with the sight instantly; all he had further to do with was the sight.

With both eyes open he never lost view of the bird for the tenth of a second. The Governor taught him to keep his eyes, both open, on the bird as it flew, and his gun came up to his line of sight. The black dot at the end of the barrel – as the sight appears in the act of shooting – had then only to cover the bird, and the finger pressed the trigger. Up to the moment that the black dot was adjusted to the mark all was automatic.

The Governor's plan was first to reduce the movements to a minimum; secondly, to obtain absolute uniformity of movement; thirdly, to secure by this absolute uniformity a perfect unconsciousness of effort of movement; in short, automatic movement; and all this in order that the continuity of glance, the look at the game, might not be interrupted for the merest fraction of a second. That glance was really the aim, the gun fitted itself to the gaze just as you thrust out your index finger and point. The body really did the work of aiming itself.

Old English Pheasant
(*Nature and the Gamekeeper*)

Pine-marten
(*Nature and the Gamekeeper*)

All the mind had to do was to effect the final adjustment of the black dot of the sight. Very often when the gun was thus brought up no such adjustment was necessary, it was already there, so that there was nothing to do but press the trigger. It then looked as if the gun touched the shoulder and was discharged instantaneously.

He was to look at the bird, to keep both eyes on it, to let his gun come to his eyes, still both open, adjust the dot and fire. There was no binocular trouble because he was never to stay to run his eyes up the barrels – that would necessitate removing his glance from the game, a thing strictly forbidden. Only the dot. He saw only the dot, and the dot gave no binocular trouble. The barrels were entirely ignored; the body had already adjusted them. Only the dot. The sight – this dot – is the secret of good shooting.

The Governor said if you shut the left eye you cannot retain your glance on the bird; the barrels invariably obscure it for a moment, and the mind has to catch itself again. He would not let Bevis take his eyes off it – he would rather he missed. Bevis was also to be careful not to let his right hand hang with all the weight of his arm on the stock, a thing which doubles the labour of the left arm, as it had to uphold the weight of the gun and of the right arm too, and thus the muzzle is apt to be depressed.

He was not to blink, but to look through the explosion. Hundreds of sportsmen blink as they pull the trigger. He was to let his gun smoothly follow the bird, even in the act of the explosion, exactly as the astronomer's clockwork equatorial follows a star. There was to be continuity of glance; and thus at last he brought down his snipes right and left, as it seemed, with a sweep of the gun.

The astronomers discovered 'personal equation.' Three men are set to observe the occultation of a satellite by Jupiter, and to record the precise time by pressing a lever. One presses the lever the hundredth of a second too soon, the second the hundredth of a second too late, the third sometimes one and sometimes the other, and sometimes is precisely accurate. The mean of these three gives the exact time. In shooting one man pulls the trigger a fraction too soon, another a fraction too late, a third is uncertain. If you have been doing your best to shoot well, and after some years still fail, endeavour to discover your 'personal equation,' and by correcting that you may succeed much better. It is a common error and unsuspected, so is blinking; you may shoot for years and never know that you blink.

Bevis's personal equation was a second too quick. In this, as in everything, he dashed at it. His snipes were cut down as if you had whipped them over; his hares were mangled; his partridges smashed. The dot was dead on them, and a volley of lead was poured in. The Governor had a difficulty to get him to give 'law' enough.

He acquired the mechanical precision so perfectly that he became careless and shot gracelessy. The Governor lectured him and hung his gun up for a week as a check. By degrees he got into the easy quiet style of finished shooting.

The two learned the better and the quicker because there were two. The Governor went through the same drill with Mark, motion for motion, word for word. Then when they were out in the field the one told the other, they compared their experiences, checked each other's faults, and commended success. They learned the better and the quicker because they had no keeper to find everything for them, and warn them when to expect a hare, and when a bird. They had to find it for themselves, like Pan. Finally, they learned the better because at first they shot at anything that took their fancy, a blackbird or a wood-pigeon, and were not restricted to one class of bird with the same kind of motion every time it was flushed.

Long before trusted with guns they had gathered from the conversation they constantly heard around them to aim over a bird that flies straight away because it usually rises gradually for some distance, and between the ears for the running hare. If the hare came towards them they shot at the grass before his paws. A bird flying aslant away needs the sight to be put in front of it, the allowance increasing as the angle approaches a right angle; till when a bird crosses straight across you must allow a good piece, especially if he comes with the wind.

Two cautions the Governor only gave them: one, to be extremely careful in getting through hedges that the muzzles of their guns pointed away, for branches are most treacherous; and secondly, never to put the forefinger inside the trigger-guard till in the act of lifting the gun to the shoulder.

For a while their territory was limited, as the Governor, who shot with Mark's, did not want the sport spoiled by these beginners. But as September drew to a close they could wander almost where they liked, and in October anywhere, on promise of not shooting pheasants should they come across any.

Upon the tops of the elms the redwings sat – high-flying thrushes with a speck of blood under each wing – and called 'kuck – kuck' as they approached. When they came to the mound Bevis went one side of the hedge and Mark the other. Then at a word Pan rushed into the mound like a javelin, splintering the dry hollow 'gix' stalks, but a thorn pierced his shaggy coat and drew a 'yap' from him.

At that the hare waited no longer, but lightly leaped from the mound thirty yards ahead. Bound! Bound! Bevis poised his gun, got the dot on the fleeting ears, and the hare rolled over and was still. So they passed October, sometimes seeing a snipe on a sandy shallow of the brook under a willow as they came round a bend. The wild-fowl began to come to the New Sea, but these were older and wilder, and therefore, not easy to shoot.

One day as they were out rowing in the Pinta they saw the magic wave, and followed it up, till Mark shot the creature that caused it, and found it to be a large diving bird. Several times Bevis fired at herons as they came over. Towards the

evening as they were returning homewards now and then one would pass, and though he knew the height was too much he could not resist firing at such a broad mark as the wide wings offered. The heron, perhaps touched, but unharmed by the pellets, whose sting had left them, almost tumbled with fright, but soon recovered his gravity and resumed his course. Somewhat later the Governor, having business in London, took Bevis and Mark with him. They stayed a week at Bevis's grandpa's, and while there, for Bevis's special pleasure, the Governor went with them one evening to see a celebrated American sportsman shoot. This pale-face from the land of the Indians quite upset and revolutionised all their ideas of how to handle a gun.

The perfection of first-rate English weapons, their accuracy and almost absolute safety, has obtained for them pre-eminence over all other firearms. It was in England that the art of shooting was slowly brought to the delicate precision which enables the sportsman to kill right and left in instantaneous succession. But why then did this one thing escape discovery? Why have so many thousands shot season after season without hitting upon it? The Governor did not like his philosophy of the gun upset in this way; his cherished traditions overthrown.

There the American stood on the stage as calm as a tenor singer, and every time the glass ball was thrown up, smash! a single rifle-bullet broke it. A single bullet, not shot, not a cartridge which opens out and makes a pattern a foot in diameter, but one single bullet. It was shooting flying with a rifle. It was not once, twice, thrice, but tens and hundreds. The man's accuracy of aim seemed inexhaustible.

Never was there any exhibition so entirely genuine: never anything so bewildering to the gunner bred in the traditionary system of shooting. A thousand rifle-bullets pattering in succession on glass balls jerked in the air would have been past credibility if it had not been witnessed by crowds. The word of a few spectators only would have been disbelieved.

'It is quite upside down, this,' said the Governor. 'Really one would think the glass balls burst of themselves.'

'He could shoot partridges flying with his rifle,' said Mark.

Bevis said nothing, but sat absorbed in the exhibition till the last shot was fired and they rose from their seats, then he said, 'I know how he did it!'

'Nonsense!'

'I'm sure I do: I saw it in a minute.'

'Well, how then?'

'I'll tell you when we get home.'

'Pooh!'

'Wait and see.'

Nothing more was said till they reached home, when half scornfully they inquired in what the secret lay?

'The secret is in this,' said Bevis, holding out his left arm.

'That's the secret.'

'How? I don't see.'

'He puts his left arm out nearly as far as he can reach,' said Bevis, 'and holds the gun almost by the muzzle. That's how he does it. Here, see – like this."

He took up his grandfather's gun, which was a muzzle-loader and had not been shot off these thirty years, and put it to his shoulder, stretching out his left arm and grasping the barrels high up beyond the stock. His long arm reached within a few inches of the muzzle.

"There!" he said.

"Well, it was like that," said Mark. "He certainly did hold the gun like that."

'But what is the difference?' said the Governor. 'I don't see how it's done now.'

'But I do,' said Bevis. 'Just think: if you hold the gun out like this, and put your left arm high up, as near the muzzle as you can, you put the muzzle on the mark directly instead of having to move it about to find it. And that's it, I'm sure. I saw that was how he held it directly, and then I thought it out."

'Let me,' said Mark. He had the gun and tried, aiming quickly at an object on the mantelpiece. 'So you can – you put the barrels right on it.'

'Give it to me,' said the Governor. He tried, twice, thrice, throwing the gun up quickly.

'Keep your left hand in one place," said Bevis. 'Not two places – don't move it.'

'I do believe he's right,' said the Governor.

'Of course I am,' said Bevis in high triumph. 'I'm sure that's it.'

'So am I,' said Mark.

'Well, really, now I come to try, I think it is,' said the Governor.

'It's like a rod on a pivot,' said Bevis. 'Don't you see the left hand is the pivot: if you hold it out as far as you can, then the long part of the rod is your side of the pivot, and the short little piece is beyond it – then you've only got to move that little piece. If you shoot in our old way then the long piece is the other side of the pivot, and of course the least motion makes such a difference. Here, where's some paper – I can see it, if you can't.'

With his pencil he drew a diagram, being always ready to draw maps and plans of all kinds. He drew it on the back of a card that chanced to lie on the table.

'There, that long straight stroke – that's the line of the gun – it's three inches long – now, see, put A at the top, and B at the bottom like they do in geometry. Now make a dot C on the line just an inch above B. Now suppose B is where the stock touches your shoulder, and this dot C is where your hand holds the gun in our old way at home. Then, don't you see, the very least mistake at C, ever so little, increases at A – ratio is the right word, increases in rapid ratio, and by the time the shot gets to the bird it's half a yard one side.'

'I see,' said Mark. 'Now do the other.'

'Rub out the dot at C,' said Bevis. 'I haven't got any india-rubber, you suppose it's rubbed out: now put the dot two inches above B, and only one inch from the top of the gun at A. That's how he held it, with his hand at this dot, say D.'

'I think he did,' said the Governor.

'Now you think,' said Bevis. 'It takes quite a sweep, quite a movement to make the top A incline much out of the perpendicular. I mean if the pivot, that's your hand, is at D, a little mistake does not increase anything like so rapidly. So it's much more easy to shoot straight quick.'

They considered this some while till they got to understand it. All the time Bevis's mind was working to try and find a better illustration, and at last he snatched up the Governor's walking stick. The knob or handle he held in his right hand, and that represented the butt of the gun which is pressed against the shoulder. His right hand he rested on the table, keeping it still, as the shoulder would be still. Then he took the stick with the thumb and finger of his left hand about one third of the length of the stick up. That was about the place where a gun would be held in the ordinary way.

'Now look,' he said, and keeping his right hand firm, he moved his left an inch or so aside. The inch at his hand increased to three or four at the point of the stick. This initial error in the aim would go on increasing till at forty yards the widest spread of shot would miss the mark.

'And now this way,' said Bevis. He slipped his left hand up the stick to within seven or eight inches of the point. This represented the new position. A small error here – or lateral motion of the hand – only produced a small divergence. The muzzle, the top of the stick, only varied from the straight line the amount of the actual movement of the left hand. In the former case a slight error of the hand multiplied itself at the muzzle. This convinced them.

'How we shall shoot!' said Mark. 'We shall beat Jack hollow!'

They returned home two days afterwards, and immediately tried the experiment with their double-barrels. It answered perfectly. As Bevis said, the secret was in the left arm.

When about to shoot, grasp the gun at once with the left hand as high up the barrel as possible without inconveniently straining the muscles, and so bring it to the shoulder. Push the muzzle up against the mark, as if the muzzle were going to actually touch it. The left hand aims, positively putting the muzzle on the game. All is centred in the left hand. The left hand must at once with the very first movement take hold high up, and must not be slid there, it must take hold high up as near the muzzle as possible without straining. The left hand is thrust out, and as it were put on the game. Educate the left arm; teach it to correspond instantaneously with the direction of the glance; teach it to be absolutely stable for the three necessary seconds; let the mind act through the left wrist. The left hand aims.

This is with the double-barrel shot gun; with the rifle at short sporting ranges the only modification is that as there is but one pellet instead of two hundred, the sight must be used and the dot put on the mark, while with the shot gun in time you scarcely use the sight at all. With the rifle the sight must never be forgotten. The left hand puts the sight on the mark, and the quicker the trigger is pressed the better, exactly reversing tradition. A slow, deliberative rifleman was always considered the most successful, but with the new system the fire cannot be delivered too quickly – the very instant the sight is on the mark, thus converting the rifleman into a snap-shooter. Of course, it is always understood that this applies to short sporting ranges; the method is for sporting only, and does not apply to long range.

One caution is necessary in shooting like this with the double-barrel. Be certain that you use a first-class weapon, quite safe. The left hand being nearly at the top of the barrel, the left hand itself, and the whole length of the left arm are exposed in case of the gun bursting. I feel that some cheap guns are not quite safe. With a good gun by a known maker there is no danger.

The American has had many imitators, but no one has reached his degree of excellence in the new art which he invented. Perhaps it is fortunate that it is not everyone who can achieve such marvellous dexterity, for such shooting would speedily empty every cover in the country.

Big Jack learned the trick from them in a very short time. His strong left arm was as steady as a rock. He tried it with his little rifle, and actually killed a hare, which he started from a furze bush, as it ran, with a single bullet. But the Governor, though convinced, would not adopt the new practice. He adhered to the old way, the way he had learned as a boy. What we learn in youth influences us through life.

But Bevis and Mark and Big Jack used it with tremendous effect in snap-shooting in lanes where the game ran or flew across, in ferreting when the rabbits bolted from hole to hole, in snipe shooting, in hedge-hunting, one each side – the best of all sport, for you do not know what may turn out next, a hare, a rabbit, a partridge from the dry ditch, or a woodcock from the dead leaves.

from *Bevis*

Chapter 11

Straight Shooting

The Squire was a good shot. He handled his double-barrel in the manner authorized by the experience of sportsmen. When a covey was flushed, or a hare started from her form, his gun came easily to the shoulder, his left hand supported it slightly in front of the trigger-guard, and, although long practice had rended aiming in the full sense of the word unnecessary, he did not fire till the sight was on the game. There was a short but appreciable interval between the levelling of the barrel and the flash, a fatal moment of adjustment, and this calm in effort seemed to control success, for he rarely missed. The bird fell without folding her wings; the hare stopped not to sit up but to lie limp and extended.

Perhaps the most eager time in shooting is when you look through the smoke to see what has been effected. Hardly any length of practice will quite efface the sense of expectation: the gunner must look, even if he know he has killed.

The Squire's anticipation was often fulfilled; yet he did miss, and that many more times in the course of a day than sportsmen in this somewhat boastful age care to acknowledge. There seems a feverish dread lest the certainty of success should be broken by the failure of a single cartridge: a tension and anxiety as if such an incident were intolerable guilt.

The Squire's field education was completed before this fierce gamble of competition began. he did not feel that he had fallen out of the front rank even if now and then both barrels sent their contents whistling wide into the uninjured air. I think he enjoyed the stubble all the more.

This old-fashioned spirit, antecedent to the modern ideas of machine-precision, rather revolted from the patent shooting recently exhibited. Curiosity was excited, but the Squire did not much admire and was entirely devoid of emulation. Yet it quite upset all his philosophy of the gun, and perhaps that was why he did not like it. The delivery of a thousand rifle bullets pattering in succession on glass balls jerked into the air, infallibly shattering these bubbles as they rose over-threw all tradition. The bitterness was in the extreme simplicity of the trick: that no one ever thought of it. Apart, of course, from practice and natural dexterity, it merely consists in extending the left arm to nearly its full reach and holding the barrel close to the muzzle. On the appearance of the game, at once grasp the gun with the left hand, as high up the barrel as possible without inconveniently straining the muscles, and lift the left hand first, so that the muzzle may come up to the 'present' a moment before the right hand brings the butt to the shoulder. All depends on the left hand, which is centre of this method, and which must be thrust out at the mark much the same as if it grasped a pistol.

To understand the new exercise correctly, try the experiment of holding the gun steady at the 'present' in this way, and, while keeping the left hand still, lower the right, letting the butt drop several inches and then raising it again. While the muzzle thus remains pointed by the left hand, the least motion of the right hand completes the position: the right, indeed, has little to do except to pull the trigger. Thumb and fingers may meet round the barrels, if preferred, for still greater stability of the left hand, as that is somewhat easier to the muscles than when the palm is hollowed but the fingers are only partly closed. Seize the barrels firmly and push the muzzle up against the mark, just as if the muzzle were going to actually touch it. Thus, the left hand aims: in the most literal sense, positively putting the muzzle on the game.

With the double-barrel shotgun no sight is required; the hand need not be bent or one eye shut, or any process of aiming gone through at all. Simply seize the barrels as near the top as convenient to the length of the arm when not unnaturally stretched, raise the barrels the fraction of a moment before the butt, look fixedly at the game, and pull the trigger: the quicker, the better. Once more let it be repeated, all is centred on the left hand: the left hand must at once, with the very first movement, take hold, high up, and must not be slid there presently; the left hand must be lifted earliest; the left hand must be thrust out at and as if it were put on the game; the left hand aims. (Educate the left arm: teach it to correspond instantaneously with the direction of the glance; teach it to be absolutely stable for the three necessary seconds; let the left hand be your top sight; let the mind act through your left wrist. With practice, such snap-shooting is possible, as has been seen in our fields.)

The trick is not in the least difficult, though so opposite to all former ideas, which attached no special value to the left hand except as a support. To attain the greatest stability consistent with ease, the usual position of the left hand is just in front of, or, with some, partly over, the trigger-guard, much about the centre of gravity of the gun. This minimizes the weight: the barrels and the stock are balanced. The new position abolishes the balance altogether - at first it seems peculiar, but soon becomes natural: and thus the most cherished traditions of shooting are put aside.

With a rifle, some little modification of these instructions is necessary. There being but one pellet, it must be delivered with accuracy, and the top sight is of the utmost importance. That a full view of it may be obtained, the thumb and fingers of the left hand must not meet, as is permissible when shooting with the double-barrel. It should be hollowed, the barrel resting on it exactly as in the old position, but must be as near the muzzle as compatible with common sense: the nearer, the better. In every other respect, the new method, with the rifle, is precisely the same as in the gun. The left hand puts the top sight at once on the mark, with such precision and ease that, with practice, a running hare or rabbit could certainly be hit. The quicker the trigger is pressed, the better: here, again, the new method directly traverses tradition. A slow, deliberative rifleman was always considered, and often with good reason, as the most successful; but, with the new position, fire cannot be delivered too quickly – the very instant the top sight is on the mark – thus converting the rifleman into a snapshooter. Instead of searching about for the mark, like an astronomer for some faint star with his telescope, as was usually the case under the old style, in the new, the muzzle, the top sight, is put immediately on it, held there rigid, and the bullet has done its work before an old style rifleman could have got his weapon comfortably settled at his shoulder.

The thing is capable of mathematical demonstration. Anyone, however, may convince himself of the fact by a simple experiment with a walking-stick.

Take the crook or knob in the right hand and place that hand upon the table. This represents the butt of the gun pressed to the shoulder, which is the fixed point. Put the thumb and finger of the left hand on the stick, about a third of its length, reckoning from the right. Then you have the gun held in the ordinary position. Now, while retaining the right hand still (as the shoulder would be), move the left hand laterally either way an inch or so. An inch of movement at the left hand causes thrice the deflection at the fore end of the stick. A mere sixteenth of an inch trebles itself there - the angle widens. This initial error in the aim goes on increasing, every yard, till at the mark forty yards away the largest spread of shot fails of effect. On a smaller scale, the same experiment may be carried out with a cedar pencil and always with the same result: the closer the left hand is placed to the right, the more a slight initial movement increases the error (or widens the angle) at the top, or muzzle.

On the reverse, the opposite effect is produced. While still holding the crook or knob of the stick steady with the right hand, extend the left arm and place the thumb and finger on the stick as near the top as you conveniently can. Then you have the new position. It now requires a large lateral motion of the left hand to produce an error or divergence equal in extent to that which previously resulted from the least movement. The muzzle, or top of the stick, only varies from the straight line to the amount of the actual movement of the left hand; in the former case, a slight error of the hand multiplied itself at the muzzle.

As the arm is not a mechanical rest of iron which can be fixed irrespective of circumstances, but is endowed with feeling, with a beating pulse, muscles that relax or contract in response to the variation of the will, and is therefore uncertain in its action, anything that reduces these vibrations to a minimum must improve the shooting. The object is to get the eye, the top sight of the rifle or the muzzle of the gun, and the game, all three distinctly in a line with each other. When holding the gun, as the walking-stick was first held, say, at a third of its length, the muzzle has to go searching about for the mark. If practice brings up the gun true in general direction, still it has to be adjusted; and when adjusted, the faintest error of the arm is doubled at the muzzle.

So that the new position is not only correct mathematically, it is best suited to the practical difficulties of shooting. You do not seem to depend on the gun, but simply on the left hand. You stretch out your left hand and, as it were, put on the mark, and immediately fire.

All this applies, of course, to sporting only: that is, to shooting at short ranges. At the long distance target it would not answer. It applies also only to quick shooting. It is not possible to shoot slowly in the new position, not meaning the number of discharges but the time occupied in aiming. If anyone wishes to make a steady, slow aim, the old position is best. Indeed, it is scarcely possible to aim long – to dwell on the aim – in the new way: the arm extended very nearly to its full length soon begins to quiver a little; and when once the vibration begins it cannot be quite stopped unless it is lowered for a moment. When first raised, the muzzle is at once put on the mark; the arm retains it there, then fire – whether shotgun or rifle.

As most sporting, even with the improved rifles, takes place at short range, the value of the new method appears very high. One caution it is as well to add: and that is, not to try this plan except with a perfectly trustworthy gun. Since breech-loading has become universal, guns burst less frequently, as it is not possible to double charge, and the barrels can be looked through lest any dirt should choke them. But, even now, guns do burst occasionally.

I have no possible grounds upon which to go, but I have long had a faint suspicion that, since breech-loading was adapted to every gun, many guns have been turned out only just thick enough in the metal to bear the expected strain, and without any provision, as it were, against the chance of extra pressure. As the left hand is much exposed in the new position, let no one use it unless quite certain of his gun.

When a lad, I often used to shoot sparrows at a trap, and became very expert at it; and I remember that my success was due to the manner in which I held the gun, grasping it before giving the signal with the left hand where that hand would have to sustain it when at the shoulder. The difference was that not a second was lost in the adjustment of the left hand or support, and it had not to be slid into position. There was nothing to do but to keep the eyes fixed on the ground about six inches in front of the trap, give the signal, fling up the gun, and pull the trigger. This was, in a measure, an approach to the new position. But then all the sparrows started from the same spot. The new position puts the muzzle of the double-barrel at once on the flying game, just as if the top touched the partridge.

'There are not ten acres on this estate,' wrote the Squire, 'that could be better farmed than at present. The woods perhaps might, theoretically, be ploughed and planted, but in fact they occupy the worst part of the property, and, if cut down, any practical farmer will tell you, would only make thin hillside grazing ground. The strip of marshy pasture in the bottom below cannot be drained unless the little lake or pond were emptied, to do which the county, or the government, must construct a canal several miles long.

'As commercial principles are to be applied to land-owning, on a balance of profit and loss, the woods, as they stand, pay well. In proportion to the labour employed, the return is high. There are, however, some outlying copses which could be spared, and which stand on a good land: in all, I think they equal about twenty acres. The tenants would object, as they would have to pay much higher for poles, flukes, hurdles, and all the endless wood used on farms, if every ash and hazel stole were grubbed.

'I have no hesitation in asserting that if the management of the estate were vested in a council of the tenants they would carefully provide for the retention of a large extent of wood.

'The American who was over here last spring told me that the farmers in his country always set aside so much of their farms for the growth of timber. It is found to be absolutely necessary.

'I keep up a good head of pheasants, but I do not think I am extravagant in proportion to the acreage of wood. Some people object to pheasants on sentimental grounds: well, they can certainly point the finger at me in this respect. But the tenants make no grievance of it – I have had no complaint whatever since I gave up the rabbits about ten years ago. They have the hares, too, after September; that is, after my party has been round. We are on the best of terms, but still there is an indefinite something in the air which pushes on the attack upon the land, and most people who have property recognize the cloud in the sky which, like the dust raised by an army, presages the assault.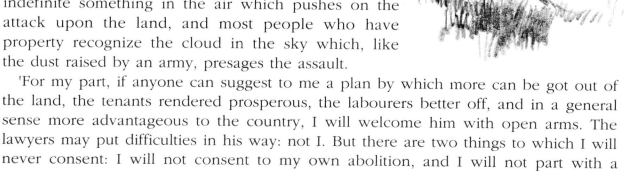

'For my part, if anyone can suggest to me a plan by which more can be got out of the land, the tenants rendered prosperous, the labourers better off, and in a general sense more advantageous to the country, I will welcome him with open arms. The lawyers may put difficulties in his way: not I. But there are two things to which I will never consent: I will not consent to my own abolition, and I will not part with a single yard of ground. That premised, I will cordially assist any attempt to increase the production.

'The advocates of Land Reform all seem to start from the supposition that the landowners are a party of obstruction: that they will oppose every project of improvement. I deny this most emphatically. If they can propose any legislation short of abolishing me, or actually taking my land from me, I shall make no opposition. A prospect of getting more out of the land would, on the contrary, fill me with delight. But I want an answer to this question: what can you do with the land more than has already been done?

'I do not believe there is a single thing that has been recommended that has not been tried on my property. The turnips come first: it is a long time ago now; still, they may be said to represent, in agriculture, what steam represents in commerce, i.e., forward motion. Certainly we have grown turnips enough, and other roots in vast quantities, and continue to do so, but we cannot do any more with them than we have done. We shall not cease to produce roots, but the limit of what can be effected with roots has been reached.

'Improvement of animal shape was the next great step: we were instructed to produce both sheep and cattle perfect in form. That too, has been done. We ourselves have done it here – Butler, up on the Downs, has taken a whole list of prizes for sheep; that American I alluded to came over on purpose to purchase some of the breed. And Thorn, whom you will remember (he's not the largest tenant but he's a monied man) has been equally successful with his shorthorns. His holding is on our arable plain. Shorthorns – what a volume of departed hope might not be written about them! They have been the Brighton 'A' Stock of Agriculture – the subject of wildest speculation, now up, now down, fluctuating not on instrinsic value but on mere opinion.

'So we have done all that can be done with sheep and cattle. We shall still keep sheep and cattle, but the limit of what can be effected with improved breeds has been reached.

'Suppose the State owned this property and brought the vast revenue collected in England to bear upon it: suppose a million per annum were spent here in improving our sheep and cattle, we should get no further. Millions have already been expended by private individuals, and, what is of more value than mere money, time, skill, and in its way, genius. The practical limit has been reached.

'Steam-ploughing ranks next. We have used the steam-plough. My father, as you know, was especially interested in the steam-plough. He spent time and money on it, and gave every facility to tenants who wished to try it. Thorn has a pair of engines and tackle, and in fine weather I constantly hear them at work. My father fancied the steam-plough particularly suited to our local arable plain; and there's no doubt it did some good. But then, you see, we have got the steam-plough, and we can't go any further. If the State itself were the owner of Thorn's farm, it could not employ more than one set of tackle on it. The limit of what can be done with the steam-plough has been reached.

'It is the same with guano. We have been rather more lavish with manure than is customary, as we found it answer as well as, or better than, anything. All the tenants used it, till their losses compelled them to reduce expenditure; and even now they are using as much as ever again in hope of recouping themselves. Still, we cannot go any further. Beyond a certain quantity it is no use putting any more.

'As for draining, all the draining that could be done has been done; in some places I am told we have overdone the draining, and we are rather discouraged with it. That is because so much of the land here drains itself sufficiently – a thing we did not appreciate until we had tried our hands at improving Nature, and failed. I say 'we' advisedly, for my father, five-and-thirty years, perhaps forty years, ago began to work with his tenants in these things. They have had to pay rent, of course; but they have practically governed the estate as much as if they had formed a council board. All their ideas have been carried out, so far as was practicable, for you know that matters are very different, when you come to deal with substantial things like land, than the theory looks on paper. I have gone on with the same system. There's nothing peculiar in it: ours is not a solitary instance; in fact, every owner I know, with the exception of two or three who are in pecuniary difficulties, is now doing the same, not from sentimental reasons but because they believe it the most profitable policy.

'Well! now I want to know what can you do with the land more than has already been done?

'Simultaneously with these purely farming steps in advance, general improvements have taken place all over the property. My father established a sort of sinking-fund for these purposes – it was (and is) the rent from two small dairy farms he chanced to inherit unexpectedly. Every year the rent from these has been steadily applied to the building of new cattle-sheds, enlargement of farm-houses, making new roads, putting up fresh cottages, and you would be surprised at what has been effected in this way in the process of time.

'Capital sums have also been expended for the same ends at intervals, and I really do not think any reasonable request has been refused: my father refused to put in some bow windows to a farmstead; and I myself refused to build a tenant a new house, in fact a villa, his idea being that his bailiff could live in the old one.

'I own that many of the cottages in...* are defective: I don't think there is any serious sanitary fault, for, fortunately, there is plenty of pure spring water – which is so great an advantage to a village. I cannot rebuild the whole place: the State itself could not do it, without heavily taxing somebody; and, even then, could not let expensive buildings at the extremely low rental within the agricultural labourers' means.

'There are plenty of allotments, and always have been ever since I can remember. Wages are not high – the tenants think them too high – but I am writing from the broadest point of view, and I must say that wages are not high. I do not think I can alter that. Even the State itself could not fix the rate of wages.

'I am not so bigoted but that I can see a great deal of creaking in the machinery of our agricultural life – hard work and not too bountiful food, and trouble, and so on. But what am I to do? Am I a demi-god? What could the State itself do? For everything human is more or less crank.

'Lastly, everybody told us that we ought to remit the rent: but I will leave that to my next letter.'

'Everybody insisted, as I said before,' the Squire continued, 'that we ought to remit the rent. We *did* remit the rent. If the State had been landlord, instead of me, what more could it have done? I remitted my rent; but one thing is quite certain, the State did *not* remit its rent. A very cruel and exacting taskmaster, *sans compassion*, is the State. In the year of deepest depression, we were called upon for rates and taxes just the same as in the most profitable season. This should not be forgotten by those who are so anxious to have the State as their landlord.

'I think you will now admit that we have tried everything; that we have done everything practicable with the land that could be done; and that the limit has been

*blank in the manuscript.

reached. Two remedies alone remain, over one of which we have no power, and to the other (if it is a remedy) I will never consent. One is the removal of the taxation which presses so heavily on the land: the other is communism. The first would undoubtedly prove a great relief, though I do not think it would effect everything (see what I shall say presently about the Market); and I want to know how long other portions of the community would consent to one class alone being freed from taxation! There would soon be an outcry. If the remission of taxation was only partial, then I say deliberately that it would not be effectual. As to communism, I will be guillotined before I will consent to it.

'How completely outside our feelings are those who talk so glibly of compensation! They say: 'You would be well paid for the land taken from you to be sub-divided among the people at large.' Now, how utterly void of understanding us must be those who suggest that money would repay us! How can they compensate us? We have held part of this estate since the time of Henry...* and the rest since Edward VI. Just consider a moment what root we have taken in all these years! If you plant shrubs in a nursery garden, you plant them to sell, and money will compensate you for their removal. But we did not plant our trees to sell. We like to see them increase and flourish, and, by and by, to watch their slow decay. I declare that a hollow old oak is a noble sight.

'Here I take my stand! By main force I may be abolished – not otherwise. Only I wish it to be well understood that I and others in my position, are not a party of obstruction, as it pleases certain people to suppose us. Any legislation, any suggestion you or anybody else can put forward to improve the condition of the tenants, the labourers, the village, the land itself, I shall welcome with open arms.

'But I do not think anything practical remains to be proposed. As for the abolition of primogeniture, the easier transfer of land, the repeal of the landlord's right as first creditor, these are mere side-issues and blind alleys, and would not, if granted, cause one single extra ear of wheat to be grown, nor give us one single extra shilling per quarter. The lawyers seem determined to fight for these matters, inch by inch: and well they may, since they obtain so rich a harvest as the custodians of our titles. I cannot say that I care much: perhaps I do not understand these subtleties. I do, however, doubt whether the repeal of my right as first creditor in case of a tenant's bankruptcy would be much to the farmer's advantage. It would only enable him to borrow a little more, and already the tenant farmers are deep enough in debt. If the only way to get more capital put into the soil is to enlarge facilities for borrowing, we had better be without it.

'So I do not think anything practical remains to be proposed. The American who came over to buy some sheep of Butler – he was quite a gentleman, and we had many conversations – well, I asked him if he could suggest anything. He went all over the place, and he considered, and said there was but one thing – would I take offence? I said: 'Certainly not.' 'Well then, Squire,' said he: 'the only thing I can see is to get rid of you!' I asked him, in reply, whether it was not true that farmers in the United States were in the hands of the money-lender and were paying him such interest that it amounted to a rent. He owned it was true, but hit me in return: for, he added, 'the tenant here pays the money-lender, as in the United States, but also pays the landlord.' But I went on to ask who, if I were abolished, was to occupy my place. He said: 'Of course, the State – that vague, impersonal corporation.' And then I asked: 'If a man emigrates to America, does he find a substantial stone or brick built homestead, ranges of solidly constructed, slated cattle-sheds, well cultivated fields, trimmed hedges, good private roads: in short, a ready-made farm waiting for

*A blank in the manuscript.

him as a free present from the State on his arrival?' My friend smiled sarcastically, and said: 'That kind of thing costs dollars.' Then I pointed out that the State here would not supply such farms for nothing: the tenants must borrow the capital to buy them, and the interest on that capital would equal the rent paid to me; they must, too, borrow the capital to put stock on and to work it, and the interest on that would represent the money-lender. I fancy they would find the State and the money-lender harder landlords than me. Money-lenders are not renowned for sympathy, or for consideration towards their debtors. They are not famous for remitting their rents, that is, their interest: still less when they deem their capital in danger - for the right of first creditor is to be repealed. Certainly the State does not remit its rent: most certainly the State insists on its right as first creditor.

'My American friend was candid enough to own that it was rather more of a tangle than it looked: the brambles grew so thick, said he, in the old country – you could not move without catching your foot in one. Still, he seemed to have a lingering desire to see me got rid of: he evidently had a feeling that I was in the way. I do not deny it. I know I am in the way. So, too, the farmer is in the way of the labourer; and the labourer, with his cottage and garden, is in the way of the tramp along the road, who has none, and would much like to take the loaf from the shelf within – only the labourer has locked the door. Just so! I am in the way; and I will not consent to my own abolition. I will not consent to communism – neither, I am certain, would my American friend, who had so high an opinion of dollars but not the slightest desire to share them with other people.

'But, though I will not consent to communism, it is a great mistake to suppose that I object to the sub-letting of the land, to the multiplication of homesteads, to the increase of the rural population. Precisely the reverse! If I could get five hundred tenants on the estate instead of fifty, my income would be trebled. I should be only too glad to split every farm up into allotments and let every single acre to a separate tenant at allotment rentals. Why, I should indeed be rich! Only let a thousand people apply to me for an acre each, and they shall have it. By Jove, I should think so! The idea is too ravishingly pleasant to dream of. Look, too, at the influence it would give me - like a colliery, or iron-works, or cotton-mills. I assure you, I will give every facility. I would go to Parliament for a Private Act, if necessary. Send me the thousand tenants quick! - But no. No such thing. The world is old, and the general sense of the public not to be so deceived. Even the masses who have had no experience of farming instinctively know better: else the mechanics from Leeds and Birmingham would come crowding down here and squat on my land, like the gold-diggers. I wish to heaven they would! A very small royalty would satisfy me. But, though they have had these things preached at them for so many years, they instinctively know better. Every man's sense tells him that my estate has nothing to offer him. Beechmast and acorns are not gold dust. if only someone could discover a plant which would yield a monetary return when cultivated in plots like large gardens, then the difficulty would be solved. The thousand tenants would soon be a fact, and the land question would settle itself. But grapes will not flourish: nor olive trees, nor figs; tobacco, they say, might be grown, to some extent, but the excise is heavy – nor could we hope to compete with Virginia. As for fruit and vegtables – fruit – is the most uncertain of crops; for vegetables there is not sufficient demand. Just in the neighbourhood of cities, it may answer: but not over the country at large. Therefore, I do not see how small tenants or acre-farmers are ever to succeed. But it is not true that I oppose their introduction.

'Our only reason in favour of large farms was, and is, that wheat and meat can best be produced on a large scale. In fact, you cannot profitably produce them on a small one. In America I read of wheat-fields so immense that it occupies a team an entire day to cross them – an entire day to plough a single furrow! How is an acre-farmer to compete with that? Large farmers with considerable capital cannot do it; and the fact is recognized by reformers, who advise us to grow strawberries, beetroot for sugar, to establish distilleries for mangold spirit, and many other things of like character, which possibly might prove successful if we could be as sure of sunshine as they are abroad. Instead of which, the more meterological observations are made, the more uncertain our climate is found to be.

'Nevertheless, it is not the weather nor the seasons that has depressed us: such seasons have happened before, and even worse, and we have risen again. But, in those days, there was practically no America. By slow degrees, the imports of corn and other foods have brought us on our knees. We cannot compete against it under any imaginable system. The wheat average, as published at this moment, is about 42s. But it is well known that the average, so-called, is fixed too high: and much corn has been sold at 36s, that is, 18s. a sack. In short, to sum up in a word, it is the Market that is the cause of our difficulties.

'The Market is down, and will remain down, and we are down with it. Sub-divide, spilt up the land as you will – drive me out by main force – but you cannot live against that Market. The greatest fallacy I have seen is the argument some have put forth that, by and by, the Americans will not find it possible to produce wheat to sell to us at a profit, on account of the increased cost of production and their own extraordinary increase of population: The reverse is the fact. The more their population increases, the more wheat and meat they send us; and at a cheaper price, because the means of communication are extended. The fact is, they must grow wheat, whether it pays or not; it is the only thing they can grow for which they can get ready cash.

'From what the American gentleman told me, I understand that for years past this has been the case. In a different way, they are in the same predicament that we are: we do not know what to produce but wheat and meat; nor do they, only they have the whip hand of us. On their immense quantities, too, a very slight percentage pays.

'I think, as the means of communication are increased, wheat and meat will come to us cheaper and cheaper, not only from America but from all parts of the world. All other matters, in comparison, are trifles – it is the Market that rules us.

'In conclusion, I have only to repeat that, if I am driven out by main force, the State will be found a harsher landlord than the Squire. If the land is divided into fractions, the produce from it will immediately be diminished by at least a third. The great wheat countries will then not only have the whip hand of us: they will put the bit in our mouths. For it is the production of English wheat and meat – produced at a terrible cost of capital, time, skill, care, and in face of every discouragement, that has hitherto compelled the foreigner to sell cheap to undersell us. He does not benevolently sell cheap for the good of Leeds and Birmingham. If he could get rid of us, if the English farmer were suppressed altogether, loud would be his rejoicings, as he could then sell dear.

'I ask: What more can be done with the land than has already been done? Give me a suggestion, and I will welcome it cordially. I am the willing agent of improvement, ready with capital; and sympathy: I am not a party of obstruction; nor am I inexorable, like the State. This is my case.'

from *The Old House at Coate*

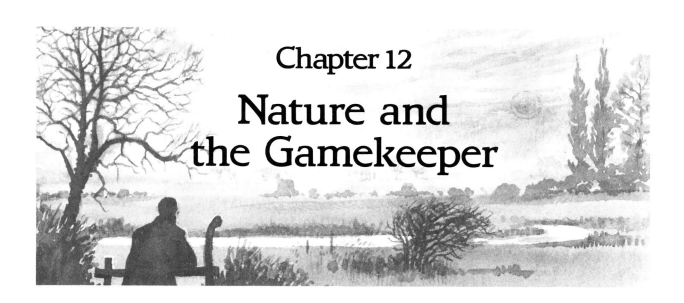

Chapter 12

Nature and the Gamekeeper

The changes in the fauna of the inland counties brought about by the favour shown to certain species are very remarkable. The alterations caused by the preservation of pheasants have reached their limit. No further effects are likely to be produced, even if pheasant-preserving should be carried to a still greater extent, which itself is improbable. One creature at least, the pine-marten, has been exterminated over Southern England, and is now only to be seen – in the stuffed state – in museums. It may be roughly described as a large tree-weasle, and was shot down on account of its habit of seizing pheasants at roost. The polecat is also practically extinct, though occasional specimens are said to occur. These two animals could not be allowed to exist in any preserve. But it is in the list of birds that the change is most striking. Eagles are gone: if one is seen it is a stray from Scotland or Wales; and so are the buzzards, except from the moors. Falcons are equally rare: the little merlin comes down from the north now and then, but the peregrine falcon as a resident or regular visitor is extinct. The hen-harrier is still shot at intervals; but the large hawks have ceased out of the daily life, as it were, of woods and fields. Horned owls are becoming rare; even the barn-owl has all but disappeared from some districts; and the wood-owl is local. The raven is extinct – quite put out. The birds are said to exist near the sea-coast; but it is certain that any one may walk over inland country for years without seeing one. These, being all more or less birds of prey, could not but be excluded from pheasant-covers. All these birds, however, would probably resume their ancient habitations in the course of five-and-twenty years if permitted to do so. They exist plentifully at no great distance – judged as such strong flyers judge distance; and if they found that they were unmolested they would soon come back from the extremities of the land.

But even more remarkable than the list of birds driven away is the list of those creatures, birds and animals, which have stood their ground in spite of traps, guns, and dogs. Stoats and weasels are always shot when seen, they are frequently trapped, and in every manner hunted to the death and their litters destroyed – the last the most effectual method of extermination. But in spite of the unceasing emnity directed against them, stoat and weasel remain common. They still take their share of game, both winged and ground. Stoat and weasel will not be killed out. As they are both defenceless creatures, and not even swift of foot, being easily overtaken in the open, their persistent continuance is curious. If any reason can be assigned for it, it must be because they spend much of their time in buries, where they are comparatively safe, and because they do not confine themselves to woods, but roam cornfields and meadows. Certainly, if man has tried to exterminate any creature, he has tried his hardest to get rid of these two, and has failed. It is even questionable whether their numbers show any appreciable diminution. Kept down to the utmost in one place, they flourish in another. Kestrel and sparrowhawk form a parallel among winged creatures. These two hawks have been shot, trapped, and their eggs destroyed unsparingly: they remain numerous just the same. Neither of them choose inaccessible places for their eyries; neither of them rear large broods. The sparrowhawk makes a nest in a tree, often in firs; the kestrel lays in old rooks,' crows', or magpies' nests. Both the parents are often shot on or near the nest, and the eggs broken. Sometimes the young are permitted to grow large enough to fly, and are then shot down after the manner of rook-shooting. Nevertheless kestrels are common, and sparrowhawks, if not quite so numerous, are in no degree uncommon. Perhaps the places of those killed are supplied by birds from the great woods, moors, and mountains of the north.

A third instance is the crow. Hated by all gamekeepers, and sportsmen, by farmers; and every one who has anything to do with country life, the crow survives. Cruel tyrant as he is to every creature smaller than himself, not a voice is raised in his favour. Yet crows exist in considerable numbers. Shot off in some places, they are recruited again from others where there is less preservation. The case of the crow, however, is less striking than that of the two hawks; because the crow is a cosmopolitan bird, and if every specimen in the British Isles were destroyed today there would be an influx from abroad in a very short time. The crow is. too, partly a sea-coast feeder, and so escapes. Still, to any one who knows how determined is the hostility to his race shown by all country people, his existence in any number must be considered remarkable. His more powerful congener the raven, as has been pointed out, is practically extinct in southern counties, and no longer attacks the shepherd's weakly lambs. Why, then, does the crow live on? Wherever a pair of ravens do exist the landowner generally preserves them now, as interesting representatives of old times. They are taken care

'Buds picked off by Tom Tits and Bullfinches'
(*Utility of Birds*)

'the farmyard afforded a supply of food to birds... all through the hardest winter'
(*Wild Fowl and Small Birds*)

of; people go to see them; the appearance of eggs in the nest is recorded. But the raven does not multiply. Barn-owls live on, though not in all districts. Influenced by the remonstrance of naturalists, many gentlemen have stopped the destruction of owls; but a custom once established is not easily put an end to.

Jays and magpies have also been subjected to a bitter warfare of extermination. Magpies are quite shot off some places; in others they exist sparingly; here and there they may be found in fair numbers. Occasionally their nests are preserved – indeed, the growing tendency is to spare. Still, they have been shot off rigorously, and have survived it. So have jays. In large woods – particularly where there is much fir – jays are so numerous that to destroy them seems almost impossible. Another bird that has defied the gun and trap is the green woodpecker, which used to be killed for alleged destruction of timber. Woodpeckers are not now so ceaselessly killed, though the old system of slaying them is common enough. They have defied not only gun and trap but the cunning noose placed at the mouth of their holes.

Twenty creatures, furred and feathered, have undergone severe persecution since

the extension of pheasant-covers, and of these the first nine have more or less succumbed – namely, pine-martin, polecat, eagle, buzzard, falcon, kite, horned owl, harrier, and raven. The remaining eleven have survived – namely, stoat, weasel, rat, crow, kestrel, sparrow, hawk, brown and barn owl, jay, magpie, and woodpecker. Pheasants of themselves are not responsible for all this warfare and all these changes, but the pheasant-cover means more than pheasants, or rather has done. Rabbits required even more protection from furred enemies; the head of rabbits kept up in many places practically paid the keeper's wages. This warfare in its fiercest form may be roughly said to be coeval with the invention of the percussion gun, and to have raged now for over half a century. The resistance, therefore, of the various species has been fairly tested, and we may reasonably conclude that no further disappearance will take place, unless by the destruction of woods themselves. One new bird only has been introduced into England since the pheasant – the red-legged partridge – which seems to be fairly established in some districts, not to the entire satisfaction of sportsmen. One new bird has also been introduced into Scotland – in this case a re-introduction. The magnificent capercailzie is now flourishing again in the north, to the honour of those who laboured for its restoration. In these notes I have not included attempts at acclimatisation, as that of the wild turkey from North America, which has partly succeeded. Beavers, too, have been induced to resume possession of their ancient streams under careful supervision, but they are outside present consideration. While England has thus lost some species and suffered a diminution of several, other countries have been supplied from our streams and woods and hedgerows. England has sent the sparrow to the United States and Australia; also the nightingale, rabbit, salmon, trout, and sweet-briar.

It is quite open to argument that pheasant-covers have saved as well as destroyed. Wood-pigeons could scarcely exist in such numbers without the quiet of preserved woods to breed in; nor could squirrels. Nor can the rarity of such birds as the little bearded tit be charged on game. The great bustard, the crane, and bittern have been driven away by cultivation. The crane, possibly, has deserted us wilfully; since civilisation in other countries has not destroyed it. And then the fashion of making natural history collections has much extended of recent years: so much so, that many blame too ardent collectors for the increasing rarity of birds like the cross bill, waxwing, hoopoe, golden oriole, and others which seem to have once visited this country more commonly than at present.

from *The Life of the Fields*

Chapter 13

The Utility of Birds

A good deal of shooting goes on before September, and the sportsmen walk, not over the stubble, but round the fields of standing corn. To pass through an arable district at this time of year, just as the wheat is fast turning to that peculiar golden-bronze tint which is so beautiful, is not unlike a visit to the scene of war; skirmishing goes on in all directions, a puff of smoke rises over the wheat, followed by a loud report, and before it has died away it is caught up and repeated by other vigilant sentries at a distance. It is true, many of these soldiers waging war with small birds are armed in a primitive manner, with a rusty old gun which was once a flintlock, and was converted years and years ago. To see an old man lugging such a weapon round the field on his shoulder, and carrying the ramrod in his hand, is not altogether a cheering spectacle to those who would fain believe in the spread of education – meaning thereby not the education of mere printed matter, but that deduced from observation. Nor is it altogether a satisfactory sight to the true sportsman who will come a month or so later on, for he has a shrewd suspicion that not a few partridges cowering in a furrow, or leverets hiding in the grass, not to speak of rabbits, are quietly knocked over under pretence of frightening chaffinches; if a bird-keeper is not supplied with shot, a handful of small splinters of flint picked up from the surface of the nearest road will answer the purpose at a short range very well. It has been abundantly shown during the present summer that all the efforts of naturalists to convince people that small birds are useful in destroying insects have practically been thrown away, for the bird-keepers are busy at work as usual. Though what the possible utility of frightening a cloud of birds out of one corner of a field of twenty acres only to see them calmly settle down in the opposite one can be, it is difficult to understand.

But, say the said sportsmen's employers – 'small birds do eat our wheat, etc., and you cannot make us disbelieve the evidence of our own eyes. Stand by the gate a moment and watch – down comes a flight of chaffinches, sparrows, and other birds into the wheat; now what do they do there if not eat it? Look there! a sparrow is hovering like a hawk just above the surface of the corn; see, he has caught hold of an ear of wheat, and bears it down with his weight. What can be clearer proof than that? Come into the rick-yard, and let us lay a train of grain along the ground, get out of sight, and in five minutes scores of birds are busy at work; with one discharge of dust shot you may destroy a dozen of fifteen in the very act. As for seeds, they will clear a whole patch in no time. In the gardens and orchards in the spring you may see the ground perfectly littered with the buds picked off the fruit-trees by those

91

worst of pests the bullfinches and tom-tits. Nothing will make us disbelieve our own eyes.' Such is the argument of the counsel for the prosecution; and it is a good one so far as it goes. It is perfectly true, whatever may be said to the contrary by too enthusiastic naturalists, that birds do eat grain. But this is only a part of the question; the fact is this, every one can see them pick up grains of wheat, and everybody does see them because they watch for and are always on the look-out to detect the act. For one who tries patiently to discover what else they live on fifty are satisfied with observing one item of food only. These birds as a matter of fact eat grain very much in the same way as at a good dinner of several courses we ourselves do not disdain a morsel of bread as a wholesome corrective to the richer dishes. A pair of sparrows feeding their young were once carefully watched, and from a few gooseberry bushes close to a window in about an hour they took off over one hundred caterpillars. These represented the meat part of the food of the family; it is not unreasonable to suppose that after such a banquet of juicy caterpillars they wanted a few grains of wheat, i.e. bread.

Chaffinches are accused of such an inordinate love of grain that they frequent the sides of roads in order to devour the half-digested or partly fermented oats in the droppings of horses. But they are equally busy at such heaps in the midst of the corn season, when the fields by the roadside are teeming with wheat, oats, corn of all kinds – when, in short, such scanty supplies as the road affords would be despised by them. Sparrows known to eat grain, rarely touch these droppings at this time of year; but tomtits, who are not accused of grain-stealing, are always at them. May we not suppose that certain forms of insect life are speedily attracted to such excrementitious matter, especially in hot weather? It is known that the buds picked off by bullfinches and tom-tits from fruit-trees contain each a tiny insect, which in the course of the season, if left on the tree, would have become the centre of a patch of blight. We asked a man who was shooting the bullfinches once, if he noticed that they did not eat the green buds, but dropped them: why, then, did they take so much trouble, if not for insects? 'Oh, bless you,' was his reply, 'they does it for mischief only!' If the chaffinches and sparrows and other birds, now being slaughtered for grain-eating, live entirely on it, as many suppose, what do they exist on in the autumn, winter, and spring, when it is absent from the fields?

The reply of a judicious counsel for the defence of the birds on their trail would be this: 'We admit that they do eat grain; but we argue, and we have proved by endless dissections of their bodies when shot as was believed in the very deed, that grain-eating is casual, and occasional, while insect-eating is incessant and continuous.' Blind indeed must the observer be who cannot see this. In pasture districts it is not unusual to see half an acre of grass pulled up by the roots in little bunches, and of course turned brown, and dead. This done by rooks in search of gnat grubs, which in some places multiply in countless numbers. What the stock and sheep-farmer would do without the starlings and rooks one cannot think; they would be literally over-run with ticks and lice were it not for those busy birds. Even the most ignorant will admit this as regards starlings. When one thinks of the extraordinary flocks of these birds, which blacken the ground where they alight, now travelling across the face of the country (in August) the imagination fails to conceive the numbers of grubs and insects, ticks, lice, and creeping things which they must destroy. The remark may perhaps be cavilled at by some, and yet it is, in part at least, true that modern agriculture has tended to increase insect life by affording it so large a variety of food upon which to exist almost all the year round. Instead of destroying the small birds in this useless manner, it were well if the children now attending school in the rural districts (to the great inconvenience of their parents in many cases) and whose heads are being crammed with all kinds of 'learning' except what will be of practical use to them, were taught to aid these very birds in the task of exterminating insect vermin. In the past, the first part of a plough boy's education was to go out bird-keeping. Let him now learn to go out and assist these very finches and birds which it was once impressed upon him as his duty to destroy, and especially now we are almost in the presence of the dreaded potato beetle from Colorado.

If reason is wholly despised, and the birds are to be driven from the fields right or wrong, at least do not kill them, let frightening be sufficient, and the only effective way to do that is by the Eastern plan. A stage is erected in the middle of the field, on which a man stands with a sling, and slings small balls of hardened clay wherever he suspects intruders to be. The chance of such a missile striking a bird sixty or a hundred yards distant is small; but he commands the whole field, and can keep it quite clear, while our bird-keeper potters round one corner, or looks over a gate at a twenty-acre field, much like a noodle or a poacher.

from *Chronicles of the Hedges*

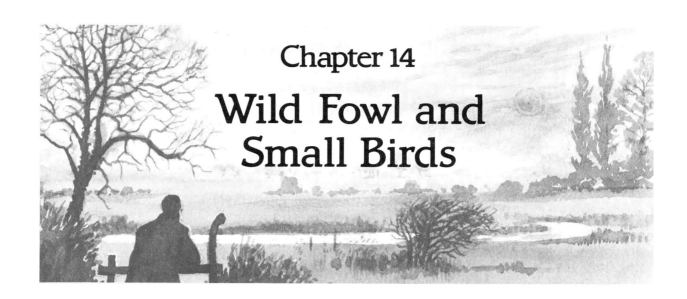

Chapter 14
Wild Fowl and Small Birds

We are glad to see that proceedings are at length being taken to enforce the observance of the Wild Birds Preservation Act, and sorry at the same time tht there shold be any difference of opinion as to the proper construction of it... We shall soon, we hope have an authoritative declaration of the meaning of the Act. At all events, it is practically useless to attempt to protect British wild fowl if foreign wild fowl, which are in every respect identical, may be sold with impunity. We may gather from the preamble that then Act is one for the protection of the wild fowl of the United Kingdom, though it is not so entitled. But then what are the 'wild fowl of the United Kingdom'? Are they wild fowl which at any given moment may be found within that area, or are they simply British birds, which do not cease to be British birds because they breed in other countries? Blackbirds and thrushes, partridges and pheasants, are none the less birds of the United Kingdom because they are found upon the Continent. Nor can it possibly be maintained that to entitle any bird to protection as a British bird it must have been bred in the United Kingdom; for nobody can say where the wild fowl were bred who haunt our coasts and inland waters. Birds found in England may have been bred in Holland, and birds found in Holland may have been bred in England. Still less is it possible to say so of birds found upon 'the high seas', where according to the 6th clause of the Act the offence may be committed. Wild fowl of the United Kingdom ought surely to mean British wild fowl; and it ought not to deprive them of protection that they happen to be caught abroad. For what we know, the duck, teal, and widgeon consigned to an English poulterer by a Dutch merchant may have been bred in the Norfolk broads or the Highland lakes, At all events if a bird loses nationality when he settles in a foreign country, he should regain it when he comes back again whether he is alive or dead...

What is being done, or shortly, we hope, will be done, for our wild fowl, ought likewise to be done for our small birds, The Act of 1876 is as systematically violated as the Act of 1872 has been; and, though it leaves out a good many birds which ought to be included in it, there is no reason why, we should not protect what we can. We look in vain in the schedule for the lark, the linnet, the greenfinch, the chaffinch, the bullfinch, and the yellowhammer, which – some for their song, some for their plumage, and some for both – are among the most delightful inhabitants of our fields and hedgegrows. Moreover, that now rare old English bird, the Cornish chough, is unaccountably omitted from it, though its skin is in cruel request for the barbarous adornment of ladies' hats. An Act which protects the hedge-sparrow, the robin, and the titmouse ought surely to protect these? But that is no reason why the law should not be properly enforced as far as it goes. Even now these birds are said to be diminishing; and if, in addition to the inevitable causes which tend to this result, we tolerate the existence of preventable ones, many species will soon become extinct. In old-fashioned times, when the corn was threshed slowly with the flail, the farmyard afforded a supply of food to birds of this description all through the hardest winter, and hundreds of finches, yellowhammers, and titmice might be seen mingling with the sparrows in front of the great barn doors, while now and then even a blackbird would so far overcome his constitutional shyness as to venture on the outskirts of the group. Now all this is at an end. Again, the destruction of hedgerows and copses, the clearing out of ditches, and generally more cleanly agriculture of the present day are not favourable to the nesting of small birds. But these are circumstances which of course we cannot help; and, on the other hand, there is one change in our habits which ought to act favourably on the preservation of these interesting species. Birds'-nesting is no longer pusued in the sweeping and indiscriminate fashion which prevailed ere the school-master was abroad. The labourer's children are now at school or at work. You nowhere see 'the strings o' heggs', which Mr. Tomlinson in *Janet's Repentance* so much admired, 'hanging up in poor people's houses.' And as for their betters, the schoolboy now is taught birds'-nesting on scientific principles, to make not strings but 'collections', and to be satisfied with a single egg out of each nest. This wholesome reform ought to tell favourably on the small birds, and do something to counteract the disappearance of barnyards and hedges.

from *Chronicles of the Hedges*

Chapter 15
The Professional Bird Catcher

The flight season having once set in, and the birds having taken to go about in flocks – generally composed of linnets for the most part, with a sprinkling of goldfinches – the fowler's first object is to ascertain what localities they most frequent. Having made himself master of this all-important information, he proceeds to the spot in the early morning; and, having set his clap-nets and placed some half-dozen small cages each containing a linnet, a goldfinch, or whatever birds he is 'setting' for, he has to wait patiently till a light comes over. Despite the most careful observation, his snares may be all in vain. For some reason best known to themselves the birds may suddenly have changed their quarters, and hour after hour may pass without his seeing a single flight. His caged decoys may warble their sweetest and loudest, but if no flight passes overhead there can be no profitable result. And when noon approaches, at which time flighting for the day generally ceases; the bird-catcher has nothing to do but pack up his traps and wait for next morning. The nets employed for the purpose are known as 'wings', and are laid flat on the ground; the size averaging about ten yards by two. They are worked by the fowler – who keeps himself as much out of sight as possible by lying down flat on the ground – by two cords, which on being pulled sharply cause one-half of the wing-net to double over the other and thus catch the birds without injuring them. As a rule, he takes up his position about thirty yards from his nets; and so intent are the flight on the decoy-birds that, as a rule, they take little or no notice of him. The fowler's success depends very much upon the state of the weather. In fine frost mornings the flights are pretty abundant; but not so in foggy or damp mornings. If there is a strong wind blowing, the birds will, as a rule, fly directly against it, or at any rate, in a slanting direction; and this knowledge enables the catcher to set his nets and take his stand with advantage. The number taken at a single draw varies considerably. Sometimes as many as fifteen or twenty birds will be caught; at other times not above three or four. Of course the prices paid by the dealers vary according to the supply. Linnets, which when scarce will fetch as much as 4s. or 5s. a dozen, are often sold when plentiful at from 1s. to 1s. 3d. a dozen. Goldfinches, which are considerably scarcer, will fetch from 4s. to 6s. per dozen, and sometimes more. Cock bullfinches bring as much as 8s. or 9s. For hen bullfinches there is hardly any demand. A few years ago, when shooting at starlings, and even sparrows, was much more frequent than it is now, the first-named birds would frequently fetch 2s. to 3s. a dozen, and the latter about a shilling. But as pets go there is no great demand for any birds except young thrushes, blackbirds, full-grown linnets, larks, goldfinches, and bullfinches.

In frosty weather, which is the best time for flighting, a good catcher will sometimes get as many as ten or twelve dozen birds a day. But against this must be put bad days, on which the catch is virtually nil; so that a man must have good luck and fair prices to earn 20s. to 25s. a week, even during the few months that the 'flighting' is on. Large as is the demand in London and other cities for singing-birds, the supply would be far in excess, were it not for the fact that an enormous proportion of the birds caught during 'flight' season die within a few days of being captured. They do not take any disease, but refuse all food; and it is not, perhaps, too much to say that not more than one in three survives. With hand-reared birds, however, the case is different, and a healthy young thrush or blackbird at six weeks or two months old will realize a higher price than a matured bird freshly caught.

When the flight season is over the catcher has another branch of his occupation to fall back upon. In the autumn and winter months large quantities of birds of every description roost in thick shrubs, in ivy-covered walls and (starlings and sparrows especially) in the thatched eaves of old-fashioned houses. The nets adopted for catching them at such seasons are called fowling or bathing nets, and are fastened to two slight poles about eight feet or ten feet long, curved at the top end and fastened together. One pole is then held in each hand, and the net is expanded and placed just in front of the eaves or ivy, a boy standing behind the fowler, with a lantern so held as to throw a light in the centre of the net. When the birds, being disturbed, make for the light, the net is folded by a quick movement of the hands. In this way, if birds are plentiful and there is plenty of cover, some hundreds may be taken in a single night. It has been whispered that pheasants, which are at times very partial to roosting in holly bushes (a favourite resort of blackbirds and thrushes), occasionally get caught in this way.

The catcher who procures birds for sale to the shop-keepers seldom or never has recourse to bird-lime: the sticky composition injures the feathers. And not often is he employed by the gamekeeper, between whom and himself no very cordial relations exist; although, except when he is after larks or sparrows, he seldom ventures upon stubble-land. The commons, where the seeds of the various grasses are most abundant, are his best pitches as a rule. Sometimes, however, the keeper is glad of his assistance in destroying hawks etc. in open and exposed districts where it is difficult to shoot them; and then, again, the 'wing' nets are brought into requisition. The lure, instead of being a decoy-bird placed in a cage, is tied down to the ground midway between the wings, with just sufficient length of string to allow him to hop and flutter when he observes his enemy the hawk soaring above him. A quick downward swoop, a jerk of the net strings, and the hawk is caught. In catching starlings, too, the tame bird is pegged down. In a cage he would escape notice, for he is not much addicted to singing. The larger birds – such as owls, magpies, jays, jackdaws, etc. – which are often exposed for sale in the dealer's windows, are in almost every instance taken from the nest when young: it would be a difficult matter to take them alive in nets.

Although the Birds Preservation Act prevents the fowler from pursuing his avocation all the year round, most of the men are decidedly in favour of the Act. They argue that during the breeding season, when there is no flight on, it is difficult to get more than a few birds a day – not enough, in fact, to make the pursuit worth following; whereas if the old birds are proctected there is a greater harvest to be made during the legitimate 'flight' season.

When not actually employed in bird-catching, the modern fowler earns a crust by fern-gathering, egg-finding, snail-picking, and in a dozen other odd ways.

Towards the end of August, the catcher may here and there turn his attention to the partridge coveys, the net used for the capture being usually composed of a kind of gauze material some twenty or thirty yards in length, which is drawn by two men lengthwise across the fields where the birds are known to resort: on their attempting to rise both ends are at once dropped. Game-keepers are thoroughly alive to this practice, and keenly on the look-out to prevent it; thorn-bushes are generally placed in different parts of such fields as are likely to be operated upon, and their presence completely frustrates the netter's plans.

To give some idea of the importance of the live-bird trade in London it may be mentioned that one shop alone in a remote district in Westminster keeps three catchers fully employed throughout the season proper. Large quantities of larks are annually caught for the table, in horsehair nooses set in the stubbles on which they are accustomed to feed; but this is an occupation in itself to a certain extent, and hardly comes under the head of professional bird-catching.

from *Chronicles of the Hedges*

Chapter 16
Decline of Partridge Shooting

That during the last five-and-twenty or thirty years partridge shooting has declined is a fact about which there can scarcely be two opinions. It is neither the same sport as it was nor does it inspire the same enthusiasm as it did in the middle of this century. And some of the causes of this, at all events, are familiar to all sportsmen. In the first place, the modern style of farming has necessitated a modern style of shooting, less favourable to real sport than the style which was in fashion when the waning generation was the rising one. These changes are so well known that it is almost unnecessary to mention them. The old wheat stubbles – which the birds, after all, loved better than anything – have entirely disappeared.

In many parts of England hedgerows, and especially double hedgerows, are fast following them, and those which remain are not such as the partridge loves: wide straggling fences, with high bushy banks full of weeds and brambles, and a deep, dry ditch along which he can run as he pleases. The land is far cleaner than it used to be; and the partridges in dry weather can run between the rows of turnips as easily as on a gravel path. Then, again, at the present day the fields seem never to be let alone. Scarcely have the gleaners disappeared before the ploughman enters on the scene. And before the middle of September comes the groaning engine, hissing and whistling in the field. Not, we mean, that the engines in particular disturb the birds; they get used to them, of course: it is the perpetual hustle on the farm at the present day compared with the old autumnal quiet which always used to reign during four or five weeks after harvest which disturbs the birds, makes them constantly on the move and not only, therefore, very difficult to find, but infinitely wilder when they are found. From these changed agricultural conditions several consequences arise. It has come nearly to this – that, as the birds will only lie in turnips, mangold-wurzels, potatoes, and cover of that description, it is waste of time to beat the stubbles for

them; a task which is left therefore to be performed by the keeper and his assistants, who drive the birds into the turnips before shooting begins. This being done, the further consequence arises that pointers and setters become not only useless, but are in the way. You know exactly where the birds are; and when you can walk them up so easily it is rather a nuisance than otherwise to be obliged to stop and turn aside to shoot at the birds which 'Old Ven' has found some sixty or eighty yards off. Hence the discarding of dogs from the shooting-field – who, unless most perfectly disciplined, are, it must be owned, liable to do as much harm as good in a modern turnip field into which five or six coveys of birds have just been driven. Hence follows a third consequence – that partridge shooting now is much more monotonous than it used to be. All the shots you get in the course of the day are very much alike; the only difference being between birds going to the right or left and birds going straight away from you. But when the sport was pursued under more natural conditions, when a scattered covey took refuge in all kinds of out-of-the-way places, and you picked up the single birds – one out of a hedge, another out of a patch of thistles, and a third, perhaps, out of an old cart-rut overgrown with rank grass and rubbish – you had a constant variety. Then, when you found a covey in the stubbles, you were able to get close up to them; and the closer you get to birds the more sure they rise. But now when birds are put off the stubbles they get up in compact body a hundred yards off; and even in turnips, as they rise much wider than they used to do, it has become by no means an easy thing to scatter a covey in the old-fashioned way, even were the variety of covers still left in which they could deposit themselves.

Surely, then, no sportsman will deny that the old style of partridge shooting was better sport than the new; and this change may, of course, account for the next which we are about to mention; though it can only account for it partially, because it shows itself in other departments of field sports as well as in partridge shooting: we mean the passion for 'pace' which is everywhere visible among sportsmen. And we are using the word 'pace' in its widest possible signification. 'A short, quick thing' is now the great charm of fox-hunting. Trout-fishing is too slow for country gentlemen, who rush off to the rivers of Norway. And all through life, both in its cares and its

pleasures, there is the same love of doing things rapidly and on a large scale, and of having the largest results to show for work done in the shortest time. Thus the old-fashioned style of shooting, whether in the field or in cover, is called 'pottering'; and it may be doubted whether, if stubble and hedges and pointers all could be restored, the fast young sportsmen of the present day would enjoy partridge shooting as their fathers did. To shoot as fast as you can load is their notion of sport. To watch dogs working or to follow up a scattered covey would bore them: and, as it is quite certain that no one who goes out partridge shooting in this frame of mind can do justice to its real merits, no wonder the sport is on the decline, independently even of the causes we have already mentioned. These causes, moreover, are not universally in operation. There are happy nooks and corners where it is still possible to shoot in the old style. But even there one is certain to hear partridge shooting depreciated; and, as this evidently cannot be owing to the deterioration of the sport itself, it must be owing to a change in the sportsman's own tastes. The general result is that, though enormous bags are made in large preserves which are shot over perhaps not more than three or four days in

the season, partridge shooting, as one of the regular amusements of a country life which every country gentleman or other person able to indulge in it looked forward to enjoying three or four days a week during the months of September and October, is at present on the wane; and as for the enthusiasm with which the 1st September was formerly anticipated, and the long and careful preparations which both man and dog underwent in order to be fit for its fatigues, they are unknown to the present generation. The pleasure of these preparations was almost equal to the sport itself; but like many other old-fashioned pleasures peculiar to a time when men stayed at home a great deal more than they do now and were obliged to make the most of such amusements as lay ready to their hand, it has vanished from the country.

There is still another cause, however, of the decline of partridge shooting which remains to be mentioned, of which it may be said, as was of another old English institution a hundred years ago, that it has increased, is increasing, and ought to be diminished – that is, if in many parts of the country partridges are to survive at all: we mean the very great increase which has taken place in late years in the number of people who shoot...

Sometimes a tenant will let his shooting; but oftener he gives leave to two or three of his neighbours, who obtain the same permission perhaps from some other adjoining farmer, and constitute a class of game-destroyers – sportsmen they cannot be called – who are the pest of every neighbourhood they frequent. Thirty years ago such persons never thought of shooting; and the ground was usually given over to the nearest landed proprietors who chose to be at the trouble of looking after it. Partridges now are ruthlessly shot down the first two weeks in the season by a whole army of gunners, who each has leave to go over a few hundred acres; and thus a good deal of sport which was once at the command of men not themselves the owner of large estates, though they were sportsmen of the true stamp, has been completely swept away. To every sportsman of mature age and well-regulated mind who has the opportunity of shooting over dogs at all, however, the "First", though shorn of its ancient glories, still presents its lasting attractions. In an average season, when the birds are not too small to shoot, and where farming has not been carried too near to perfection, good sport may still be had with dogs. The partridges will lie a little at first over the short stubble, provided a few tares have considerately been left among the wheat; and if there has been rain enough to bring on the turnips without injuring the young broods, the old system of beating up coveys and killing them one by one may still be pursued with success. The worst of it is that it is so difficult, except on very light land, to combine these two conditions – rain enough, that is, for the root crops, without too much for the newly hatched partridges. On heavy clay lands the wet soon becomes injurious to the birds while, unfortunately, on such ground the turnips require more than elsewhere. The result is that not more than one season out of three or four, if that, is a really good one on land of this description; the sportsman being doomed at other times to see turnip fields dotted over with occasional plants, from which covey after covey fly harmlessly and defiantly away; or else to plod knee-deep through luxuriant cover to find nothing for his pains but a trace or two of birds.

from *Chronicles of the Hedges*

Chapter 17

The Sacrifice to Trout

How much the breeding of pheasants has told upon the existence of other creatures in fur and feathers I have already shown; and much the same thing is true of the preservation of trout. There is this difference, however: that while the pheasant has now produced its utmost effect, the alterations due to trout are increasing. Trout are now so highly and so widely preserved that the effect cannot but be felt. Their preservation in the numbers now considered necessary entails the destruction of some and the banishment of other creatures. The most important of these is the otter. Guns, dogs, traps set under water so as not to be scented; all modes of attack are pressed into the service, and it is not often that he escapes. When traces of an otter were found, a little while since, in the Kennet – he had left his mark on the back of a trout – the fact was recorded with as much anxiety as if a veritable wolf had appeared. With such animosity has the otter been hunted that he is becoming one of the rarest of wild animals here in the south. He is practically extinct on the majority of southern streams, and has been almost beaten off the Thames itself. But the otter is not likely to be exterminated in the sense that the wolf has been. Otters will be found elsewhere in England long after the last of them has disappeared from the south. Next the pike must be ousted from trout-streams. Special nets have been invented by which pike can be routed from their strongholds. Much hunting about quickens the intelligence of the pike to such a degree that he cannot be secured in the ordinary manner; he baffles the net by keeping close to the bank, behind stones, or by retiring to holes under roots. Perch have to go as well as pike; and then comes the turn of birds.

Herons, kingfishers, moorhens, coots, grebes, ducks, teal, various divers, are all proscribed on behalf of trout. Herons are regarded as most injurious to a fishery. As was observed a century ago, a single heron will soon empty a pond or a stretch of brook. As their long necks give them easy command of a wide radius in spying round them, it is rather difficult to shoot them with a shot-gun; but with the small-bore rifles now made no heron is safe. They are generally shot early in the morning. Were it not for the fact that herons nest; like rooks, and that heronries are valued appurtenances in parks, they would soon become scarce. Kingfishers prey on smaller fish, but are believed to eat almost as many as herons. Kingfishers

103

resort in numbers to trout nurseries, which are as traps for them: and there they are more than decimated. Owls are known to take fish occasionally, and are therefore shot. The greatest loss sustained in fisheries takes place in the spawning season, and again when the fry are about. Some students of fish-life believe that almost all wild-fowl will swallow the ova and fry of trout. It must be understood that I am not here entering into the question whether all these are really so injurious; I am merely giving a list of the 'dogs with a bad name.' Moorhens and coots are especially disliked because they are on or near the water day and night, and can clear off large quantities of fry. Grebes (di-dappers or dabchicks) are similar in habit, but less destructive because fewer. Ducks are ravenous devourers; teal are equally hated. The various divers which occasionally visit the streams are also guilty. Lastly, the swan is a well-known trout-pirate. Besides these, the two kinds of rat – land and water – have a black mark against them. Otter, pike, perch, heron, kingfisher, owl, moorhen, coot, grebe, diver, wild-duck, swan, teal, dipper, land-rat, and water-rat – altogether sixteen creatures – are killed in order that one may flourish. Although none of these, even in the south of England – except the otter – has yet been excluded, the majority of them are so thinned down as to be rarely seen unless carefully sought.

To go through the list: otters are practically excluded; the pike is banished from trout streams but is plentiful in others; so too with perch; herons, much reduced in numbers; owls, reduced; kingfishers, growing scarce; coots, much less numerous because not permitted to nest; grebes, reduced; wild-duck, seldom seen in summer, because not permitted to nest; teal same; swan, not permitted on fisheries unless ancient rights protect it; divers, never numerous, now scarcer; moorhens, still fairly plentiful because their ranks are constantly supplied from moats and ponds where they breed under semi-domestic conditions. The draining of marsh-lands and levels began the exile of wild-fowl; and now the increasing preservation of trout adds to the difficulties under which these birds strive to retain a hold upon inland waters. The Thames is too long and wide for complete exclusion; but it is surprising how few moorhens even are to be seen along the river. Lesser rivers are still more empty, as it were, of life. The great osier-beds still give shelter to some, but not nearly so many as formerly. Up towards the spring-heads, where the feeders are mere runlets, the scarcity of wild-fowl has long been noticed. Hardly a wild-duck is now seen; one or two moorhens or a dabchick seem all. Coots have quite disappeared in some places: they are shot on ponds, having an ill reputation for the destruction of the fry of coarse or pond fish, as well as of trout. Not all these changes, indeed, are attributable to trout alone; but the trout holds a sort of official position and leads the van. Our southern rivers, with the exception of the Thames, are for the most part easily preserved.

They run through cultivated country, with meadows or cornfields, woods or copses, and rarely far through open, unenclosed land. A stranger, and without permission, would often find it difficult to walk half a mile along the bank of such a stream as this. Consequently, if it is desired to preserve it, riparian owners can do so to the utmost, and the water-fowl considered injurious to fish can as easily be kept down. It is different in the north, for instance, where the streams have a background of moors, mountains, tarns, and lakes. In these their fastnesses birds find some security. From the coast they are also recruited; while on our southern coasts it is a source of lament that wild-fowl are not nearly so plentiful as formerly. Of course in winter it often happens that a flock of wild-fowl alight in passing; but how long do they stay? The real question is, how many breed? Where trout are carefully preserved, very few indeed; so that it is evident trout are making as much difference as the pheasants. Trout preservation has become much more extended since the fish

'... the trout holds a sort of official position...'
(*The Sacrifice to Trout*)

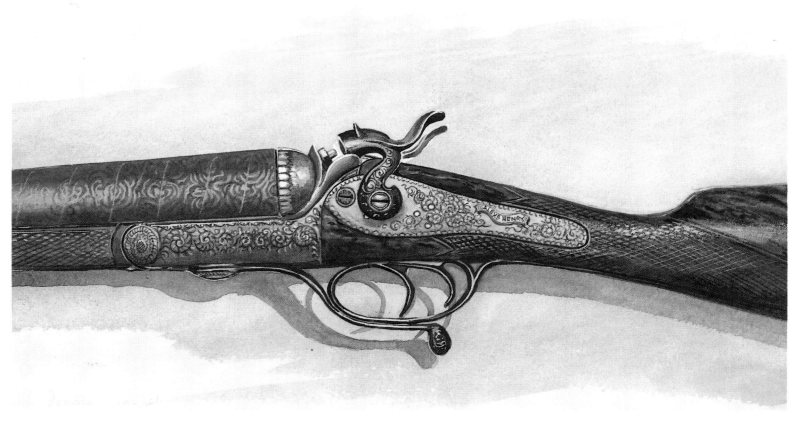

'... the double barrel is the gun of the time.'
(*The Single-Barrel Gun*)

'… kingfishers, growing scarce…'
(*The Sacrifice to Trout*)

has been studied and found to be easily bred. Advertisements are even put forward recommending people to keep trout instead of poultry, since they can be managed with certainty. It seems reasonable, therefore, to suppose that the influence of trout on wild creatures will continue to extend for some time yet. Already where trout preservation has been carefully carried out it has produced a visible impression upon their ranks. In ten years, if it were abandoned, most of these creatures would be plentiful again on the waters from which they have been driven; I should myself be very glad to see many of them back again.

But if preservation has excluded many creatures, it has also saved many. Badgers, in all probability, would be extinct – really extinct, like the wolf – were it not for the seclusion of covers. Without the protection which hunting afford them, foxes would certainly have disappeared. The stag and fallow-deer are other examples; so too, the wild white cattle maintained in a few parks. In a measure the rook owes its existence to protection; for although naturalists have pointed out its usefulness, the rook is no favourite with agriculturists. Woodcocks, again, are protected, and are said to have increased, though it is open to question if their increased numbers may not be due to other causes. Cultivation banishes wild geese and snipe, but adds to the numbers of small birds, I fancy, and very probably to the number of mice. When the country was three-fourths champaign – open, unenclosed, and uncultivated – it cannot be supposed that so many grain-eating birds found sustenance as now. The subject is capable of much development. Enough, however, has been said to show that Nature at present is under artificial restraints; but her excluded creatures are for the most part ready to return if ever those restraints are removed.

from *The Life of the Fields*

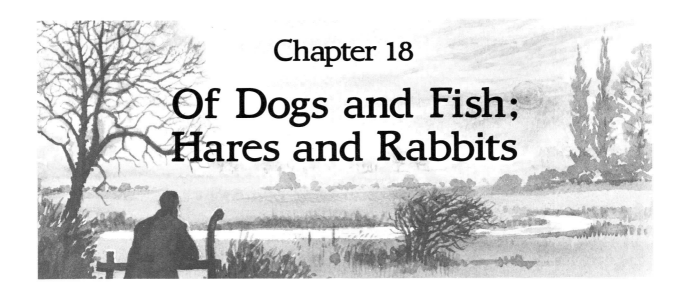

Chapter 18
Of Dogs and Fish; Hares and Rabbits

The gamekeeper, with dogs around him from morning till night, associated with them from childhood, has no doubts upon the matter whatever, but with characteristic decision is perfectly certain that they think and reason in the same way as human beings, though of course in a limited degree. Most of his class believe, likewise, in the reasoning power of the dog: so do shepherds; and so, too, the labourers who wait on and feed cattle are fully persuaded of their intelligence, which, however, in no way prevents them throwing the milking-stool at their heads when unruly. But the concession of reason is no guarantee against ill-usage, else the labourer's wife would escape.

The keeper, without thinking it perhaps, affords a strong illustration of his own firm faith in the mind of the dog. His are taught their proper business thoroughly; but there it ends. 'I never makes them learn no tricks,' says he, 'because I don't like to see'em made fools of.' I have observed that almost all those whose labour lies in the field, and who go down to their business in the green meadows, admit the animal world to a share in the faculty of reason. It is the cabinet thinkers who construct a universe of automations.

No better illustration of the two modes of observation can be found than in the scene of Goethe's 'Faust' where Faust and Wagner walking in the field are met by a strange dog. The first sees something more than a mere dog; he feels the presence of an intelligence within the outward semblance – in this case an evil intelligence, it is true, but still a something beyond mere tail and paws and ears. To Wagner it is a dog and nothing more – that will sit at the feet of his master and fawn on him if spoken to, who can be taught to fetch and carry or bring a stick; the end, however, proves different. So one mind sees the outside only; another projects itself into the mind of the creature, be it dog, or horse, or bird.

Experience certainly educates the dog as it does the man. After long acquaintance and practice in the field we learn the habits and ways of game - to know where it will or not be found. A young dog in the same way dashes swiftly up a hedge, and misses the rabbit that, hearing him coming, doubles back behind a tree or stole; an old dog leaves nothing behind him, searching every corner. This is acquired knowledge. Neither does all depend upon hereditary predisposition as exhibited in the various breeds – the setter, the pointer, the spaniel, or greyhound – and their especial drift of brain; their capacity is not wholly confined to one sphere. They possess an initiating power – what in man is called originality, invention, discovery: they make experiments.

I had a pointer that exhibited this faculty in a curious manner. She was weakly when young, and for that reason, together with other circumstances, was never properly trained: a fact that may perhaps have prevented her 'mind' from congealing into the stolidity of routine. She became an outdoor pet, and followed at heel everywhere. One day some ponds were netted, and of the fish taken a few chanced to be placed in a great stone trough from which cattle drank in the yard - a common thing in the country. Some time afterwards, the trough being foul, the fish – they were roach, tench, perch, and one small jack – were removed to a shallow tub while it was being cleansed. In this tub, being scarcely a foot deep though broad, the fish were of course distinctly visible, and at once became an object of the most intense interest to the pointer. She would not leave it; but stood watching every motion of the fish, with her head now on one side, now on the other. There she must have remained some hours, and was found at last in the act of removing them one by one and laying them softly, quite unhurt, on the grass.

I put them back into the water, and waited to see the result. She took a good look, and then plunged her nose right under the surface and half-way up the neck, completely submerging the head, and in that position groped about on the bottom till a fish came in contact with her mouth and was instantly snatched out. Her head must have been under water each time nearly a minute, feeling for the fish. One by one she drew them out and placed them on the ground, till only the jack remained. He puzzled her, darting away swift as an arrow and seeming to anticipate the enemy. But after a time he, too, was captured.

They were not injured – not the mark of a tooth was to be seen - and swam as freely as ever when restored to the water. So soon as they were put in again the pointer recommenced her fishing, and could hardly be got away by force. The fish were purposely left in the tub. The next day she returned to the amusement, and soon became so dexterous as to pull a fish out almost the instant her nose went under water. The jack was always the most difficult to catch, but she managed to conquer him sooner or later. When returned to the trough, however, she was done – the water was too deep. Scarcely anything could be imagined apparently more opposite to the hereditary intelligence of a pointer than this; and certainly no one attempted to teach her, neither did she do it for food. It was an original motion of her own: to what can it be compared but mind proceeding by experiment? They can also adjust their conduct to circumstances, as when they take to hunting on their own account: they then generally work in couples.

If a spaniel, for instance, one of those allowed to lie loose about farmhouses, takes to hunting for herself, she is almost always found to meet a canine friend at a little distance from the homestead. It is said that spaniels when they go off like this never bark when on the heels of a rabbit, as they would do if a sportsman was with them and the chase legitimate. This suppression of what must be an almost uncontrollable inclination shows no little intelligence. If they gave tongue, they would be certainly detected, and as certainly thrashed. To watch the sneaking way in which a spaniel will come home after an unlawful expedition of this kind is most amusing. She makes her appearance on the road or footpath so as not to look as if coming from the hedges, and enters at the back; or if any movement be going on, as the driving of cattle, she will join in it, displaying extraordinary zeal in assisting: anything to throw off suspicion.

Of all sport, if a man desires to widen his chest, and gain some idea of the chase as it was in ancient days, let him take two good greyhounds and 'uncouple at the timorous flying hare', following himself on foot. A race like this over the elastic turf of the downs, inhaling with expanded lungs air which acts on the blood as strong drink on the brain, stimulating the pulse, and strengthening every fibre of the frame, is equal to another year of life. Coursing for the coursing's sake is capital sport. A hare when sorely tried with the hot breath from the hounds' nostrils on his flanks, will sometimes puzzle them by dashing round and round a rick. Then in sweeping circles the trio strain their limbs, but the hare, having at the corners the inner side and less ground to cover, easily keeps just ahead. This game lasts several minutes, till presently one of the hounds is sharp enough to dodge back and meet the hare the opposite way. Even then his quick eye and ready turn often give him another short breathing space by rushing away at a tangent.

Rabbits, although of 'low degree' in comparison with the pheasant, really form an important item in the list of the keeper's charges. Shooting generally commences with picking out the young rabbits about the middle or towards the end of the hay harvest, according as the season is early or late. Some are shot by the farmers, who have the right to use a gun, earlier than this, while they still disport in the mowing grass. It requires experience and skill to select the young rabbit just fit for table from the old bucks, the does which may yet bring forth another litter, and those little bunnies that do not exceed the size of rats.

The grass conceals the body of the animal, and nothing is visible beyond the tips of the ears; and at thirty yards distance one pair of ears is very like another pair. The developed ear is, however, less pointed than the other; and in the rabbit of a proper size they are or seem to be wider apart. The eye is also guided by the grass itself and the elevation of the rabbit's head above it when lifted in alarm at chance sound: if the animal is full grown of course the head stands higher. In motion the difference is at once seen; the larger animal's back and flanks show boldly, while the lesser seems to slip through the grass. By these signs, and by a kind of instinct which grows upon one when always in the field, it is possible to distinguish between them even in tall grass and in the gloaming.

This sort of shooting, if it does not afford the excitement of the pheasant battue, or require the alertness necessary in partridge killing, is not without its special pleasures. These are chiefly to be attributed to the genial warmth of the weather at that season, when the reapers have only just begun to put the tall corn to the edge of their crooked swords, and one can linger by the hedge-side without dread of wintry chills.

The aftermath in which the rabbits feed is not so tall as the mowing grass, and more easy and pleasant to walk through, though it is almost devoid of flowers. Neither does it give so much shelter; and you must walk close to the hedge, gliding gently from bush to bush, the slower the better. Rabbits feed several times during the day – i.e. in the very early morning, next about eleven o'clock, again at three or four, and again at six or seven. Not that every rabbit comes out to nibble at those hours, but about that time some will be seen moving outside the buries.

As you stroll beside the hedge, brushing the boughs, a rabbit feeding two hundred yards away will lift his head inquiringly from the grass. Then stop, and remain still as the elm tree hard by. In a minute or two, reassured, the ears perked up so sharply fall back, and he feeds again. Another advance of ten or twenty yards, and up go the ears – you are still till they drop once more. The rabbit presently turns his back towards you, sniffing about for the tenderest blades; this is an opportunity, and an advance of forty or fifty paces perhaps is accomplished. Now, if you have a rook-rifle you are near enough; if a smooth-bore, the same system of stalking must be carried farther yet. If you are patient enough to wait when he takes alarm, and only to advance when he feeds, you are pretty sure to 'bag' him.

Sometimes, when thus gliding with stealthy tread, another rabbit will suddenly appear out of the ditch within easy reach; it is so quiet he never suspected the presence of an enemy. If you pause and keep quite still, which is the secret of all stalking, he will soon begin to feed, and the moment he turns his back towards you up goes the gun; not before, because if he sees your arm move he will be off to the ditch. True, a snap-shot might be made as he runs, which at first sight would appear more sportsmanlike than 'potting'; but it is not so, for it is ten chances to one that you do not kill him dead on the spot in the short distance he has to traverse. Perhaps the hind legs will be broken; well, then he will drag them along behind him, using the fore paws with astonishing rapidity and power. Before the second barrel can be emptied he will gain the shelter of the fern that grows on the edge of the bank and dive into a burrow, there to die in misery. So that it is much better to steadily 'pot' him. Besides which, if a rabbit dies in a burrow all the other animals in that particular burrow desert it till nature's scavengers have done their work. A dog cannot well be taken while stalking – not that dogs will not follow quietly, but because a rabbit, catching sight of a dog, is generally stricken with panic even if a hundred yards away, and bolts immediately.

I have seen a rabbit whose back was broken by shot drag itself ten yards to the ditch. If the forelegs are broken, then he is helpless: all the kicks of the hind legs only tumble him over and over without giving him much progress. The effects of shot are very strange, and sometimes almost inexplicable; as when a hare which has received a pellet through the edge of the heart runs a quarter of mile before dropping. It is noticed that hares and rabbits, hit in the vital organs about the heart, often run a considerable distance, and then, suddenly in the midst of their career, roll head over heels dead. Both hares and rabbits are occasionally killed with marks of old shot wounds, but not very often, and they are but of a slight character – the pellets are found just under the skin, with a kind of lump round them. Shot holes through the ears are frequently seen, of course doing no serious harm.

Now and then a rabbit hit in the head will run round and round in circles, making not the slightest attempt to escape. The first time I saw this, not understanding it, I gave the creature the second barrel; but next time I let the rabbit do as he would. He circled round and round, going at a rapid pace. I stood in his way, and he passed between my legs. After half a dozen circles the pace grew slower. Finally, he stopped, sat up quite still for a minute or so, and then drooped and died. The pellet had struck some portion of the brain.

I once, while looking for snipe with charges of small shot in the barrels, roused a fine hare, and fired without apparent effect. But after crossing about half of the field with a spaniel tearing behind, he began to slacken speed, and I immediately followed. The hare dodged the spaniel admirably, and it was with the utmost difficulty I secured him (refraining from firing the second barrel on purpose). He had been stopped by one single little pellet in the great sinew of the hind leg, which had partly cut it through. Had it been a rabbit he would certainly have escaped into a bury, and there perhaps died, as shot wounds frequently fester: so that in stalking rabbits, or waiting for them behind a tree or bush, it is much better to take a steady aim at the head, and so avoid torturing the creature.

'Potting' is hardly sport, yet it has an advantage to those who take a pleasure in observing the ways of bird and animal. There is just sufficient interest to induce one to remain quiet and still, which is the prime condition of seeing anything; and in my own case the rabbits so patiently stalked have at last often gone free, either from their own amusing antics, or because the noise of the explosion would disturb something else under observation. In winter it is too cold; then you step quietly and yet briskly up to a fence or gateway, and glance over, and shoot at once; or with the spaniels hunt the bunnies from the fern upon the banks, yourself one side of the hedge and the keeper the other.

In excavating his dwelling, the rabbit, thoughtless of science, constructs what may be called a natural auditorium singularly adapted for gathering the expiring vibrations of distant sound. His round tunnel bored in a sandy bank is largest at the opening, like the mouth of a trumpet, and contracts within – a form which focusses the undulations of the air. To obtain the full effect the ear should listen some short way within; but the sound, as it is thrown backwards after entering, is often sufficiently marked to be perceptible when you listen outside. The great deep ditches are dry in summer; and though shooting be not the object, yet a gun for knocking over casual vermin is a pleasant excuse for idling in a reclining position shoulder-high in fern hidden like a skirmisher in such an entrenchment. A mighty root bulging from the slope of the bank forms a natural seat. There is a cushion of dark green moss to lean against, and the sand worked out from the burrows – one nearly on a level with the head and another lower down – has here filled up the ditch to some height, making a footstool.

In the ditch lie numbers of last year's oak leaves, which so sturdily resist decay. All the winter and spring they were soaked by the water from the 'land-springs' – as those which only run in wet weather are called – draining into it, and to that water they communicated a peculiar flavour, slightly astringent. Even moderate-size streamlets become tainted in the latter part of the autumn by the mass of leaves they carry down, or filter through, in woodland districts. Often the cottagers draw their water from a small pool filled by such a ditch, and coated at the bottom with a thick layer of decomposing leaves. The taste of this water is strong enough to overcome the flavour of their weak tea, yet they would rather use such water than walk fifty yards to a brook. It must, however, be admitted that the brooks at that time are also tinctured with leaf, and there seems to be no harm in it.

Out from among these dead leaves in the ditch protrudes a crooked branch fallen long since from the oak, and covered with grey lichen. On the right hand a tangled thicket of bramble with its uneven-shaped stems closes the spot in, and on the left a stole of hazel rises with the parasitical 'hardy fern' fringing it near the earth. The outer bark of the hazel is very thin; it is of a dark mottled hue; bruise it roughly, and the inner bark shows a bright green. The lowly ivy creeps over the bank – its leaves with five angles and variegated with grey streaks. Through the hawthorn bushes above comes a faint but regular sound – it is the parting fibres of the grass-blades in the meadow on the other side as the cows tear them apart, steadily eating their way onwards. The odour of their breath floats heavy on the air. The sun is sinking and there is a hush and silence.

But the rabbit-burrow here at my elbow is not silent; it seems to catch and heighten faint noises from a distance. A man is walking slowly home from his work up the lane yonder; the fall of his footsteps is distinctly rendered by the hole here. The dull thuds of a far-off mallet or 'bitel' (beetle) driving in a stake are plainly audible. The thump-thump of a horse's hoofs cantering on the sward by the roadside, though deadened by the turf, are reproduced or sharpened. Most distinct of all comes the regular sound of oars against the tholepins or rowlocks of a boat moving on the lake many fields away. So that in all probability to the rabbit his hole must be a perfect 'Ear of Dionysius', magnifying a whisper – unless, indeed, its turns and windings confuse the undulations of sound. It is observable that before the rabbit ventures forth he stays and listens just within the entrance of his burrow, where he cannot see any danger unless absolutely straight before him – a habit that may have unconsciously grown up from the apparent resonance of sound there.

Sitting thus silently on the root of the oak, presently I hear a slight rustling among the dead leaves at the bottom of the ditch. They heave up as if something was pushing underneath; and after a while, as he comes to the heap of sand thrown out by the rabbits, a mole emerges, and instantly with a shiver, as it were, of his skin throws off the particles of dust upon his fur as a dog fresh from the water sends a shower from his coat. The summer weather having dried the clay under the meadow turf and made it difficult to work, he has descended into the ditch, beneath which there is still a certain moistness, and where he can easily bore a tunnel.

It is rather rare to see a mole above ground; fortunately for him he is of diminutive size, or so glossy a fur would prove his ruin. As it is, every other old pollard willow tree along the hedge is hung with miserable moles, caught in traps, and after death suspended – like criminals swinging on a gibbet – from the end of slender willow boughs. Moles seem to breed in the woods: first perhaps because they are less disturbed there, next because under the trees the earth is usually softer, retains its moisture longer, and is easier to work. From the woods their tracks branch out, ramifying like the roads which lead from a city. They have in addition main arteries of traffic, king's highways, along which they will journey one after the other; so that the mole-catcher, if he can discover such a road, slaughters many in succession. The heaps they throw up are awkward in mowing grass, the scythe striking against them; and in consequence of complaints of their rapid multiplication in the woods the keeper has to employ men to reduce their numbers. It is curious to note how speedily the mole buries himself in the soil; it is as if he suddenly dived into the earth.

Another slight rustling – a pause, and it is repeated; this time on the bank, among the dry grass. It is mice; they have a nervous habit of progressing in sharp, short stages. They rush forward seven or eight inches with lightning-like celerity – a dun streak seems to pass before your eye; then they stop short a moment or two, and again make another dash. This renders it difficult to observe them, especially as a single dead brown leaf is sufficient to hide one. It is so silent that they grow bold, and play their antics freely, darting to and fro, round and under the stoles, chasing each other. Sometimes they climb the bushes, running along the upper surface of the boughs that chance to be nearly horizontal. Once on a hawthorn branch in a hedge I saw a mouse descending with an acorn; he was, perhaps, five feet from the ground, and how and from whence he had got his burden was rather puzzling at first. Probably the acorn, dropping from the tree, had been caught and held in the interlacing of the bush till observed by the keen, if tiny, eyes below.

Mice have a magical way of getting into strange places. In some farmhouses they still use the ancient, old-fashioned lanterns made of tin – huge machines intended for a tallow candle, and with plates of thin translucent horn instead of glass. They are not wholly despicable; since if set on the ground and kicked over by a recalcitrant cow in the sheds, the horn does not break as glass would. These lanterns, having a handle at the top, are by it hung up to the beam in the kitchen; and sometimes to the astonishment of the servants in the quiet of the evening, they are found to be animated by some motive power, swinging to and fro and partly turning round. A mouse has got in – for the grease; but how? that is the 'wonderment', as the rustic philosophers express it; for, being hung from the beam, eight or nine feet from the stone-flagged floor, there seems no way of approach for the mouse except by 'walking' on the ceiling or along and partly underneath the beam itself. If so, it would seem to be mainly by the propulsive power exerted previous to starting on the trip – just as a man can get a little way up the perpendicular side of a rick by running at it. Occasionally, no doubt, the mouse has entered when the lantern has been left opened while lighted on the ground, and so got shut in; but mice have been found in lanterns cobwebbed from long disuse.

Suddenly there peeps out from the lower rabbit-hole the stealthy reddish body of a weasel. I instinctively reach for the gun leaning against the bank, and immediately the spell is broken. The mice rush to their holes, the weasel darts back into the bowels of the earth, a rabbit that has quietly slipped out unseen into the grass bounds with eager haste to cover, and out of the oak over-head there rises, with a great clatter of wings, a wood-pigeon that had settled there.

When the pale winter sunshine falls upon the bare branches of an avenue of elms – such as so often ornament parks - they appear lit up with a faint rosy colour, which instantly vanishes on the approach of a shadow. This shimmering mirage in the boughs seems due to the myriads of lesser twigs, which at the extremities have a tinge of red, invisible at a distance till the sunbeams illuminate the trees. Beyond this passing gleam of colour, nothing relieves the blackness of the January landscape, except here and there the bright silvery bark of the birch.

For several seasons now in succession the thrush has sung on the shortest days, as though it were spring; a little later, in the early mornings, the blackbird joins, filling the copse with a chorus at the dawn. But, if the wind turns to east or north, the rooks perch on the oaks in the hedgerows in the middle of the day, puffing out their feathers and seeming to abandon all search for food, as if seized with uncontrollable melancholy. Hardy as these birds are, a long frost kills them in numbers, principally by slow starvation. They die during the night, dropping suddenly from their roosting-place on the highest boughs of the great beech-trees, with a thud distinctly heard in the silence of the woods. The leaves of the beech decay so gradually as to lie in heaps beneath for months, filling up the hollows, so that an unwary passer-by may plunge knee-deep in leaves. Rooks when feeding usually cross the field facing the wind, perhaps to prevent the ruffling of their feathers.

Wood-pigeons have apparently much increased in numbers of recent years; they frequent sheltered spots where the bushes diminish the severity of the frost. Sometimes on the hills at a lonely farmhouse, where the bailiff has a long-barrelled ancient fowling-piece, he will lay a train of grain for them, and with a double charge of shot, kill many at a time.

Men have boasted of shooting twenty at once. But with an ordinary gun it is not credible; and the statement, without wilful exaggeration, may arise from confusion in counting, for it is a fact that some of the older uneducated country labourers cannot reckon correctly. It is not unusual in parishes to hear of a cottage woman who has had twenty children. Upon investigation the real number is found to be sixteen or seventeen, yet nothing on earth will convince the mother that she has not given birth to a score. They get hazy in figures when exceeding a dozen.

A pigeon is not easily brought down – the quills are so stiff and strong that the shot, if it comes aslant, will glance off. Many pigeons roost in the oaks of the hedges, choosing by preference one well hung with ivy, and when it is a moonlit night afford tolerable sport. It requires a gun on each side of the hedge. A stick flung up awakes the birds; they rise with a rush and clatter, and in the wildness of their flight and the dim light are difficult to hit. There is a belief that pigeons are partially deaf. If stalked in the daytime they take little heed of footsteps or slight noises which would alarm other creatures; but, on the other hand, they are quick of eye, and are gone directly anything suspicious appears in sight. You may get quite under them and shoot them on the bough at night. It is not their greater wakefulness but the noise they make in rising which renders them good protectors of preserves; it alarms other birds and can be heard at some distance.

When a great mound and hedgerow is grubbed up, the men engaged in the work often anticipate making a considerable bag of the rabbits, whose holes riddle it in every direction, thinking to dig them out even of those innermost chambers whence the ferret has sometimes been unable to dislodge them. But this hope is almost always disappointed; and when the grub-axe and spade have laid bare the 'buries' only recently teeming with life, not a rabbit is found. By some instinct they have discovered the approach of destruction, and as soon as the first few yards of the hedge are levelled secretly depart. After a 'bury' has been ferreted it is some time before another colony takes possession: this is seemingly from the intense antipathy of the rabbit to the smell of the ferret. Even when shot at and pressed by dogs, a rabbit in his hasty rush will often pass a hole which would have afforded instant shelter because it has been recetly ferreted.

At this season the labourers are busy with 'beetle' (pronounced 'bitel') - a huge mallet - and iron wedges, splitting the tough elm-butts and logs for firewood. In old times a cottager here and there with a taste for astrology used to construct an almanack by rule of thumb, predicting the weather for the ensuing twelve months from the first twelve days of January. As the wind blew on those days, so the prevailing weather of the months might be foretold. The aged men, however, say that in this divination the old style must be adhered to, for the sequence of signs and omens still follows the ancient reckoning, which ought never to have been interfered with.

from *The Gamekeeper at Home*

Chapter 19

Wiltshire Labourers

LETTER I
(To the editor of the "Times.")

Sir,

The Wiltshire agricultural labourer is not so highly paid as those of Northumberland, nor so low as those of Dorset; but in the amount of his wages, as in intelligence and general position, he may fairly be taken as an average specimen of his class throughout a large portion of the kingdom.

As a man, he is usually strongly built, broad-shouldered, and massive in frame, but his appearance is spoilt by the clumsiness of his walk and the want of grace in his movements. Though quite as large in muscle, it is very doubtful if he possesses the strength of the seamen who may be seen lounging about the ports. There is a want of firmness, a certain disjointed style, about his limbs, and the muscles themselves have not the hardness and tension of the sailor's. The labourer's muscle is that of a cart-horse, his motions lumbering and slow. His style of walk is caused by following the plough in early childhood, when the weak limbs find it a hard labour to pull the heavy nailed boots from the thick clay soil. Ever afterwards he walks as if it were an exertion to lift his legs. His food may, perhaps, have something to do with the deadened slowness which seems to pervade everything he does – there seems a lack of vitality about him. It consists chiefly of bread and cheese with bacon twice or thrice a week varied with onions, and if he be a milker (on some farms) with a good 'tuck-out' at his employer's expense on Sundays. On ordinary days he dines at the fashionable hour of six or seven in the evening – that is, about that time his cottage scents the road with a powerful odour of boiled cabbage, of which he eats an immense quantity. Vegetables are his luxuries, and a large garden, therefore, is the greatest blessing he can have. He eats huge onions raw; he has no idea of flavouring his food with them, nor of making those savoury and inviting messes or vegetable soups at which the French peasantry are so clever. In Picardy I have often dined in a peasant's cottage, and thoroughly enjoyed the excellent soup he puts upon the table for his ordinary meal. To dine in an English labourer's cottage would be impossible. His bread is generally good, certainly; but his bacon is the cheapest he can buy at small second-class shops – oily, soft, wretched stuff; his vegetables are cooked in detestable style, and eaten saturated with the pot liquor. Pot liquor is a favourite soup. I have known cottagers actually apply at farmers' kitchens not only for the pot liquor in which meat has been soddened, but for the water in which potatoes have been boiled – potato liquor – and sup it up with avidity. And this is not in times of dearth or scarcity, but rather as a relish. They never buy anything but bacon; never butchers' meat. Philanthropic ladies, to my knowledge, have demonstrated over and over again even to their limited capacities that certain parts of butchers' meat can be bought just as cheap, and will make more savoury and nutritive food; and even now, with the present high price of meat, a certain proportion would be advantageous. In vain; the labourers obstinately adhere to the pig, and the pig only. When, however, an opportunity does occur the amount of food they will eat is something astonishing. Once a year, at the village club dinner, they gormandise to repletion. In one instance I knew of a man eating a plate of roast beef (and the slices are cut enormously thick at these dinners), a plate of boiled beef, then another of boiled mutton, and then a fourth of roast mutton,and a fifth of ham. He said he could not do much to the bread and cheese; but didn't he go into the pudding! I have even heard of men stuffing to the fullest extent of their powers, and then retiring from the table to take an emetic of mustard and return to a second gorging. There is scarcely any limit to their powers of absorbing beer. I have known reapers and mowers make it their boast that they could lie on their backs and never take the wooden bottle (in the shape of a small barrel) from their lips till they had drunk a gallon, and from the feats I have seen I verily believe it a fact. The beer they get is usually poor and thin, though sometimes in harvest the farmers bring out a taste of strong liquor, but not till the work is nearly over; for from this very practice of drinking enormous quantities of small beer the labourer cannot drink more than a very limited amount of good liquor without getting tipsy. This is why he so speedily gets inebriated at the alehouse. While mowing and reaping many of them lay in a small cask.

They are much better clothed now than formerly. Corduroy trousers and slops are the usual style. Smock-frocks are going out of use, except for milkers and faggers. Almost every labourer has his Sunday suit, very often really good clothes, sometimes glossy black, with the regulation 'chimney-pot'. His unfortunate walk betrays him, dress how he will. Since labour has become so expensive it has become a common remark among the farmers that the labourer will go to church in broadcloth and the masters in smock-frocks. The labourer never wears gloves – that has to come with the march of the times; but he is particularly choice over his necktie. The women must dress in the fashion. A very respectable draper in an agricultural district was complaining to me the other day that the poorest class of women would have everything in the fashionable style, let it change as often as it would. In former times, if he laid in a stock of goods suited to tradesmen, and farmers' wives and daughters, if the fashion changed, or they got out of date, he could dispose of them easily to the servants. Now no such thing. The quality did not matter so much, but the style must be the style of the day – no sale for remnants. The poorest girl, who had not got two yards of flannel on her back, must have the same style of dress as the squire's daughter – Dolly Vardens, chignons, and parasols for ladies who can work all day reaping in the broiling sun of August! Gloves, kid, for hands that milk the cows!

The cottages now are infinitely better than they were. There is scarcely room for further improvement in the cottages now erected upon estates. They have three bedrooms, and every appliance and comfort compatible with their necessarily small size. It is only the cottages erected by the labourers themselves on waste plots of ground which are open to objection. Those he builds himself are, indeed, as a rule, miserable huts, disgraceful to a Christian country. I have an instance before me at this moment where a man built a cottage with two rooms and no staircase or upper apartments, and in those two rooms eight persons lived and slept – himself and wife, grown-up daughters, and children. There was not a scrap of garden attached, not enough to grow half-a-dozen onions. The refuse and sewage was flung into the road, or filtered down a ditch into the brook which supplied part of the village with water. In another case at one time there was a cottage in which twelve persons lived. This had upper apartments, but so low was the ceiling that a tall man could stand on the floor with his head right through the opening for the staircase, and see along the upper floor under the beds! These squatters are the curse of the community. It is among them that fever and kindred infectious diseases break out; it is among them that wretched couples are seen bent double with rheumatism and affections of the joints caused by damp. They have often been known to remain so long, generation after generation, in these wretched hovels, that at last the lord of the manor, having neglected to claim quit-rent, they can defy him, and claim them as their own property, and there they stick, eyesores and blots, the fungi of the land. The cottages erected by farmers or by landlords are now, one and all, fit and proper habitations for human beings; and I verily believe it would be impossible throughout the length and breadth of Wiltshire to find a single bad cottage on any large estate, so well and so thoroughly have the landed proprietors done their work. On all farms gardens are attached to the cottages, in many instances very large, and always sufficient to produce enough vegetables for the resident. In villages the allotment system has been greatly extended of late years, and has been found most beneficial, both to owners and tenants. As a rule the allotments are let at a rate which may be taken as £4 per annum – a sum which pays the landlord very well, and enables the labourer to remunerate himself. In one village which came under my observation the clergyman of the parish has turned a portion of his glebe land into allotments – a most excellent and noble example, which cannot be too widely followed or too much extolled. He is thus enabled to benefit almost every one of his poor parishioners, and yet without destroying that sense of independence which is the great characteristic of a true Englishman. He has issued a book of rules and conditions under which these allotments are held, and he thus places a strong check upon drunkeness and dissolute habits, indulgence in which is a sure way to lose the portions of ground. There is scarcely an end to the benefits of the allotment system. In villages there cannot be extensive gardens, and the allotments supply their place. The extra produce above that which supplies the table and pays the rent is easily disposed of in the next town, and places many additional comforts in the labourer's reach. The refuse goes to help support and fatten the labourer's pig, which brings him in profit enough to pay the rent of his cottage, and the pig, in turn, manures the allotment. Some towns have large common lands, held under certain conditions; such are Malmesbury, with 500 acres, and Tetbury (the common land of which extends two miles), both these being arable, &c. These are not exactly in the use of labourers, but they are in the hands of a class to which the labourer often rises. Many labourers have fruit-trees in their gardens, which, in some seasons, prove very profitable. In the present year, to my knowledge, a labourer sold £4 worth of apples; and another made £3, 10s. off the produce of one pear-tree, pears being scarce.

To come at last to the difficult question of wages. In Wiltshire there has been no extended strike, and very few meetings upon the subject, for the simple reason that the agitators can gain no hold upon a country where, as a mass, the labourers are well paid. The common day-labourer receives 10s, 11s., and 12s. a week, according to the state of supply and demand for labour in various districts; and, if he milks, 1s. more, making 13s. a week, now common wages. These figures are rather below the mark; I could give instances of much higher pay. To give a good idea of the wages paid I will take the case of a hill farmer (arable, Marlborough Downs), who paid this last summer during harvest 18s. per week per man. His reapers often earned 10s. a day – enough to pay their year's rent in a week. These men lived in cottages on the farm, with three bedrooms each, and some larger, with every modern appliance, each having a garden of a quarter of an acre attached and close at hand, for which cottage and garden they paid 1s. per week rent. The whole of these cottages were insured by the farmer himself, their furniture, &c., in one lump, and the insurance policy cost him, as nearly as possible, 1s.3d. per cottage per year. For this he deducted 1s. per year each from their wages. None of the men would have insured unless he had insisted upon doing it for them. These men had from six to eight quarts of beer per man (over and above their 18s. a week) during harvest every day. In spring and autumn their wages are much increased by piece-work, hoeing, &c. In winter the farmer draws their coal for them in his waggons, a distance of eight miles from the nearest wharf, enabling them to get it at cost price. This is no slight advantage, for, at the present high price of coal, it is sold, delivered in the villages, at 2s. per cwt. Many who cannot afford it in the week buy a quarter of a cwt. on Saturday night, to cook their Sunday's dinner with, for 6d. This is at the rate of £2 per ton. Another gentleman, a large steam cultivator in the Vale, whose name is often before the public, informs me that his books show that he paid £100 in one year in cash to one cottage for labour, showing the advantage the labourer possesses over the mechanic, since his wife and child can add to his income. Many farmers pay £50 and £60 a year for beer drunk by their labourers – a serious addition to their wages. The railway companies and others who employ mechanics do not allow them any beer. The allowance of good cottage and a quarter of an acre of garden for 1s. per week is not singular. Many who were at the Autumn Manoeuvres of the present year may remember having a handsome row of houses, rather than cottages, pointed out to them as inhabited by labourers at 1s. per week. In the immediate neighbourhood of large manufacturing towns 1s. 6d. a week is sometimes paid; but then these cottages would in such positions readily let to mechanics for 3s., 4s., and even 5s. per week. There was a great outcry when the Duke of Marlborough issued an order that the cottages on his estate should in future only be let to such men as worked upon the farms where those cottages were situated. In reality this was the very greatest blessing the Duke could have conferred upon the agricultural labourer; for it ensured him a good cottage at a nearly nominal rent and close to his work; whereas in many instances previously the cottages on the farms had been let at a high rate to the mechanics, and the labourer had to walk miles before he got to his labour. Cottages are not erected by landowners or by farmers as paying speculations. It is well known that the condition of things prevents the agricultural labourer from being able to pay a sufficient rent to be a fair percentage upon the sum expended. In one instance a landlord has built some cottages for his tenant, the tenant paying a certain amount of interest on the sum invested by the landlord. Now, although this is a matter of arrangement, and not of speculation – that is, although the interest paid by the tenant is a low percentage upon the money laid out, yet the rent paid by the labourers inhabiting these cottages to the tenant does not reimburse him when he pays his landlord as interest – not by a considerable margin. But then he has the advantage of his labourers close to his work, always ready at hand.

Over and above the actual cash wages of the labourer, which are now very good, must be reckoned his cottage and garden, and often a small orchard, at a nominal rent, his beer at his master's expense, piece-work, gleaning after harvest, &c., which alter his real position very materially. In Gloucestershire, on the Cotswolds, the best-paid labourers are the shepherds, for in that great sheep-country much trust is reposed in them. At the annual auctions of shearlings which are held upon the large farms a purse is made for the shepherd of the flock, into which every one who attends is expected to drop a shilling, often producing £5. The shepherds on the Wiltshire Downs are also well paid, especially in lambing-time, when the greatest watchfulness and care are required. It has been stated that the labourer has no chance of rising from his position. This is sheer cant. He has very good opportunities of rising, and often does rise, to my knowledge. At this present moment I could mention a person who has risen from a position scarcely equal to that of a labourer, not only to have a farm himself, but to place his sons in farms. Another has just entered on a farm; and several more are on the high-road to the desirable consummation. If a labourer possesses any amount of intelligence he becomes a head-carter or head-fagger, as the case may be; and from that to be assistant or under-bailiff, and finally bailiff. As a bailiff he has every opportunity to learn the working of a farm, and is often placed in entire charge of a farm at a distance from his employer's residence. In time he establishes a reputation as a practical man, and being in receipt of good wages, with very little expenditure, saves some money. He has now little difficulty in obtaining the promise of a farm, and with this can readily take up money. With average care he is a made man. Others rise from petty trading, petty dealing in pigs and calves, till they save sufficient to rent a small farm, and make the basis of larger dealing operations. I question very much whether a clerk in a firm would not find it much more difficult, as requiring larger capital, to raise himself to a level with his employer than an agricultural labourer does to the level of a farmer.

Many labourers now wander far and wide as navvies, &c., and perhaps when these return home, as most of them do to agricultural labour, they are the most useful and intelligent of their class, from a readiness they posses to turn their hand to anything. I know one at this moment who makes a large addition to his ordinary wages by brewing for the small inns, and very good liquor he brews, too. They pick up a large amount of practical knowledge.

The agricultural women are certainly not handsome; I know no peasantry so entirely uninviting. Occasionally there is a girl whose nut-brown complexion and sloe-black eyes are pretty, but their features are very rarely good, and they get plain quickly, so soon as the first flush of youth is past. Many have really good hair in abundance, glossy and rich, perhaps from its exposure to the fresh air. But on Sundays they plaster it with strong-smelling pomade and hair-oil, which scents the air for yards most unpleasantly. As a rule, it may safely be laid down that the agricultural women are moral, far more so than those of the town. Rough and rude jokes and language are, indeed, too common; but that is all. No evil comes of it. The fairs are the chief cause of immorality. Many an honest, hard-working servant-girl owes her ruin to these fatal mops and fairs, when liquor to which she is unaccustomed overcomes her. Yet it seems cruel to take from them the one day or two of the year on which they can enjoy themselves fairly in their own fashion. The spread of friendly societies, patronised by the gentry and clergy, with their annual festivities, is a remedy which is gradually supplying them with safe, and yet congenial, amusement. In what may be termed lesser morals I cannot accord either them or the men the same phrase. They are too ungrateful for the many great benefits which are bountifully supplied them – the brandy, the soup, and fresh meat readily extended without stint from the farmer's home in sickness to the cottage are too quickly forgotten. They who were most benefited are often the first to most loudly complain and to backbite. Never once in all my observation have I heard a labouring man or woman make a grateful remark; and yet I can confidently say that there is no class of persons in England who receive so many attentions and benefits from their superiors as the agricultural labourers. Stories are rife of their even refusing to work at disastrous fires because beer was not immediately forthcoming. I trust this is not true; but it is too much in character. No term is too strong in condemnation for those persons who endeavour to arouse an agitation among a class of people so short-sighted and so ready to turn against their own benefactors and their own interest. I am credibly informed that one of these agitators, immediately after the Bishop of Gloucester's unfortunate but harmlessly intended speech at the Gloucester Agricultural Society's dinner – one of these agitators mounted a platform at a village meeting and in plain language incited and advised the labourers to duck the farmers! The agricultural women either go out to field-work or become indoor servants. In harvest they hay-make – chiefly light work, as raking – and reap, which is much harder labour; but then, while reaping they work their own time, as it is done by the piece. Significantly enough, they make longer hours while reaping. They are notoriously late to arrive, and eager to return home, on the hay-field. The children help both in haymaking and reaping. In spring and autumn they hoe and do other piece-work. On pasture farms they beat clots or pick up stones out of the way of the mowers' scythes. Occasionally, but rarely now, they milk. In winter they wear gaiters, which give the ankles a most ungainly appearance. Those who go out to service get very low wages at first from their extreme awkwardness, but generally quickly rise. As dairymaids they get very good wages indeed. Dairymaids are scarce and valuable. A dairymaid who can be trusted to take charge of a dairy will sometimes get £20 besides her board (liberal) and sundry perquisites. These often save money, marry bailiffs, and help their husbands to start a farm.

In the education provided for children Wiltshire compares favourably with other counties. Long before the passing of the recent Act in reference to education the clergy had established schools in almost every parish, and their exertions have enabled the greater number of places to come up to the standard required by the Act, without the assistance of a School Board. The great difficulty is the distance children have to walk to school, from the sparseness of population and the number of outlying hamlets. This difficulty is felt equally by the farmers,

who, in the majority of cases, find themselves situated far from a good school. In only one place has anything like a cry for education arisen, and that is on the extreme northern edge of the county. The Vice-Chairman of the Swindon Chambers of Agriculture recently stated that only one-half of the entire population of Inglesham could read and write. It subsequently appeared that the parish of Inglesham was very sparsely populated, and that a variety of circumstances had prevented vigorous efforts being made. The children, however, could attend schools in adjoining parishes, not farther than two miles, a distance which they frequently walk in other parts of the country.

Those who are so ready to cast every blame upon the farmer, and to represent him as eating up the earnings of his men and enriching himself with their ill-paid labour, should remember that farming, as a rule is carried on with a large amount of borrowed capital. In these days, when £6 an acre has been expended in growing roots for sheep, when the slightest derangement of calculation in the price of wool, meat, or corn, or the loss of a crop, seriously interferes with a fair return for capital invested, the farmer has to sail extremely close to the wind, and only a little more would find his canvas shaking. It was only recently that the cashier of the principal bank of an agricultural county, after an unprosperous year, declared that such another season would make almost every farmer insolvent. Under these circumstances it is really to be wondered at that they have done as much as they have for the labourer in the last few years, finding him with better cottages, better wages, better education, and affording him better opportunities of rising in the social scale. – I am, Sir, faithfully yours,
Richard Jefferies.
Coate Farm, Swindon, Nov. 12, 1872

Lord Shaftesbury, in the *Times*, Dec. 6th, says:-

'It is our duty and our interest to elevate the present condition of the labourer, and to enable him to assert and enjoy every one of his rights. But I must agree with Mr. Jefferies that, even under the actual system of things, numerous instances have occured of a rise in the social scale as the result of temperance, good conduct, and economy. He has furnished some examples. I will give only one from my own estate:– 'T.M. was for many years shepherd to Farmer P–; he bought with his savings a small leasehold property at – for £170, and he had accumulated £100 besides. He had brought up a son and three daughters, and his son now occupies the leasehold.' This is the statement as given to me in writing.'

LETTER II
(To the Editor of the "Times.")

Sir,
I did not intend to make any reply to the numerous attacks made upon my letter published in the *Times* of the 14th inst., but the statements made by 'The Son of a Wiltshire Labourer' are such as I feel bound to resent on the part of the farmers of this county.

He says he wishes the landed proprietors would take as much care to provide cottages for their labourers as I represent them as doing. I repeat what I said, that the cottages on large estates are now, one and all, fit habitations for human beings. The Duke of Marlborough is a large proprietor of cottages in this neighbourhood, and his plan has been, whenever a cottage did not appear sufficiently commodious, to throw two into one. The owner of the largest estate near Swindon has been engaged for many years past in removing the old thatched mud hovels, and replacing them with substantial, roomy, and slate-roofed buildings. Farmers are invariably anxious to have good cottages. There is a reluctance to destroy the existing ones, both from the inconvenience and the uncertainty sometimes of others being erected. Often too, the poor have the strongest attachment to the cabin in which they were born and bred, and would strongly resent its destruction, though obviously for their good. Farmers never build bad cottages now. When a tenement falls in, either from decay or the death of the tenant, the cottage which is erected on its site is invariably a good one. A row of splendid cottages has recently been erected at Wanborough. They are very large, with extensive gardens attached. Some even begin to complain that the cottages now erected are in a sense 'too good' for the purpose. The system of three bedrooms is undoubtedly the best from a sanitary point of view, but it is a question whether the widespread belief in that system, and that system alone, has not actually retarded the erection of reasonably good buildings. It is that third bedroom which just prevents the investment of building a cottage from paying a remunerative percentage on the capital expended. Two bedrooms are easily made – the third puzzles the builder where to put it with due regard to economy. Nor is a third bedroom always required. Out of ten families perhaps only two require a third bedroom; in this way there is a large waste in erecting a row. It has been suggested that a row should consist of so many cottages with two bedrooms only for families who do not want more, and at each end a building with three bedrooms for larger families. In one instance two cottages were ordered to be erected on an estate, the estimate for which was £640; these when completed might have left for £10 per annum, or 1³/₄ per cent. on the capital invested! The plans for these cottages had so many dormer windows, porches, intricacies of design in variegated tiles, &c., that the contractor gave it up as a bad job. I mention this to show that the tendency to build good cottages has gone even beyond what was really required, and ornamentation is added to utility.

Then it is further stated that the labourer cannot build cottages. I could name a lane at this moment the cottages in which were one and all built by labourers; and there are half-a-dozen in this village which were erected by regular farm labourers. The majority of these are, as I said before, wretched hovels, but there are two or three which demonstrate that the labourer, if he is a thrifty man, earns quite sufficient to enable him to erect a reasonably good building. The worst hovel I ever saw (it was mentioned in my letter of the 14th) was built by a man who is notorious for his drinking habits. Some forty years ago, when wages were much lower than they are now, two labourers, to my knowledge, took possession of a strip of waste land by the roadside, and built themselves cottages. One of these was a very fair building; the other would certainly be condemned now-a-days. The lord of the manor claimed these; and the difficulty was thus adjusted:– The builders were to receive the value of their tenements from the lord of the manor, and were to remain permanent tenants for life on payment of a small percentage, interest upon the purchase-money, as quit-rent. On their deaths the cottages were to become the property of the lord of the manor. One man received £40 for his cottage, the other £20, which sums forty years ago represented relatively a far higher value than now, and demonstrate conclusively that the labourer, if he is a steady, hard-working man, can build a cottage. Another cottage I know of, built by a farm labourer, is really a very creditable building – good walls, floors, staircase, sashes, doors, it stands high, and appears very comfortable, and even pleasant, in summer, for they are a thrifty family, and can even display flower-pots in the window. Other cottages have been built or largely added to in my memory by labourers. On these occasions they readily obtain help from the farmers. One lends his team and waggons to draw the stones; another supplies wood for nothing; but of late I must admit there has been some reluctance to assist in this way (unless for repairs) because it was so often found that the buildings thus erected were not fit habitations. The Boards of Guardians often find a difficulty from the limited ownership of some of the labourers, who apply for relief, of their cottages. Perhaps they have not paid quit-rent for a year or two; but still they cannot sell, and yet it seems unjust to the ratepayers to assist a man who has a tenement which he at least calls his own, and from which he cannot be ejected. I know a labourer at this moment living in a cottage originally built by his father, and added to by himself by the assistance of the neighbouring farmers. This man has been greatly assisted by one farmer in particular, who advanced him money by which he purchased a horse and cart, and was enabled to do a quantity of hauling, flint-carting for the waywardens, and occasionally to earn money by assisting to carry a farmer's harvest. He rents a large piece of arable land, and ought to be comparatively well off.

'The Son of a Wiltshire Labourer' complains that the farmers or proprietors do not make sufficient efforts to supply the cottages with water. The lord of the manor and the tenant of the largest farms in this immediate neighbourhood have but just sunk a well for their cottages; previously they had got their supply from a pump in an adjacent farmyard thrown open by the proprietor to all the village.

It is the labourer himself who will not rise. In a village with which I am acquainted great efforts have been made by a farmer and a gentleman living near to provide proper school instruction for the children. One labourer was asked why he did not send his children to school. He replied, 'Because he could not afford it.' 'But,' said the farmer, 'it is only threepence altogether.' 'Oh, no; he could not afford it.' 'The farmer explained to him that the object was to avoid a School Board, which, in other places, had the power to fine for not sending children to school. 'No, he could not afford it.' The farmer's books show that his labourer, his wife, and two children received 28s. 6d. per week, his cottage rent free, and a very large garden at a low rent. Yet he could not afford the 3d. a week which would enable his children ultimately to take a better position in the world! The same farmer, who is a liberal and large-minded man, has endeavoured, without success, to introduce the practice of paying in cash instead of beer, and also the system of payment for overtime. The men say no, they would rather not. 'In wet weather,' they say, 'we do no work, but pay us; and if we work a little later in harvest, it only makes it fair.' They would not take money instead of beer. In another case which came under my personal observation in the middle of last summer, a farmer announced his intention of paying in cash instead of allowing beer. In the very press of the haymaking, with acres upon acres of grass spoiling, his men, one and all, struck work because he would not give them beer, and went over to a neighbour's field adjacent and worked for him for nothing but their share in the beer. If labourers work longer hours in harvest (corn), it is because it is piece-work, and they thereby make more money. I contend that the payment in kind, the beer, the gleanings, the piece-work, the low and nominal cottage rent, the allotment ground and produce, and the pig (not restricted to one pig in a year), may fairly be taken as an addition to their wages. I am informed that in one parish the cottage rents vary from 10d. to 1s. 2d. per week; nearly all have gardens, and all may have allotments up to a quarter of an acre each at 3d. per lug, or 40s. per acre. I am also informed of a labourer renting a cottage and garden at 1s. per week, the fruit-trees in whose garden produced this year three sacks of damsons, which he sold at 1. 6d. per gallon, or £6.18s. I know of a case in which a labourer – an earnest, intelligent, hard-working man – makes £2 a week on an average all the year round. But then he works only at piece-work, going from farm to farm, and this is, of course, an exceptional case. The old men, worn out with age and infirmity, are kept on year after year by many farmers out of charity, rather than let them go to the workhouse, though totally useless and a dead loss, especially as occupying valuable cottage-room. There is a society, the annual meetings of which are held at Chippenham, and which is supported by the clergy, gentry, and farmers generally of North Wilts, for the object of promoting steady habits among the labourers and regarding cases of long and deserving services. There is also a friendly society on the best and most reliable basis, supported by the gentry, and introduced as far as possible into villages. The labourers on the Great Western Railway works at Swindon earn from 15s. a week upwards, according as they approach to skilled workmen. Attracted by the wages, most of the young men of the neighbourhood try the factory, but usually, after a short period return to farm-work, the result of their experience being that they are better off as agricultural labourers. Lodgings in the town close to the factory are very expensive, and food in proportion; consequently they have to walk long distances to their labour – some from Wanborough, five miles; Wroughton, three and a half miles; Purton, four miles; and even Wootton Bassett, six miles, which twice a day is a day's work in itself. Add to this the temptations to spend money in towns, and the severe labour, and the man finds himself better off with his quiet cottage and garden on a farm at 12s. a week and 1s. for milking, with beer, and a meal on Sundays. The skilled mechanics, who earn 36s. to £2 per week, rent houses in the town at 6s. to 8s.; and in one case I knew of 12s. per week paid by a lodger for two rooms. These prices cannot be paid out of the mechanic's wage; consequently he sub-lets, or takes lodgers, and sometimes these sub-let, and the result is an overcrowding worse than that of the agricultural cottages, around which there is at least fresh air and plenty of light (nearly as important), which are denied in a town. The factory labourer and the mechanic are liable to instant dismissal. The agricultural labourers (half of them at least) are hired by the year or half-year, and cannot be summarily sent along unless for misconduct. Wages have recently been increased by the farmers of Wiltshire voluntarily and without pressure from threatened strikes, It is often those who receive the highest wages who are the first to come to the parish for relief. It is not uncommon for mechanics and others to go for relief where it is discovered that they are in receipt of sick pay from the yard club, and sometimes from two friendly societies, making 18s. a week. A manufacturing gentleman informed me that the very men whom he had been paying £8 a week to were the first to apply for relief when distress came and the mills stopped. It is not low wages, then, which causes improvident habits. The only result of deporting agricultural labourers to different counties is to equalise the wages paid all over England. This union-assisted emigration affords the improvident labourer a good opportunity of transporting himself to a distant county, and leaving deeply in debt with the tradesmen with whom he has long dealt. I am informed that this is commonly the case with emigrating labourers. A significant fact is noted in the leader of the Labour News of the 16th of November; the return of certain emigrants from America is announced as 'indicative that higher quotations are not always representative of greater positive advantages.' The agricultural labourer found that out when he returned from the factory at 15s. per week to farm labour at 12s. I am positive that the morality of the country compares favourably with that of the town. I was particularly struck with this fact on a visit to the Black Country. One of the worst parishes for immorality in Wiltshire is one where glovemaking is carried on; singularly enough, manufactures and immorality seem to go together. 'The Son of a Labourer' says that all the advantages the labourer does possess are owing to the exertions of the clergy; pray who support the clergy but the farmers?

I think that the facts I have mentioned sufficiently demonstrate that the farmers and the landlords of Wiltshire have done their duty, and more than their mere duty, towards the labourers; and only a little investigation will show that at present it is out of their power to do more. Take the case of a farmer entering a dairy-farm of, say, 250 acres, and calculate his immediate outgoings – say fifty cows at £20, £1000; two horses at £25, £50; waggons, carts, implements, £100; labour, three men at 12s. per week, £94; harvest labour, £20; dairymaid £10; tithe, taxes, rates, &c., £100; rent, £2 per acre, £500. Total, £1874. In other words (exclusive of the capital invested in stock), the outgoings amount to £724 per annum; against which put – fifty cows' milk, &c., at £10 per head, £500; fifty calves, £100; fifty tons of hay at £3.10s., £175. Total income £775; balance in hand £51. Then comes the village school subscription; sometimes a church rate (legally voluntary, but morally binding),&c.

So that, in hard figures (all these are below the mark, if anything), there is positively nothing left for the farmer but a house and garden free. How, then, is money made? By good judgement in crops, in stock, by lucky accidents. On a dairy-farm the returns begin immediately; on an arable one there is half a year at least to wait. The care, the judgement, required to be exercised is something astonishing, and a farmer is said to be all his life learning his trade. If sheep are dear and pay well, the farmer plants roots; then, perhaps after a heavy expenditure for manure, for labour, and seed, there comes the fly, or a drought, and his capital is sunk. On the other hand, if the season be good, roots are cheap and over-plentiful, and where is his profit then? He works like a labourer himself in all weathers and at all times; he has the responsibility and the loss, yet he is expected to find the labourer, not only good cottages, allotments, schooling, good wages, but Heaven knows what besides. Supposing the £1874 (on the dairy-farm) be borrowed capital for which he must pay at least 4 per cent – and few, indeed, are there who get money at that price – it is obvious how hard he must personlly work, how hard, too, he must live, to make both ends meet. And it speaks well for his energy and thrift that I heard a bank director not long since remark that he had noticed after all, with every drawback, the tenant farmers had made as a rule more money in proportion than their landlords. A harder-working class of men does not exist than the Wiltshire farmers.

Only a few days ago I saw in your valuable paper a list, nearly a column long, of the millionaires who had died in the last ten years. It would be interesting to know how much they had spent for the benefit of the agricultural labourer. Yet no one attacks them. They pay no poor-rates, no local taxation, or nothing in proportion. The farmer pays the poor-rate which supports the labourer in disease, accident, and old age; the highway rates on which the millionaire's carriage rolls; and very soon the turnpike trusts will fall in, and the farmers – i.e., the land – will have to support the imperial roads also. With all these heavy burdens on his back, having to compete against the world, he has yet no right to compensation for his invested capital if he is ordered to quit. Without some equalisation of local taxation – as I have shown, the local taxes often make another rent almost – without a recognised tenant-right, not revolutionary, but for unexhausted improvements, better security, so that he can freely invest capital, the farmer cannot – I reiterate it, he cannot – do more than he has done for the labourer. He would then employ more skilled labour, and wages would be better. And, after all that he does for them, he dares not find fault, or he may find his ricks blazing away – thanks to the teaching of the agitators that the farmer are tyrants, and, by inference, that to injure them is meritorious. There is a poster in Swindon now offering £20 reward for the discovery of the person who maliciously set fire to a rick of hay in Lord Bolingbroke's park at Lydiard.

If any farmers are hard upon their men, it is those who have themselves been labourers and have risen to be employers of labour. These very often thoroughly understand the art of getting the value of a man's wage out of him. I deliberately affirm that the true farmers, one and all, are in favour of that maxim of a well-known and respected agriculturist of our county – 'A fair day's wage for a fair day's work.'

I fear the farmers of Wiltshire would be only too happy to ride thorough-breds to the hunt, and see their daughters driving phaetons, as they are accused of doing; but I also fear that very, very few enjoy that privilege. Most farmers, it is true, do keep some kind of vehicle; it is necessary when their great distance from a town is considered, and the keep of a horse or two comes to nothing on a large farm. It is customary for them to drive their wives or daughters once a week on market-days into the nearest town. If here and there an energetic man succeeds in making money, and is able to send his son to a university, all honour to him. I hope the farmers will send their sons to universities; the spread of education in their class will be of as much advantage to the community as among the labouring population, for it will lead to the more general application of science to the land and a higher amount of production. If the labourer attempted to rise he would be praised; why not the farmer?

It is simply an unjustifiable libel on the entire class to accuse them of wilful extravagance. I deliberately affirm that the majority of farmers in Wiltshire are exactly the reverse; that, while they practise a generous hospitality to a friend or a stranger, they are decidedly saving and frugal rather than extravagant, and they are compelled to be so by the condition of their finances. To prove that their efforts are for the good of the community I need only allude to the work of the late Mr. Stratton, so crowned with success in improving the breed of cattle – a work in the sister county of Gloucester so ably carried on at this present moment by Mr. Edward Bowly, and by Mr. Lane and Mr. Garne in the noted Cotswold sheep. The breeds produced by these gentlemen have in a manner impregnated the whole world, imported as they have been to America and Australia. It was once ably said that the readings of the English Bible Sunday after Sunday in our churches had preserved our language pure for centuries, and, in the same way, I do verily believe that the English (not the Wiltshire only, but the English) farmer as an institution, with his upright, untainted ideas of honour, honesty, and morality, has preserved the tone of society from that corruption which has so miserably degraded France – so much so that Dumas recently scientifically predicted that France was *en route à prostitution générale*. Just in the same way his splendid constitution as a man recruits the exhausted, pale, nervous race who dwell in cities, and prevents the Englishman from physically degenerating. – I am, Sir, faithfully yours,

Richard Jefferies

Coate Farm, Swindon, November 21, 1872.

from *The Toilers of the Field*

Chapter 20

The Squire and the Land

'A man should be straight, like a gun,' said the Squire, looking into the lock he was cleaning, and carefully running some oil which had become thick from absorbing particles of dust. 'But good form is not much regarded in these days. A high score is the one great aim and object, and if you cannot make a high score there seems a feeling abroad that you may as well at once disappear. In fact, you do disappear. Whether it is shooting, or cricket, or lawn tennis, or boating, or swimming, or walking, you must do something that nobody else has ever done. You must kill every pigeon, or finish the mile in two seconds less time than all who have tried before. How you walk, or how you shoot, in good style or not, matters not the least. The record is everything. Nobody looks at you – the public look at the scoring board. But I like to see a man himself, as straight as a gun; what do I care about figures on the telegraph! I never could back a horse unless I had seen him, and felt him, and watched him at exercise and got to know him. There are thousands put on horses which the backers have never seen and never will see. I do not protest against it: all I say is, it is not my feeling. In the ferocious competition of our times, the competitor himself is quite forgotten. Why should everyone compete? Why enter every colt for the Derby? We seem to be all rubbed out – ourselves, I mean – and merely ticketed with a number, like the convicts: a number indicating our position in the huge rush for a place. It is open to me to grumble, since I am nowhere: merely an 'O' in the world's estimation.'

He polished away at the lock-plate till it shone like silver.

'As you dislike competition, some people would say you are an enemy to progress.' said his visitor.

'That is the popular opinion, I know,' replied the Squire. 'To be a landowner is to be the bodily presentment of ignorance and anti-civilization. I utterly deny it. I say I am an agent of rural advancement. I have done everything I could to get the school at... into working order, short of teaching myself. I have subscribed a considerable sum towards the new railway, to meet the preliminary expenses, and parted with my land for nothing – practically nothing. Besides all my personal efforts, there's a heap of letters on the table there now waiting to be answered. Country railways would never be made without the assistance of landowners: how could the little villages and market towns pay for them? Sir Anthony N. put down a thousand, to begin with. Of course, we shall reap a benefit from it, but not nearly so much in proportion as the labouring people, whose wages will rise: they know that; they are most eager for it. My great hope is that the population will increase. I mean, our country population.

There might then be a market for vegetables and garden produce, and a better demand for land to cultivate. There can scarcely be said to be a demand for land at all at the present moment.'

"But, I thought,' said his visitor, 'that you country gentlemen hated all innovation, and change, and would not have the railway near your parks and covers.'

'Well, I cannot deny that that was the case some fifty years ago,' said the Squire; 'but you must, in justice, own that our ancestors had no knowledge of the rail. We can look back on it; we have had fifty years' experience, and thoroughly understand it. Is it not extremely unjust, to say the least, to visit me with opprobrium because my predecessor could not foresee steam? Who could have foreseen it? – I doubt if a Bacon could. The present generation of landowners, I assure you, think very differently. You see, I am simply a capitalist whose capital consists of land instead of cash. My class of capital has not advanced so rapidly as other kinds, and I am anxious to increase the yield from it.'

'Still, you are exclusive – you stand aloof from the people; you don't assist popular movements.'

'I forgive you for saying that,' said the Squire, 'because that also is a sort of article of belief among you City gentlemen. The truth is precisely the reverse: I assist every popular movement, from a cottage flower show to a new railway. I have just subscribed to the new Chapel schools at Latten* (I am a Churchman, you know). I really do not think I am exclusive – I mean, personally: not so much as many wealthy employers of labour in London, who give liberal wages to their men but, beyond that, know nothing of them, or of anyone else except their own class. Now, I know almost everyone in the parish; really, I think I may say, every one, and quite three-fourths of the people round the place, and I take a great interest in them, too. Do you know, I do not think the ploughman who touches his hat to me is half so servile as many well-educated persons I have met in town who seem able to descend to any depth of adulation to secure an invitation to a millionaire's table.'

'But you would not speak to the ploughman.'

'Not speak to a ploughman!' exclaimed the Squire, dropping a tiny screwdriver with which he was replacing the lock on the stock, in amazement, and laughing. 'I should rather think I would. I would shake hands with any honest or decent fellow in the parish; there are not many cottages I have not been in, at one time or another; I, or Geraldine. But then, you City people, who know everything, do not seem to have the least idea of the natural condition of things in the country. You seem to think we have stood still here these last two generations, and are, morally and socially, still in kneebuckles and powder!'

'No, no! not quite so bad as that; but, still, there is a wide gulf between you and the ploughman.'

'I differ,' said the Squire: 'the social relations are not nearly so sharply defined in our village as in cities and their suburbs. We have all more or less a community of interest and a common subject to talk about: the weather, the crops, and the state of farming. The labourers, the farmers, the dealers – everybody has something to say about it; I take the deepest interest in it, of course. In cities and town life there is a diversity of trade and business; you are not all concerned in one business, and therefore, you are more distant, having no public topic of conversation. But please understand me: I am not criticizing your manners, far from it; what I wish is to remove some of the curious misunderstanding which exists concerning us. You must excuse me for saying that I think the prejudice is on your side, not ours. We have no prejudice against you, or against progress and improvement, as you wrongly assume; but you have a strong prejudice against us, as if we were survivals of the barbarous ages.'

'Well,' said his visitor, smiling and glancing meaningly around the gun-room at the racks, and bench, and arms. 'You are looking at the old guns,' said the Squire: 'you consider them symptoms of barbarous tastes. There I meet you face to face to the battle – I differ from you altogether. I am for all improvements and all kinds of progress – your railways, and telegraphs, and telephones, and tramways, and education, and sanitation; your artisic propaganda, even; every scientific, and artistic, and moral, and social, step forward has my hearty good wishes. At the same time, I want a man to be a man. How can he be a man without some speck of nature in him? I don't like the idea of our becoming altogether artificial. I hope something of the forest feeling – the spirit of the forest – will survive in everyone. I am sure sport is morally good for us. Whether it is hunting, or shooting, or coursing, or racing, there is something in it which lifts one out of the vapidness of life. It braces up the body, and sets the heart beating, and lights up a sparkle in the eye. Something comes out of the woods and hills and brooks and fills you inwardly with an exaltation. You feel like a man. Fortunately, no amount of artificiality is likely to drive the love of sport out of us – out of the masses, I mean. Racing is more popular than ever; so is coursing; so is hunting; so is shooting – where one hunted years ago, ten hunt now; where one gun was sold then, twenty are sold now. People burst out every autumn; away they go to moor and loch, and sea and mountain (for climbing comes within what I call sport), to get their manhood back again.

'If ever it should happen that our forests and hills should be cultivated, and every trace of wildness smoothed out of the country, do you know, I verily believe it would become necessary to plant forests and lay down hills with turf: in short, to make national preserves – just as it is found necessary now to preserve open spaces. No: you can't rub manhood out of the English people, as the latter Romans rubbed away their beards with pumice stone.

'There is, I think, nothing so grand as the way in which the nation starts to its feet the moment there is a call to arms: let it but suppose itself insulted: let the trumpet sound, and every man is up in a second. I verily believe that in case of real danger we could raise a million men in a week.'

'Horrible!' his visitor exclaimed, shutting his eyes and waving his hands: 'most horrible; don't speak of anything so dreadful. I see you are as barbarian as ever.'

'Not so barbarous as you and your artificiality,' said the Squire, warmly, bringing down his fist with a bang on the bench and making the tools jump from their places. 'Your modern ideal of women is disgraceful. I never pick up a paper without finding some evil insinuation about women. It is false, sir, false – utterly false. I say you may go into a hundred houses, one after the other, and be certain that the women are not only pure but beyond reproach. I mean to say that the tone of female society is higher and purer now than ever it was.'

from *The Old House at Coate*

Chapter 21
The Gentleman-Farmer

He comes striding over the fallow, a gun on his arm, a pipe in his mouth, and a dog at his heels. A tall loose-jointed young fellow – for his bones are not yet 'set', and the country air prolongs the period of growth – with plentiful indications of whiskers and moustache. His trousers are turned up (your old-fashioned farmer always wore gaiters) to preserve them from getting soiled; his cuffs are somewhat wrinkled, but he will change them before dinner; and 'There's the bell, by Jove!' – for his tutor, the big tenant-farmer, or rather agricultural capitalist, sits down at six, rings in his guests, and has a man-servant to wait at table and fill his pupil's glass with wine. If the new novels have not come up from Messrs. Smith & Son's bookstall and library at the station – whither the groom rides daily to fetch them – and if the squire or the rector has not sent round a pressing invitation, the pupil mounts his bicycle, and takes a 'run' into the market-town. As he glides along the smooth road (which, by the bye, in a year or two will not be quite so smooth, now the turnpikes have dropped in, and the parish has to repair it) a ploughman remarks to his master, a *working* farmer – observe that – as they lean against a gate,

He be a spruck un!

Ay, ay, John; I allers zed it 'ud come to no good when um zet up a aggericulturul college!

At the market-town our friend meets a few choice spirits at the billiard-table, and 'knocks the balls' about at pool. At a quarter-past eleven, when the house by law should be shut, he quits the green cloth for the bar, where the favoured habitués are sipping the sweetest, i.e. forbidden, glass of the evening; and after glancing at the sporting-paper, consults in a corner with the landlord, who is a bookmaker on a pretty extensive scale under the rose. Having made an entry or two in a certain small pocket-book, chaffed the barmaid, and gallantly lifted his hat to the buxom landlady (who pronounces him '*such* a gentleman!') he starts for home as the church-clock tolls midnight, while the policeman on the beat carefully looks round the corner the other way, mindful of many a fee. Slipping in by a latchkey, our studious pupil finishes his pipe in bed, and drops off to sleep, perhaps dreaming of the old song,

'We be all jolly fellows what follows the plough!'

Breakfast about ten – the raw mists have rolled away by then – in his own special corner by the bay-window looking out on the lawn and flower-beds. His letters are there on a silver salver, and the morning paper, unopened and smelling of printer's ink, lies beside them. His host's daughter is there, and laughingly pours out his coffee, and contrives to make it precisely to his fancy. There are the breast of a pheasant, some kidneys, a ham, and a few other trifles to pick up from, or pitch at Jip, who sits at his feet and 'yaps', if his lips are dry and palate parched after last night. A glance at the sporting correspondent's news, a yawn or so, and then – to business. Throwing the breechloader over his shoulder, he stalks through the turnips, zigzagging towards a noise of panting and puffing, and a column of black smoke yonder. Bang, bang! right and left, by Jove! Picking up the partridges with a passing thought of bread-sauce, he makes his way to where the steam-ploughing engines are at work, and, choosing a comfortable sheltered corner under an oak, sits down upon the dry bank in the warm sunshine to study the operations. There is something very soothing in the hum of the flywheels, and gradually the scene fades out of sight; sweet slumber settles upon him, till a tall greyhound dashes up and licks a fly off his nose, and a jovial voice cries, 'Now, Tom; lunch-time, my boy!' So they stroll home together, Tom and his master, who tells him a sly story, and jerks his thumb in his ribs, while they shout with laughter, and the startled rooks rise with a loud 'Caw!'

After lunch Tom thinks he will stretch the mare on the downs; and returning about four finds lawn-tennis in full swing, and three or four ladies charmingly attired, who form a very pretty foreground to the ancient rambling, red-tiled, and ivy-hidden house. There is some decent champagne at dinner; and, on the whole, things are tolerably comfortable. You would hardly think, if you sat at the well-appointed table and glanced at the furniture and the pictures on the walls and the silver prize-cups yonder, sipping your champagne and trifling with fish or game, that agriculture was going to the dogs. But you might perhaps begin to realize that the big agricultural capitalist is a latter-day plant, which his landlord, even though he have a title, finds it necessary to cultivate skilfully and conciliate socially. Tom, having just returned from his holiday ramble to Paris, or some other continental pleasure centre, has plenty to talk of, and presently is in request at the piano, and does not acquit himself badly.

When these things come to pall a little the season grows cooler, and the scent begins to lie, and our friend becomes very busy indeed, for he has to attend a meet of the hounds almost every morning. The capitalist, his tutor, has three or four, or even six, hunters in his stable, and Tom has to keep them up to their work; the tutor rides a stone or so too heavy for the younger horses. Besides which Tom has a mare of his own, which he is 'making', and which he risks his neck to show off, with a shrewd notion of selling and clearing a fifty before long. For although an idle dog in the eyes of the working farmers round about, our pupil is far sharper in the ways of this modern world than they are, and is wide awake to the advantage of making a circle of acquaintances at the Hunt who may be useful to him hereafter. Should frost interfere with these pursuits, there are the snipes to be knocked over in the water-meadows, and that woodcock they flushed in the double mound, where the spring bubbles up and does not freeze, to be looked after. Or better still, there is the rabbit-ferreting going on in the squire's covers, which affords first-class practice, and plenty of it. There are few places more lively than the end of a great sandy bank riddled with burrows when three or four 'pugs' are busy inside, with their red eyes and somewhat butcher-like tastes. The bunnies come tumbling out here, there, and everywhere – popping from one hole to the other, darting across to the wood there, slipping up the ditch, dodging behind trees and stumps and boulder-stones, and doing everything in fact, except giving you time to take aim. The keeper stands on one side of the hedge, Tom watches the other, two assistants are in the ditches attending to 'pug', and the firing is something to listen to – a perfect Plevna for the brown-coated creatures. In the rear, note a mighty jar of October ale, and altogether, even in frosty weather, Tom contrives to keep warm.

But it is not all play. You should see him in a slop-jacket, with a black face, and a bundle of cotton-waste in one hand, driving the traction engine with the greatest *sang-froid,* fetching up a load of coal in the wagon behind from the railway-station, or working the ploughing tackle, and in the interim, while his engine is slacking, i.e. the wire-rope uncoiling and the plough travelling towards the opposite engine, cracking filberts with the spanner. You should see him at the annual sale of shorthorns or ram-lambs, or whatever the speciality of the place may be, busy with the dinner-tickets, showing the big men over the pens, and hinting confidentially that this ram or that bull is 'a splendid thing, sir, and sure to make your money twice over'. Then behold him rising at the inevitable dinner to propose the toast of 'the buyers', and rolling out well-balanced periods, which make the company feel what a thing it is to have 'eddication'. To be able to hold forth glibly, and strike the popular nails on the head with a sprinkling of jocularity, is an essential accomplishment to the 'coming' agriculturist. Without a good speech or two nothing can be done. Upstairs in his room Tom has a box crammed full of scientific knowledge – books on geology, botany, mathematics (!) physiology, &c., which he had to scan pretty closely at 'college', and which are supposed to fit youth for the plough and the cattle-stall, but which box has never been opened since he arrived on the farm. He looks upon them with intense scorn, and prides himself on being a 'practical' man. He sees that good sherry well plied has an amazing influence on the price of shorthorns. He notes that a brace of pheasants or a hare judiciously left at the local newspaper-office is usually followed by 'extensive' accounts of the wonderful animals or extraordinary crops to be found at a certain spot. Free champagne has been known to oil quills with a wider scope than that of the local editor; and the agricultural capitalist who would get a cosmopolitan fame and bring bidders from the United States and Australia must keep open house to the press. Tom has a shrewd idea that certain pieces of oblong paper with a stamp on them are continually passing between his tutor, the auctioneer (who should in these days rather be called the agricultural stockbroker – not punningly either) and the Bank. The meaning of which is that these great concerns of three and four thousand acres require a good deal of 'financing', and also that more money is made by judicious speculation – buying and selling and making a price with advertising – than by the simple husbandry of sowing the seed and waiting till it ripens. Nor does he forget to observe that a 'silver tongue' and good address will get a young fellow a first-class farm much more surely than any solid experience. For though the squire's lady may sneer at his lack of pedigree, and so forth, yet somehow there is more pleasure in seeing a tall, well-dressed, gentlemanly young man, who can talk and knows how to behave, in the pew at church every Sunday than the cumbrous old style of rude and yet sheepish tenant-farmer. So Tom is by no means such a fool as he may seem to the slow-coaches of the parish. He has a note-book, in which he jots down briefly and in cipher these and similar observations upon the ways of mankind; and when he draws on his snow-white cuffs and gold links, and adjusts a stray curl over his forehead before he goes down to dinner, where he will meet somebody from 'the Hall', he is wiser in his generation than those crotchety college-tutors with their jargon of superphosphates. To all the rectors' daughters (who seldom have curates to keep up to their duty) round about, to the big gentlemen farmers' girls, and even to the ladies at 'the Hall', bored to death half their time, Tom and his kind are a positive blessing. As for his hunting and shooting, a heavy sum has been paid as a premium, and stiff amount annually for his board, &c., and why should he not have it out of the soil?

These youths of late years have become quite a feature in rural society. Who are they? It would be hard to say, as they are drawn from so many sources. When men have accumulated great fortunes in trade or commerce, as the years go on they find their boys growing up, and what is to be done with them? One is destined to carry on the City concern; another goes into the Church or the Army or the Bar, places once only filled from the country gentlemen's families; and the third – 'Well, he's fond of out-door exercise, let's make him a farmer!' That is the history in many cases; but occasionally the pupil is a cadet from a higher social grade – a grade which sees the necessity of putting the fellows to do something to get money or at least their living, and yet cannot overcome the repugnance to trade. Now in the position of the big agriculturist there exists a certain parallelism, as it were, with the gentry; there is nothing degrading or pettifogging about it, and so this new profession powerfully recommends itself. And the free open-air life is a great inducement.

These young men not infrequently go off to the colonies after they have finished their time, and grow into mighty sheep-masters in Australia, or own a hundred thousand acres in Natal, and so do good work in the world. For the young fellow who gets through his billiards and petty bookmaking, stable propensities, and so forth, early in life, is generally found to possess more knowledge of men and to succeed better than the mere studious book-worm or milk-sop, who is ever at the edge of a petticoat, cannot soil his boots after a hare, and thinks croquet an exciting game.

from *Landscape and Labour*

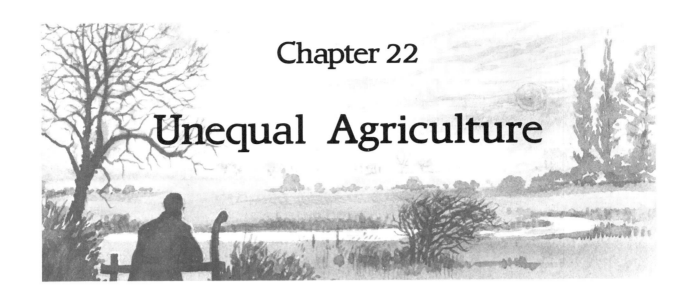

Chapter 22

Unequal Agriculture

In the way of sheer, downright force few effects of machinery are more striking than a steam-ploughing engine dragging the shares across a wide expanse of stiff clay. The huge engines used in our ironclad vessels work with a graceful ease which deceives the eye; the ponderous cranks revolve so smoothly, and shine so brightly with oil and polish, that the mind is apt to underrate the work performed. But these ploughing engines stand out solitary and apart from other machinery, and their shape itself suggests crude force, such force as may have existed in the mastodon or other unwieldy monster of the prehistoric ages. The broad wheels sink into the earth under the pressure; the steam hissing from the escape valves is carried by the breeze through the hawthorn hedge, hiding the red berries with a strange, unwonted cloud; the thick dark brown smoke, rising from the funnel as the stoker casts its food of coal into the fiery mouth of the beast, falls again and floats heavily over the yellow stubble, smothering and driving away the partridges and hares. There is a smell of oil, and cotton-waste, and gas, and steam, and smoke, which overcomes the fresh,sweet odour of earth and green things after a shower. Stray lumps of coal crush the delicate pimpernel and creeping convolvulus. A shrill, short scream rushes forth and echoes back from an adjacent rick – puff ! the fly-wheel revolves, and the drum underneath tightens its hold upon the wire rope. Across yonder a curious, shapeless thing, with a man riding upon it, comes jerking forward, tearing its way through stubble and clay, dragging its iron teeth with sheer strength deep through the solid earth. The thick wire rope stretches and strains as if it would snap and curl up like a

tortured snake; the engine pants loudly and quick; the plough now glides forward, now pauses, and, as it were, eats its way through a tougher place, then glides again, and presently there is a pause, and behold the long furrow with the upturned subsoil is completed. A brief pause, and back it travels again, this time drawn from the other side, where a twin monster puffs and pants and belches smoke, while the one that has done its work uncoils its metal sinews. When the furrows run up and down a slope, the savage force, the fierce, remorseless energy of the engine pulling the plough upwards, gives an idea of power which cannot but impress the mind.

This is what is going on upon one side of the hedge. These engines cost as much as the fee-simple of a small farm; they consume expensive coal, and water that on the hills has to be brought long distances; they require skilled workmen to attend to them, and they do the work with a thoroughness which leaves little to be desired. Each puff and pant echoing from the ricks, each shrill whistle rolling along from hill to hill, proclaims as loudly as iron and steel can shout, 'Progress! Onwards!' Now step through this gap in the hedge and see what is going on in the next field. It is a smaller ground, of irregular shape and uneven surface. Steam-ploughs mean *plains* rather than fields – broad, square expanses of land without awkward corners – and as level as possible, with mounds that may have been tumuli worked down, rising places smoothed away, old ditch-like drains filled up, and fairly good roads. This field may be triangular or some indescribable figure, with narrow corners where the high hedges come close together, with deep furrows to carry away the water, rising here and sinking there into curious hollows, entered by a narrow gateway leading from a muddy lane where the ruts are a foot deep. The plough is at work here also, such a plough as was used when the Corn Laws were in existence, chiefly made of wood – yes, actually wood, in this age of iron – bound and strengthened with metal, but principally made from the tree – the tree which furnishes the African savage at this day with the crooked branch with which to scratch the earth, which furnished the ancient agriculturists of the Nile Valley with their primitive implements. It is drawn by dull, patient oxen, plodding onwards now just as they were depicted upon the tombs and temples, the graves and worshipping places, of races who had their being three thousand years ago. Think of the suns that have shone since then; of the summers and the bronzed grain waving in the wind, of the human teeth that have ground that grain, and are now hidden in the abyss of earth; yet still the oxen plod on, like slow Time itself, here this day in our land of steam and telegraph. Are not these striking pictures, remarkable contrasts? On the one side steam, on the other the oxen of the Egyptians, only a few thorn-bushes between dividing the nineteenth century B.C. from the nineteenth century A.D. After these oxen follows an aged man, slow like themselves, sowing the seed. A basket is at his side, from which at every stride, regular as machinery, he takes a handful of that corn round which so many mysteries have gathered from the time of Ceres to the hallowed words of the great Teacher, taking His parable from the sower. He throws it with a peculiar steady jerk, so to say, and the grains, impelled with the exact force and skill, which can only be attained by long practice, scatter in an even shower. Listen! On the other side of the hedge the rattle of the complicated drill resounds as it drops the seed in regular rows – and, perhaps, manures it at the same time – so that the plants can be easily thinned out, or the weeds removed after the magical influence of the despised clods has brought on the miracle of vegetation. These are not extreme and isolated instances; no one will need to walk far afield to witness similar contrasts. There is a medium between the two – a third class – an intermediate agriculture. The pride of this farm is in its horses, its teams of magnificent animals, sleek and glossy of skin, which the carters spend hours in feeding lest they should lose their appetites – more hours than ever they spend in feeding their own children. These noble creatures, whose walk is power and whose step is strength; work a few hours daily, stopping early in the afternoon, taking also an ample margin for lunch. They pull the plough also like the oxen, but it is a modern implement, of iron, light, and with all the latest improvements. It is typical of the system itself – half and half – neither the old oxen nor the new steam, but midway, a compromise. The fields are small and irregular in shape, but the hedges are cut, and the mounds partially grubbed and reduced to the thinnest of banks, the trees thrown, and some draining done. Some improvements have been adopted, others have been omitted.

Upon those broad acres where the steam-plough was at work, what tons of artificial manure, superphosphate, and guano, liquid and solid, have been sown by the progressive tenant! Lavishly and yet judiciously, not once, but many times, have the fertilizing elements been restored to the soil, and more than restored – added to it till the earth itself has grown richer and stronger. The scarifier and the deep plough have turned up the subsoil and exposed the hard, stiff under-clods to the crumbling action of the air and the mysterious influence of light. Never before since Nature deposited those earthy atoms there in the slow process of some geological change has the sunshine fallen on them, or their latent power been called forth. Well-made and judiciously laid drains carry away the flow of water from the winter rains and floods – no longer does there remain a species of reservoir at a certain depth, chilling the tender roots of the plants as they strike downwards, lowering the entire temperature of the field. Mounds have been levelled, good roads laid down, nothing left undone that can facilitate operations or aid in the production of strong, succulent vegetation. Large flocks of well-fed sheep, folded on the corn lands, assist the artificial manure and perhaps even surpass it. When at last the plant comes to maturity and turns colour under the scorching sun, behold a widespread ocean of wheat, an English gold-field, a veritable Yellow Sea, bowing in waves before the southern breeze – a sight full of peaceful poetry. The stalk is tall and strong, good in colour, fit for all purposes. The ear is full, large; the increase is truly a hundredfold. Or it may be roots. By these means the progressive agriculturist has produced a crop of swedes or mangolds which in individual size and collective weight per acre would seem to an old-fashioned farmer perfectly fabulous. Now, here are many great benefits. First, the tenant himself reaps his reward, and justly adds to his private store. Next, the property of the landlord is improved, and increases in value. The labourer gets better house accommodation, gardens, and higher wages. The country at large is supplied with finer qualities and greater quantities of food, and those who are engaged in trade and manufactures, and even in commerce, feel an increased vitality in their various occupations.

On the other side of the hedge, where the oxen were at plough, the earth is forced to be self-supporting – to restore to itself how it can the elements carried away in wheat and straw and root. Except a few ill-fed sheep, except some small quantities of manure from the cattle-yards, no human aid, so to say, reaches the much-abused soil. A crop of green mustard is sometimes ploughed in to decompose and fertilize, but as it had to be grown first the advantage is doubtful. The one object is to spend as little as possible upon the soil, and to get as much out of it as may be. Granted that in numbers of cases no trickery be practised, that the old rotation of crops is honestly followed, and no evil meant, yet even then, in course of time, a soil just scratched on the surface, never fairly manured, and always in use, must of necessity deteriorate. Then, when such an effect is too patent to be any longer overlooked, when the decline of the produce begins to alarm him, the farmer, perhaps, buys a few hundredweight of artificial manure, and frugally scatters it abroad. This causes "a

'The partridges will lie a little at first over the short stubble...'
(*Decline of Partridge Shooting*)

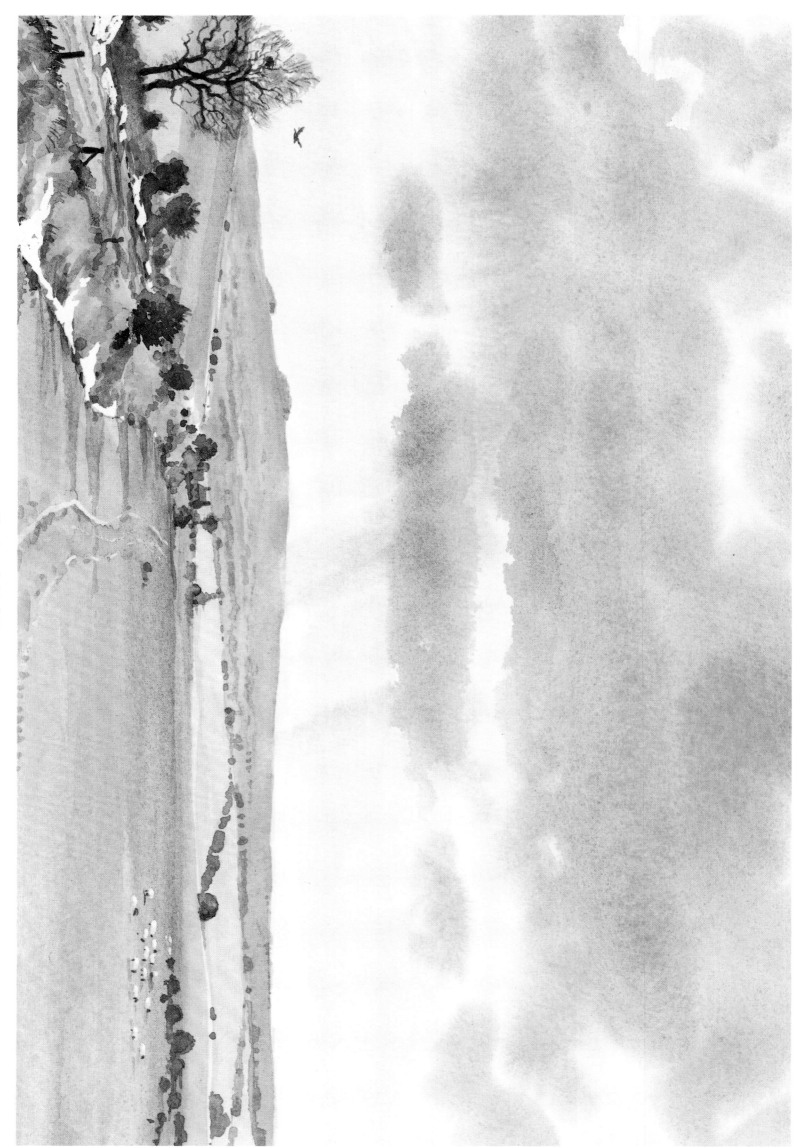

The dawn behind Coate
(*The Squire and the Land*)

flash in the pan"; it acts as a momentary stimulus; it is like endeavouring to repair a worn-out constitution with doses of strong cordial; there springs up a vigorous vegetation one year, and the next the earth is more exhausted than before. Soils cannot be made highly fertile all at once even by superphospahtes; it is the inability to discern this fact which leads many to still argue in the face of experience that artificial manures are of no avail. The slow oxen, the lumbering wooden plough, the equally lumbering heavy waggon, the primitive bush-harrow, made simply of a bush cut down and dragged at a horse's tail – these are symbols of a standstill policy utterly at variance with the times. Then this man loudly complains that things are not as they used to be – that wheat is so low in price it will not yield any profit, that labour is so high and everything so dear; and, truly, it is easy to conceive that the present age, with its competition and eagerness to advance, must really press very seriously upon him.

Most persons have been interested enough, however little connected with agriculture, to at least once in their lives walk round an agricultural show, and to express their astonishment at the size and rotundity of the cattle exhibited. How easy, judging from such a passing view of the finest products of the country centred in one spot, to go away with the idea that under every hawthorn hedge a prize bullock of enormous girth is peacefully grazing! Should the same person ever go across country, through gaps and over brooks, taking an Asmodeus-like glance into every field, how marvellously would he find that he had been deceived! He might travel miles, and fly over scores of fields, and find no such animals, nor anything approaching to them. By making inquiries he would perhaps discover in most districts one spot where something of the kind could be seen – an oasis in the midst of a desert. On the farm he would see a long range of handsome outhouses, tiled or slated, with comfortable stalls and every means of removing litter and manure, tanks for liquid manure, skilled attendants busy in feeding, in preparing food, storehouses full of cake. A steam-engine in one of the sheds – perhaps a portable engine, used also for threshing – drives the machinery which slices up or pulps roots, cuts up chaff, pumps up water, and performs a score of other useful functions. The yards are dry, well paved, and clean; everything smells clean; there are no foul heaps of decaying matter breeding loathsome things and fungi; yet nothing is wasted, not even the rain that falls upon the slates and drops from the eaves. The stock within are worthy to compare with those magnificent beasts seen at the show. It is from these places that the prize animals are drawn; it is here that the beef which makes England famous is fattened; it is from here that splendid creatures are sent abroad to America or the Colonies, to improve the breed in those distant countries. Now step forth again over the hedge, down yonder in the meadows.

This is a cow-pen, one of the old-fashioned style; in the dairy and pasture countries you may find them by hundreds still. It is pitched by the side of a tall hedge, or in an angle of two hedges, which themselves form two walls of the enclosure. The third is the cow-house and shedding itself; the fourth is made of willow rods. These rods are placed upright, confined between horizontal poles, and when new this simple contrivance is not wholly to be despised; but when the rods decay, as they do quickly, then gaps are formed, through which the rain and sleet and bitter wind penetrate with ease. Inside this willow paling is a lower hedge, so to say, two feet distant from the other, made of willow work twisted – like a continuous hurdle. Into this rude manger, when the yard is full of cattle, the fodder is thrown. Here and there about the yard, also stand cumbrous cribs for fodder, at which two cows can feed at once. In one corner there is a small pond, muddy, stagnant, covered with duckweed, perhaps reached by a steep, 'pitched' descent, slippery, and difficult for the cattle to get down. They foul the very water they drink. The cow-house, as it is called, is really merely adapted for one or two cows at a time, at the period of calving – dark, narrow, awkward. The skilling, or open house where the cows lie and chew the cud in winter, is built of boards or slabs at the back, and in front supported upon oaken posts standing on stones. The roof is of thatch, green with moss; in wet weather the water drips steadily from the eaves, making one long gutter. In the eaves the wrens make their nests in the spring, and roost there in winter. The floor here is hard, certainly, and dry; the yard itself is a sea of muck. Never properly stoned or pitched, and without a drain, the loose stones cannot keep the mud down, and it works up under the hoofs of the cattle in a filthy mass. Over this there is litter and manure a foot deep; or if the fogger does clean up the manure, he leaves it in great heaps scattered about, and on the huge dunghill just outside the yard he will show you a fine crop of mushrooms cunningly hidden under a light layer of litter. It is his boast that the cow-pen was built in the three sevens; on one ancient beam, worm-eaten and cracked, there may perhaps be seen the inscription '1777' cut deep into the wood. Over all, at the back of the cow-pen, stands a row of tall elm-trees, dripping in wet weather upon the thatch, in the autumn showering their yellow leaves into the hay, in a gale dropping dead branches into the yard. The tenant seems to think even this shelter effeminate, and speaks regretfully of the old hardy breed which stood all weathers, and wanted no more cover than was afforded by a hawthorn bush. From here a few calves find their way to the butcher, and towards Christmas one or two moderately fat beasts.

Near by lives a dairy farmer, who, without going to the length of the famous stock-breeder whose stalls are the pride of the district, yet fills his meadows with a handsome herd of productive short-horns, giving splendid results in butter, milk, and cheese, and who sends to the market a succession of animals which, if not equal to the gigantic prize beasts, are nevertheless valuable to the consumer. This tenant does good work, both for himself and for the labourers, the landlord, and the country. His meadows are a sight in themselves to the experienced eye – well drained, great double mounds thinned out, but the supply of wood not quite destroyed – not a rush, a 'bullpoll', a thistle or a 'rattle', those yellow pests of mowing grass to be seen. They have been weeded out as carefully as the arable farmer weeds his plants. Where broad deep furrows used to breed those aquatic grasses which the cattle left, drains have been put in and soil thrown over till the level was brought up to the rest of the field. The manure carts have evidently been at work here, perhaps the liquid manure tank also, and some artificial aid in places where required, both of seed and manure. The number of stock kept is the fullest tale the land will bear, and he does not hesitate to help the hay with cake in the fattening stalls. For there are stalls, not so elaborately furnished as those of the famous stock-breeder, but comfortable, clean, and healthy. Nothing is wasted here either. So far as practicable the fields have been enlarged by throwing two or three smaller enclosures together. He does not require so much machinery as the great arable farmer, but here are mowing machines, haymaking machines, horse-rakes, chain harrows, chaff-cutters, light carts instead of heavy waggons – every labour-saving appliance. Without any noise or puff this man is doing good work, and silently reaping his reward. Glance for a moment at an adjacent field: it is an old 'leaze' or ground not mown, but used for grazing. It has the appearance of a desert a wilderness. The high, thick hedges encroach upon the land; the ditches are quite arched over by the brambles and briars which trail out far into the grass. Broad deep furrows are full of tough, grey aquatic grass, 'bullpolls', and short brown rushes; in the winter they are so many small brooks. Tall bennets from last year and thistle abound – half the growth is useless for cattle; in autumn the air here is white with the clouds of thistle-down. It is a tolerably large field but the meadows held by the same tenant are small, with double mounds and trees, rows of spreading oaks and tall elms; these meadows run up into the strangest nooks and corners. Sometimes, where they follow the course of a brook which winds and turns, actually an area equal to about half the available field is occupied by the hedges. Into this brook the liquid sewage from the cow-pens filtrates, or, worse still, accumulates in a hollow, making a pond, disgusting to look at, but which liquid, if properly applied, is worth almost its weight in gold. The very gateways of the fields in winter are a Slough of Despond, where the wheels sink in up to the axles, and in summer great ruts jolt the loads almost off the waggons.

Where the steam-plough is kept, where first-class stock are bred, there the labourer is well housed, and his complaints are few and faint. There cottages with decent and even really capital accommodation for the families spring up, and are provided with extensive gardens. It is not easy, in the absence of statistics, to compare the difference in the amount of money put in circulation by these contrasted farms, but it must be something extraordinary. First comes the capital expenditure upon machinery – ploughs, engines, drills, what not – then the annual expenditure upon labour, which, despite the employment of machinery, is as great or greater upon a progressive farm as upon one conducted on stagnant principle. Add to this the cost of artificial manure, of cake and feeding-stuffs, etc., and the total will be something very heavy. Now, all this expenditure, this circulation of coin, means not only gain to the individual, but gain to the country at large. Whenever in a town a great manufactory is opened and gives employment to several hundred hands, at the same time increasing the production of a valuable material, the profit – the *outside* profit, so to say – is as great to others as to the proprietors. But these half-cultivated lands, these tons upon tons of wasted manure, these broad hedges and weed-grown fields, represent upon the other hand an equal loss. The labouring classes in the rural districts are eager for more work. They may popularly be supposed to look with suspicion upon change, but such an idea is a mistaken one. They anxiously wait the approach of such works as new railways or extension of old ones in the hope of additional employment. Work is their gold-mine, and the best mine of all. The capitalist, therefore, who sets himself to improve his holding is the very man they most desire to see. What scope is there for work upon a stagnant dairy farm of one hundred and fifty acres? A couple of foggers and milkers, a hedger and ditcher, two or three women at times, and there is the end. And such work! – mere animal labour, leading to so little result. The effect of constant, of lifelong application in such labour cannot but be deteriorating to the mind. The master himself must feel the dull routine. The steam-plough teaches the labourer who works near it something; the sight must react upon him, utterly opposed as it is to all the traditions of the past. The enterprise of the master must convey some small spirit of energy into the mind of the man. Where the cottages are built of wattle and daub, low and thatched – mere sheds, in fact – where the gardens are small, and the allotments, if any, far distant, and where the men wear a sullen, apathetic look, be sure the agriculture of the district is at a low ebb.

Are not these few pictures sufficient to show beyond a cavil that the agriculture of this country exhibits the strangest inequalities? Anyone who chooses can verify the facts stated, and may perhaps discover more curious anomalies still. The spirit of science is undoubtedly abroad in the homes of the English farmers, and immense are the strides that have been taken; but still greater is the work that remains to be done. Suppose anyone had a garden, and carefully manured, and dug over and over again, and raked, and broke up all the larger clods, and well watered one particular section of it, leaving all the rest to follow the dictates of wild nature, could he possibly expect the same amount of produce from those portions which, practically speaking, took care of themselves? Here are men of intellect and energy employing every possible means to develop the latent powers of the soil, and producing extraordinary results in grain and meat. Here also are others who, in so far as circumstances permit, follow in their footsteps. But there remains a large area in the great garden of England which, practically speaking, takes care of itself. The grass grows, the seed sprouts and germinates, very much how they may, with little or no aid from man. It does not require much penetration to arrive at the obvious conclusion that the yield does not nearly approach the possible production. Neither in meat nor corn is the tale equal to what it well might be. All due allowance must be made for barren soils of sand or chalk with thinnest layers of earth; yet then there is an enormous area, where the soil is good and fertile, not properly productive. It would be extremely unfair to cast the blame wholly upon the tenants. They have achieved wonders in the past twenty years; they have made gigantic efforts and bestirred themselves right manfully. But a man may wander over his farm and note with discontented eye the many things he would like to do – the drains he would like to lay down, the manure he would like to spread abroad, the new stalls he would gladly build, the machine he so much wants – and then, shrugging his shoulders, reflect that he has not got the capital to do it with. Almost to a man they are sincerely desirous of progress; those who cannot follow in great things do in little. Science and invention have done almost all that they can be expected to do; chemistry and research have supplied powerful fertilizers. Machinery has been made to do the work which at first sight seems incapable of being carried on by wheels and cranks. Science and invention may rest awhile: what is wanted is the universal application of their improvements by the aid of more capital. We want the great garden equally highly cultivated everywhere.

from *The Hills and the Vale*

Chapter 23

The Idle Earth

The bare fallows of a factory are of short duration, and occur at lengthened intervals. There are the Saturday afternoons – four or five hours' shorter time; there are the Sundays – fifty-two in number; a day or two at Christmas, at Midsummer, at Easter. Fifty-two Sundays, plus fifty-two half days on Saturdays; eight days more for bona-fide holidays – in all, eighty-six days on which no labour is done. This is as near as may be just one quarter of the year spent in idleness. But how fallacious is such a calculation! for overtime and night-work make up far more than this deficient quarter; and therefore it may safely be said that man works the whole year through, and has no bare fallow. But earth – idle earth – on which man dwells, has a much easier time of it. It takes nearly a third of the year out in downright leisure, doing nothing but inchoating; a slow process indeed, and one which all the agricultural army have of late tried to hasten, with very indifferent success. Winter seed sown in the fall of the year does not come to anything till the spring; spring seed is not reaped till the autumn is at hand. But it will be argued that this land is not idle, for during those months the seed is slowly growing – absorbing its constituent parts from the atmosphere, the earth, the water; going through astonishing metamorphoses; outdoing the most wonderful laboratory experiments with its untaught, instinctive chemistry. All true enough; and hitherto it has been assumed that the ultimate product of these idle months is sufficient to repay the idleness, that in the *coup* of the week of reaping there is a dividend recompensing the long, long days of development. Is it really so? This is not altogether a question which a practical man used to City formulas of profit and loss might ask. It is a question to which, even at this hour, farmers themselves – most unpractical of men – are requiring an answer. There is a cry arising throughout the country that farms do not pay; that a man with a moderate 400 acres and a moderate £1,000 of his own, with borrowed money added, cannot get a reasonable remuneration from those acres. These say they would sooner be hotel-keepers, tailors, grocers – anything but farmers. These are men who have tried the task of subduing the stubborn earth, which is no longer bountiful to her children. Much reason exists in this cry, which is heard at the market ordinary, in the lobby, at the club meetings – wherever agriculturists congregate, and which will soon force itself out upon the public. It is like this. Rents have risen. Five shillings per acre makes an enormous difference, though nominally only an additional £100 on 400 acres. But as in agricultural profits one must not reckon more than 8 per cent, this 5s. per acre represents nearly another £1,000 which must be invested in the business, and which must be made to return interest to pay the additional rent. If that cannot be done, then it represents a dead £100 per annum taken out of the agriculturist's pocket.

Then – labour, the great agricultural *crux*. If the occupier pays 3s. per week more to seven men, that adds more than another £50 per annum to his out-goings, to meet which you must somehow make your acres represent another £500. Turnpikes fall in, and the roads are repaired at the ratepayers' cost. Compulsory education – for it is compulsory in reality, since it compels voluntary schools to be built – comes next, and as generally the village committee mull matters, and have to add a wing, and rebuild, and so forth, till they get in debt, there grows up a rate which is a serious matter, not by itself, but added to other things. Just as in great factories they keep accounts in decimals because of the vast multitude of little expenses which are in the aggregate serious – each decimal is equivalent to a rusty nail or so – here on our farm threepence or fourpence in the pound added to threepence or sixpence ditto for voluntary Church-rate puts an appreciable burden on the man's back. The tightness, however, does not end here; the belt is squeezed closer than this. No man had such long credit as the yeoman of yore (thirty years ago is 'of yore' in our century). Butcher and baker, grocer, tailor, draper, all gave him unlimited credit as to time. As a rule, they got paid in the end; for a farmer is a fixture, and does not have an address for his letters at one place and live in another. But modern trade manners are different. The trader is himself pressed. Competition galls his heel. He has to press upon his customers, and in place of bills sent in for payment once a year, and actual cash transfers in three, we have bills punctually every quarter, and due notice of county court if cheques are not sent at the half-year. So that the agriculturist wants more ready cash; and as his returns come but once a year, he does not quite see the fairness of having to swell other men's returns four times in the same period. Still a step further, and few words will suffice to describe the increased cost of all the materials supplied by these tradesmen. Take coals, for instance. This is a fact so patent that it stares the world in the face. A farmer, too, nowadays has a natural desire to live as other people in his station of life do. He cannot reconcile himself to rafty bacon, cheese, radishes, turnip-tops, homespun cloth, smock frocks. He cannot see why his girls should milk the cows or wheel out manure from the yards any more than the daughters of tradesmen; neither that his sons should say 'Ay' and 'Noa,' and exhibit a total disregard of grammer and ignorance of all social customs. The piano, he thinks, is quite as much in its place in his cool parlour as in the stuffy so-called drawing-room at his grocer's in the petty town hard by, where they are so particular to distinguish the social ranks of 'professional tradesmen' from common tradesmen. Here in all this, even supposing it kept down to economical limits, there exists a considerable margin of expenditure greater than in our forefathers' time. True, wool is dearer, meat dearer; but to balance that put the increased cost of artificial manure and artificial food – two things no farmer formerly bought – and do not forget that the seasons rule all things, and are quite as capricious as ever, and when there is a bad season the loss is much greater than it used to be, just as the foundering of an ironclad costs the nation more than the loss of a frigate.

Experience every day brings home more and more the fatal truth that moderate farms do not pay, and there are even ominous whispers about the 2,000 acres system. The agriculturist says that, work how he may, he only gets 8 per cent. per annum; the tradesman, still more the manufacturer, gets only 2 per cent. each time, but he turns his money over twenty times a year, and so gets 40 per cent. per annum. Eight per cent. is a large dividend on one transaction, but it is very small for a whole year – a year, the one-thirtieth of a man's whole earning period, if we take him to be in a business at twenty-five, and to be in full work till fifty-five, a fair allowance. Now, why is it that this cry arises that agriculture will not pay? and why is it that the farmer only picks up 8 per cent.? The answer is simple enough. It is because the earth is idle a third of the year. So far as actual cash return is concerned, one might say it was idle eleven out of the twelve months. But that is hardly fair. Say a third of the year.

The earth does not continue yielding a crop day by day as the machines do in the manufactory. The nearest approach to the manufactory is the dairy, whose cows send out so much milk per diem; but the cows go dry for their calves. Out of the tall chimney shaft there floats a taller column of dark smoke hour after hour; the vast engines puff and snort and labour perhaps the whole twenty-four hours through; the drums hum round, the shafts revolve perpetually, and each revolution is a penny gained. It may be only steel-pen making – pens, common pens, which one treats as of no value and wastes by dozens; but the iron-man thumps them out hour after hour, and the thin stream of daily profit swells into a noble river of gold at the end of the year. Even the pill people are fortunate in this: it is said that every second a person dies in this huge world of ours. Certain it is that every second somebody takes a pill; and so the millions of globules disappear, and so the profit is nearer 8 per cent. per hour than 8 per cent. per annum. But this idle earth takes a third of the year to mature its one single crop of pills; and so the agriculturist with his slow returns cannot compete with the quick returns of the tradesman and manufacturer. If he cannot compete, he cannot long exist; such is the modern law of business. As an illustration, take one large meadow on a dairy farm; trace its history for one year, and see what an idle workshop this meadow is. Call it twenty acres of first-class land at £2 15s. per acre, or £55 per annum. Remember that twenty acres is a large piece on which some millions multiplied by millons of cubic feet of air play on a month, and on which an incalculable amount of force in the shape of sunlight is poured down in the summer. January sees this plot of dull, dirty green, unless hidden by snow; the dirty green is short, juiceless herbage. The ground is as hard as a brick with the frost. We will not stay now to criticize the plan of carting out manure at this period, or dwell on the great useless furrows. Look carefully round the horizon of the twenty acres, and there is not an animal in sight, not a single machine for making money, not a penny being turned. The cows are all in the stalls. February comes, March passes; the herbage grows slowly; but still no machines are introduced, no pennies roll out at the gateways. The farmer may lean on the gate and gaze over an empty workshop, twenty acres big, with his hands in his pockets, except when he pulls out his purse to pay the hedge-cutters who are clearing out the ditches, the women who have been stone-picking, and the carters who took out the manure, half of which stains the drains, while the volatile part mixes with the atmosphere. This is highly profitable and gratifying. The man walks home, hears his daughter playing the piano, picks up the paper, sees himself described as a brutal tyrant to the labourer, and ten minutes afterwards in walks the collector of the voluntary rate for the village school, which educates the labourers' children. April arrives; grass grows rapidly. May comes; grass is now long. But still not one farthing has been made out of that twenty acres. Five months have passed, and all this time the shafts in the manufactories have been turning, and the quick coppers accumulating. Now it is June, and the mower goes to work; then the haymakers, and in a fortnight if the weather be good, a month if it be bad, the hay is ricked. Say it cost £1 per acre to make the hay and rick it – i.e., £20 – and by this time half the rent is due, or £27 10s. = total expenditure (without any profit as yet), £47 10s, exclusive of stone-picking, ditch-cleaning, value of manure, etc. This by the way. The five months' idleness is the point at present. June is now gone. If the weather be showery the sharp-edged grass may spring up in a fortnight to a respectable height; but if it be a dry summer – and if it is not a dry summer the increased cost of haymaking runs away with profit – then it may be fully a month before there is anything worth biting. Say at the end of July (one more idle month) twenty cows are turned in, and three horses. One cannot estimate how long they may take to eat up the short grass, but certain it is that the beginning of November will see that field empty of cattle again; and fortunate indeed the agriculturist who long before that has not had to 'fodder' (feed with hay) at least once a day. Here, then, are five idle months in spring, one in summer, two in winter; total, eight idle months. But, not to stretch the case, let us allow that during a part of that time, though the meadow is idle, its produce – the hay – is being eaten and converted into milk, cheese and butter, or meat, which is quite correct; but, even making this allowance, it may safely be said that the meadow is absolutely idle for one-third of the year, or four months. That is looking at the matter in a mere pounds, shillings, and pence light. Now look at it in a broader, more national view. Does it not seem a very serious matter that so large a piece of land should remain idle for that length of time? It is a reproach to science that no method of utilizing the meadow during that eight months has been discovered. To go further, it is very hard to require of the agriculturist that he should keep pace with a world whose maxims day by day tend to centralize and concentrate themselves into the one canon, Time is Money, when he cannot buy any ingenuity get his machinery to revolve more than once a year. In the old days the farmer belonged to a distinct class, a very isolated and independent class, little affected by the progress or retrogression of any other class, and not at all by those waves of social change which sweep over Europe. Now the farmer is in the same position as other producers: the fall or rise of prices, the competition of foreign lands, the waves of panic or monetary tightness, all tell upon him quite as much as on the tradesman. So that the cry is gradually rising that the idle earth will not pay.

On arable land it is perhaps even more striking. Take a wheat crop, for instance. Without going into the cost and delay of the three years of preparation under various courses for the crop, take the field just before the wheat year begins. There it lies in November, a vast brown patch, with a few rooks here and there hopping from one great lump to another; but there is nothing on it – no machine turning out materials to be again turned into money. On the contrary, it is very probable that the agriculturist may be sowing money on it, scarifying it with steam ploughing-engines, tearing up the earth to a great depth in order that the air may penetrate and the frost disintegrate the strong, hard lumps. He may have commenced this expensive process as far back as the end of August, for it is becoming more and more the custom to plough up directly after the crop is removed. All November, December, January, and not a penny from this broad patch, which may be of any size from fifteen to ninety acres, lying perfectly idle. Sometimes, indeed, persons who wish to save manure will grow mustard on it and plough it in, the profit of which process is extremely dubious. At the latter end of February or beginning of March, just as the season is early or late, dry or wet, in goes the seed – another considerable expense. Then April, May, June, July are all absorbed in the slow process of growth – a necessary process, of course, but still terribly slow, and not a penny of ready-money coming in. If the seed was sown in October, as is usual on some soils, the effect is the same – the crop does not arrive till next year's summer sun shines. In August the reaper goes to work, but even then the corn has to be threshed and sent to market before there is any return. Here is a whole year spent in elaborating one single crop, which may, after all, be very unprofitable if it is a good wheat year, and the very wheat over which such time and trouble have been expended may be used to fat beasts, or even to feed pigs. All this, however, and the great expense of preparation, though serious matters enough in themselves, are beside our immediate object. The length of time the land is useless is the point. Making every possible allowance, it is not less than one-third of the year – four months out of the twelve. For all practical – i.e., monetary – purposes it is longer than that. No wonder that agriculturists aware of this fact are so anxious to get as much as possible out of their one crop – to make the one revolution of their machinery turn them out as much money as possible. If their workshop must be enforcedly idle for so long, they desire that when in work there shall be full blast and double tides. Let the one crop be as heavy as it can. Hence the agitation for compensatory clauses, enabling the tenant to safely invest all the capital he can procure in the soil. How else is he to meet the increased cost of labour, of rent, of education, of domestic materials; how else maintain his fair position in society? The demand is reasonable enough; the one serious drawback is the possibility that, even with this assistance, the idle earth will refuse to move any faster.

We have had now the experience of many sewage-farms where the culture is extremely 'high'. It has been found that these farms answer admirably where the land is poor – say, sandy and porous – but on fairly good soil the advantage is dubious, and almost limited to growing a succession of rye-grass crops. After a season or two of sewage soaking the soil becomes so soft that in the winter months it is unapproachable. Neither carts nor any implements can be drawn over it; and then in the spring the utmost care has to be exercised to keep the liquid from, touching the young plants, or they wither up and die. Sewage on grass lands produces the most wonderful results for two or three years, but after that the herbage comes so thick and rank and 'strong' that cattle will not touch it; the landlord begins to grumble, and complains that the land, which was to have been improved, has been spoilt for a long time to come. Neither is it certain that the employment of capital in other ways will lead to a continuous increase of profit. There are examples before our eyes where capital has been unsparingly employed, and upon very large areas of land, with most disappointing results. In one such instance five or six farms were thrown into one; straw, and manure, and every aid lavishly used, till a fabulous number of sheep and other stock was kept; but the experiment failed. Many of the farms were again made separate holdings, and grass laid down in the place of glowing cornfields. Then there is another instance, where a gentleman of large means and a cultivated and business mind, called in the assistance of the deep plough, and by dint of sheer subsoil ploughing grew corn profitably several years in succession. But after a while he began to pause, and to turn his attention to stock and other aids. It is not for one moment contended that the use of artificial manure, of the deep plough, of artifical food, and other improvements will not increase the yield, and so the profit of the agriculturist. It is obvious that they do so. The question is, Will they do so to an extent sufficient to repay the outlay? And, further, will they do so sufficiently to enable the agriculturist to meet the ever-increasing weight which presses on him? It would seem open to doubt. One thing appears to have been left quite out of sight by those gentlemen who are so enthusiastic about compensation for unexhausted improvements, and that is, if the landlord is to be bound down so rigidly, and if the tenant really is going to make so large a profit, most assuredly the rents will rise very considerably. How then? Neither the sewage system, nor the deep plough, nor the artificial manure has, as yet, succeeded in overcoming the *vis inertiæ* of the idle earth. They cause an increase in the yield of the one revolution of the agriculturist machine per annum; but they do not cause the machine to revolve twice or three times. Without a decrease in the length of this enforced idleness any very great increase of profit does not seem possible. What would any manufacturer think of a business in which he was compelled to let his engines rest for a third of the year? Would he be eager to sink his capital in such an enterprise?

The practical man will, of course, exclaim that all this is very true, but Nature is Nature, and must have its way, and it is useless to expect more than one crop per annum, and any talk of three or four crops is perfectly visionary. 'Visionary', by the way, is a very favourite word with so-called practical men. But the stern logic of figures, of pounds, shillings, and pence, proves that the present condition of affairs cannot last much longer, and they are the true 'visionaries' who imagine that it can. This enormous loss of time, this idleness, must be obviated somehow. It is a question whether the millions of money at present sunk in agriculture are not a dead loss to the country; whether they could not be far more profitably employed in developing manufacturing industries, or in utilizing for home consumption the enormous resources of Southern America and Australasia; whether we should not get more to eat, and cheaper, if such was the case. Such a low rate of interest as is now obtained in agriculture – and an interest by no means secure either, for a bad season may at any time reduce it, and even a too good season – such a state of things is a loss, if not a curse. It is questionable whether the million or so of labourers representing a potential amount of force almost incalculable, and the thousands of young farmers throbbing with health and vigour, eager *to do*, would not return a far larger amount of good to the world and to themselves if, instead of waiting for the idle earth at home to bring forth, they were transported bodily to the broad savannahs and prairies, and were sending to the mother-country innumerable shiploads of meat and corn – unless, indeed, we can discover some method by which our idle earth shall be made to labour more frequently. This million or so of labourers and these thousands of young, powerfully made farmers literally do nothing at all for a third of the year but wait, wait for the idle earth. The strength, the will, the vigour latent in them is wasted. They do not enjoy this waiting by any means. The young agriculturist chafes under the delay, and is eager *to do*. They can hunt and course hares, 'tis true, but that is feeble excitement indeed, and feminine in comparison with the serious work which brings in money.

The idleness of arable and pasture land is as nothing compared to the idleness of the wide, rolling downs. These downs are of immense extent, and stretch through the very heart of the country. They maintain sheep, but in how small a proportion to the acreage! In the spring and summer the short herbage is cropped by the sheep; but it is short, and it requires a large tract to keep a moderate flock. In the winter the down is left to the hares and field-fares. It has just as long a period of absolute idleness as the arable and pasture land, and when in work the yield is so very, very small.

After all, the very deepest ploughing is but scratching the surface. The earth at five feet beneath the level has not been disturbed for countless centuries. Nor would it pay to turn up this subsoil over large areas, for it is nothing but clay, as many a man has found to his cost who, in the hope of a heavier crop, has dug up his garden half a spade deeper than usual. But when the soil really is good at that depth, we cannot get at it so as to turn it to practical account. The thin stratum of artificial manure which is sown is no more in comparison than a single shower after a drought of months; yet to sow too much would destroy the effect. No blame, then, falls upon the agriculturist, who is only too anxious to get a larger produce. It is useless charging him with incompetency. What countless experiments have been tried to increase the crop: to see if some new system cannot be introduced! With all its progress, how little real advance has agriculture made! All because of the stubborn, idle earth. Will not science some day come to our aid, and show how two crops or three may be grown in our short summers; or how we may even overcome the chill hand of winter? Science has got as far as this: it recognizes the enormous latent forces surrounding us – electricity, magnetism; some day, perhaps, it may be able to utilize them. It recognizes the truly overwhelming amount of force which the sun of summer pours down upon our fields, and of which we really make no use. To recognize the existence of a power is the first step towards employing it. Till it was granted that there was a power in steam the locomotive was impossible.

It would be easy to swell this notice of idle earth by bringing in all the waste lands, now doing nothing – the parks, deer forests, and so on. But that is not to the purpose. If the wastes were reclaimed and the parks ploughed up, that would in nowise solve the problem how to make the cultivated earth more busy. It is no use for a man who has a garden to lean on his spade, look over his boundary wall, and say, 'Ah, if neighbour Brown would but dig up his broad green paths how many more potatoes he would grow!' That would not increase the produce of the critic's garden by one single cabbage. Certainly it is most desirable that all lands capable of yielding crops should be reclaimed, but one great subject for the agriculturist to study is, how to shorten the period of idleness in his already cultivated plots. At present the earth is so very idle.

from *The Hills and the Vale*

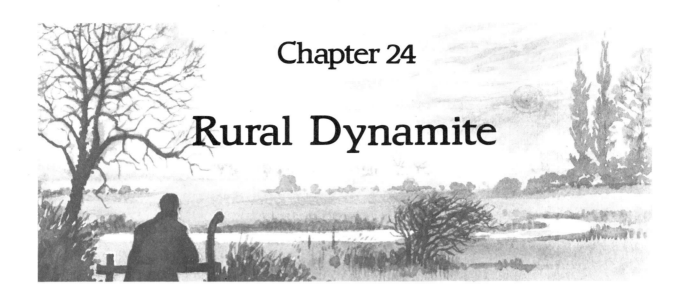

Chapter 24

Rural Dynamite

In the cold North men eat bread of fir-bark; in our own fields the mouse, if pressed for food in winter, will gnaw the bark of sapling trees. Frost sharpens the teeth like a file, and hunger is keener than frost. If any one used to more fertile scenes had walked across the barren meads Mr. Roberts rented as the summer declined, he would have said that a living could only be gained from them as the mouse gains it in frost-time. By sharp-set nibbling and paring; by the keenest frost-bitten meanness of living; by scraping a little bit here, and saving another trifle yonder, a farmer might possibly get through the year. At the end of each year he would be rather worse off than before, decending a step annually. He must nibble like a frost-driven mouse to merely exist. So poor was the soil, that the clay came to the surface, and in wet weather a slip of the foot exposed it – the heel cut through the veneer of turf into the cold, dead, moist clay. Nothing grew but rushes. Every time a horse moved over the marshy land his hoof left deep holes which never again filled up, but remained the year through, now puddles, full of rain water, and now dry holes. The rain made the ground a swamp; the sun cracked it as it does paint. Who could pay rent for such a place? – for rushes, flags, and water.

Yet it was said, with whisper and nod, that the tenant, Mr. Roberts, was a warm man as warm men go after several years of bad seasons, falling prices, and troubles of all kinds. For one thing, he hopped, and it is noted among country folk, that, if a man hops, he generally accumulates money. Mr. Roberts hopped, or rather dragged his legs from rheumatics contracted in thirty years' hardest of hard labour on that thankless farm. Never did any man labour so continually as he, from the earliest winter dawn when the blackbird, with puffed feathers, still tried to slumber in the thornbush, but could not for cold, on till the latest summer eve, after the white barn owl had passed round the fir copse. Both with his hands, and with his eyes, now working, now watching, the man ceased not, and such was his dogged pertinacity that, like the mouse, he won a living. He did more, he saved. At what price? At the price of a fireless life: I mean without cheer, by denial of everything which renders human life superior to that of the rabbit in his burrow. No wife, no children, no niece, or any woman to see to his comforts; no comfort and no pleasure; a bare house and-rheumatism. Bill, his principal labourer, Dolly's brother, slept with him in the same bed, master and man, a custom common in old times, long since generally disused.

Yet Mr. Roberts was not without some humanism, if such a word may be used; certainly he never gave away a penny, but as certainly he cheated no man. He was upright in conduct, and not unpleasant in manner. He could not have been utterly crabbed for this one labourer, Bill, to stay with him five-and-twenty years. This was the six-and-twentieth year they had dwelt there together in the gaunt, grey, lonely house, with woods around them, isolated from the world, and without a hearth. A hearth is no hearth unless a woman sit by it. This six-and-twentieth year, the season then just ended, had been the worst of the series; rain had spoiled the hay, increased the payment of wages by lengthening the time of hay-making; ruin, he declared, stared him in the face; he supposed at last he must leave the tenancy. And now the harvest was done, the ricks thatched with flags from the marsh (to save straw), the partridges were dispersed, the sportsmen having broken up the coveys, the black swifts had departed - they built every year in the grey stone slates on the lonely house – and nothing was left to be done but to tend the cattle morning and evening, to reflect on the losses, and to talk ceaselessly of the new terror which hung over the whole district.

It was rick-burning. Probably, gentlemen in London, who 'sit at home at ease,' imagine rick-burning a thing of the past, impossible' since insurance robbed the incendiary of his sting, unheard of and extinct. Nothing of the kind. That it is not general is true, still to this day it breaks out in places, and rages with vehemence, placing the countryside under a reign of terror. The thing seems inexplicable, but it is a fact; the burning of ricks and farm- sheds every now and then, in certain localities, reaches the dimensions of a public disaster.

One night from the garret window, Mr. Roberts, and Bill, his man, counted five fires visible at once. One was in full sight, not a mile distant, two behind the wood, above which rose the red glow, the other two dimly illumined the horizon on the left like a rising moon. While they watched in the dark garret the rats scampered behind them, and a white barn owl floated silently by. They counted up fourteen fires that had taken place since the beginning of the month, and now there were five together. Mr. Roberts did not sleep that night. Being so near the woods and preserves it was part of the understanding that he should not keep a gun – he took a stout staff, and went to his hayricks, and there stayed till daylight. By ten o'clock he was trudging into the town; his mind had been half-crazed with anxiety for his ricks; he was not insured, he had never insured, just to save the few shillings it cost, such was the nibbling by which he lived. He had struggled hard and kept the secret to himself – of the non-insurance – he foresaw that if known he should immediately suffer. But at the town the insurance agent demurred to issue a policy. The losses had been so heavy, there was no knowing how much farther the loss might extend, for not the slightest trace of the incendiary had yet been discovered, notwithstanding the reward offered, and this was a new policy. Had it been to add to an old one, had Mr. Roberts insured in previous years, it would have been different. He could not do it on his own responsibility, he must communicate with the head office; most likely they would do it, but he must have their authority. By return of post he should know. Mr. Roberts trudged home again, with the misery of two more nights confronting him; two more nights of exposure to the chance of utter ruin. If those ricks were burned, the savings – the nibblings of his life – were gone. This intense, frost-bitten economy, by which alone he had been able to prosper, now threatened to overwhelm him with destruction.

There is nothing that burns so resolutely as a hayrick; nothing that catches fire so easily. Children are playing with matches; one holds the ignited match till it scorches the fingers, and drops it. The expiring flame touches three blades of dry grass, of hay fallen from the rick, these flare immediately; the flame runs along like a train of gun powder, rushes up the side of the rick, singeing it as a horse's coat is singed, takes the straw of the thatch which blackens into a hole, cuts its way through, the draught lifts it up the slope of the thatch, and in five minutes the rick is on fire irrecoverably. Unless beaten out at the first start, it is certain to go on. A spark from a pipe, dropped from the mouth of a sleeping man, will do it. Once well alight, and the engines may come at full speed, one five miles, one eight, two ten; they may pump the pond dry, and lay hose to the distant brook - it is in vain. The spread of the flames may be arrested, but not all the water that can be thrown will put out the rick. The outside of the rick where the water strikes it turns black, and dense smoke arises, but the inside core continues to burn till the last piece is charred. All that can be done is to hastily cut away that side of the rick – if any remains – yet untouched, and carry it bodily away. A hayrick will burn for hours, one huge mass of concentrated, glowing, solid fire, not much flame, but glowing coals, so that the farmer may fully understand, may watch and study and fully comprehend the extent of his loss. It burns itself from a square to a dome, and the red dome grows gradually smaller till its lowest layer of ashes strews the ground. It burns itself as it were in blocks: the rick was really homogeneous; it looks while aglow as if it had been constructed of large bricks or blocks of hay. These now blackened blocks dry and crumble one by one till the dome sinks. Under foot the earth is heated, so intense is the fire; no one can approach, even on the windward side, within a pole's length. A widening stream of dense white smoke flows away upwards, flecked with great sparks, blackening the elms, and carrying flakes of burning hay over outhouses, sheds, and farmsteads. Thus from the clouds, as it seems, drops further destruction. Nothing in the line of the wind is safe. Fine impalpable ashes drift and fall like rain half a mile away. Sometimes they remain suspended in the air for hours, and come down presently when the fire is out, like volcanic dust drifting from the crater. This dust lies soft and silky on the hand. By the burning rick, the air rushing to the furnace roars aloud, coming so swiftly as to be cold; on one side intense heat, on the other cold wind. The pump, pump, swing, swing of the manual engines; the quick, short pant of the steam fire-engines; the steam and hiss of the water; shouts and answers; gleaming brass helmets; frightened birds; crowds of white faces, whose frames are in shadow; a red glow on the black, wet mud of the empty pond; rosy light on the walls of the homestead, crossed with vast magnified shadows; windows glistening; men dragging sail-like tarpaulins and rick cloths to cover the sheds; constables upright and quiet, but watchful, standing at intervals to keep order; if by day, the strangest mixture of perfect calm and heated anxiety, the smoke bluish, the floating flakes visible as black specks, the flames tawny, pigeons fluttering round, cows grazing in idol-like indifference to human fears. Ultimately, rows of flattened and roughly circular layers of blackened ashes, whose traces remain for months.

This is dynamite in the hands of the village ruffian.

This hay, or wheat, or barley, not only represents money; it represents the work of an entire year, the sunshine of a whole summer; it is the outcome of man's thought and patient labour, and it is the food of the helpless cattle. Besides the hay, there often go with it buildings, implements, waggons, and occasionally horses are suffocated. Once now and then the farmstead goes.

Now, has not the farmer, even if covered by insurance, good reason to dread this horrible incendiarism? It is a blow at his moral existence as well as at his pecuniary interests. Hardened indeed must be that heart that could look at the old familiar scene, blackened, fire-spoilt, trodden, and blotted, without an inward desolation. Boxes and barrels of merchandise in warehouses can be replaced, but money does not replace the growth of nature.

Hence the brutality of it – the blow at a man's heart. His hay, his wheat, his cattle, are to a farmer part of his life; coin will not replace them. Nor does the incendiary care if the man himself, his house, home, and all perish at the same time. It is dynamite in despite of insurance. The new system of silos – burying the grass when cut at once in its green state, in artifical caves – may much reduce the risk of fire if it comes into general use.

These fire invasions almost always come in the form of an epidemic; not one but three, five, ten, fifteen fires follow in quick succession. Sometimes they last through an entire winter, though often known to take place in summer, directly after harvest.

Rarely does detection happen; to this day half these incendiary fires are never followed by punishment. Yet it is noted that they generally occur within a certain radius; they are all within six or seven, or eight miles, being about the distance that a man or two bent on evil could compass in the night time. But it is not always night; numerous fires are started in broad daylight. Stress of winter weather, little food, and clothing, and less fuel at home have been put forward as causes of a chill desperation, ending in crime. On the contrary, these fires frequently occur when labourers' pockets are full, just after they have received their harvest wages. Bread is not at famine prices; hard masters are not specially selected for the gratification of spite; good masters suffer equally. What then is the cause?

There is none but that bitter, bitter feeling which I venture to call the dynamite disposition, and which found in every part of the civilised world; in Germany, Italy, France, and our own mildly ruled England. A brooding, morose, concentrated hatred of those who possess any kind of substance or comfort; landlord, farmer, every one. An unsparing vendetta, a merciless shark-like thirst of destructive vengeance; a monomania of battering, smashing, crushing, such as seizes the Lancashire weaver, who kicks his woman's brains out without any special reason for dislike, mingled with and made more terrible by this unchangeable hostility to property and those who own it. No creed, no high moral hopes of the rights of man and social regeneration, no true sans culottism even, nothing at all but set teeth and inflated nostrils; blow up, smash, annihilate! A disposition or character which is not imaginary but a fact, as proved abundantly by the placing of rails and iron chairs on lines to upset trains, by the dynamite explosions at Government offices, railway stations, and even at newspaper offices, the sending of letters filled with explosives, firing dynamite in trout streams just to destroy the harmless fish; a character which in the country has hitherto manifested itself in the burning of ricks and farm buildings. Science is always putting fresh power into the hands of this class. In cities they have partly awakened to the power of knowledge; in the country they still use the match. If any one thinks that there is no danger in England because there are no deep-seated causes of discontent, such as foreign rule, oppressive enactments, or conscription, I can assure him that he is woefully

mistaken. This class needs no cause at all; prosperity cannot allay its hatred, and adversity does not weaken it. It is certainly unwise to the last degree to provoke this demon, to control which as yet no means have been found. You cannot arrest the invisible; you cannot pour Martini-Henry bullets into a phantom. How are you going to capture people who blow themselves into atoms in order to shatter the frame of a Czar?

In its dealings with the lower class this generation is certainly far from wise. Never was the distinction so sharp between the poor – the sullen poor who stand scornful and desperate at the street corners – and the well-to-do. The contrast now extends to every one who can afford a black coat. It is not confined to the millionaire. The contrast is with every black coat. Those who only see the drawing-room side of society, those who move, too, in the well-oiled atmosphere of commercial offices, are quite ignorant of the savage animosity which watches them to and fro the office or the drawing-room from the street corner. Question it is if any mediaeval soldiery bursting abroad in Sinigaglia were so brutal as is the street rough, that blot and hideous product of modern civilisation. How easy it is to point to the sobriety and the good sense of the working class and smile in assumed complacency! What have the sober mass of the working class to do with it? No more than you or I, or the Rothschilds, or dukes of blood royal. There the thing is, and it requires no great sagacity to see that the present mode of dealing with it is a failure and likely to be worse. If you have gunpowder, you should not put it under hydraulic pressure. You should not stir it up and hold matches to it to see if it is there. That is what prosecutions and imprisonments on charges of atheism and so on do. It is stirring up the powder and trying it with a match.

Nor should you put it under hydraulic pressure, which is now being done all over the country, under the new laws which force every wretch who enters a workhouse for a night's shelter to stay there two nights; under the cold-blooded cruelty which, in the guise of science, takes the miserable quarter of a pint of ale from the lips of the palsied and decrepit inmates; which puts the imbecile – even the guiltless imbecile – on what is practically bread and water. Words fail me to express the cruelty and inhumanity of this crazed legislation.

Sometimes we see a complacent paragraph in the papers, penned by an official doubtless, congratulating the public that the number relieved under the new regulations had dropped from, say, six hundred to a hundred and fifty. And what, oh blindest of the blind, do you imagine has become of the remaining four hundred and fifty? Has your precious folly extinguished them? Are they dead? No, indeed. All over the country, hydraulic pressure, in the name of science, progress, temperance, and similar perverted things, is being put on the gunpowder – or the dynamite, if you like – of society. Every now and then some individual member of the Army of Wretches turns and becomes the Devil of modern civilisation. Modern civilisation has put out the spiritual Devil and produced the Demon of Dynamite. Let me raise a voice, in pleading for more humane treatment of the poor – the only way, believe me, by which society can narrow down and confine the operations of this new Devil. A human being is not a dog, yet is treated worse than a dog.

Force these human dogs to learn to read with empty stomachs – stomachs craving for a piece of bread while education is crammed into them. In manhood, if unfortunate, set them to break stones. If imbecility supervene give them bread and water. In helpless age give them the cup of cold water. This is the way to breed dynamite. And then at the other end of the scale let your Thames Embankment Boulevard be the domain of the street rough; let your Islington streets be swept by bands of brutes; let the well dressed be afraid to venture anywhere unless in the glare

Morning on Coate water
(*The Squire and the Land*)

The Squire and the Land

'After the white barn owl had passed around the fir copse'
(*Rural Dynamite*)

of gas and electric light! Manufacture it in one district, and give it free scope and play in another. Yet never was there an age in which the mass of society, from the titled to the cottager, was so full of real and true humanity, so ready to start forward to help, so imbued with the highest sentiments. The wrong is done in offical circles. No steel-clad baron of Norman days, no ruthless red-stockinged cardinal, with the Bastile in one hand and the tumbril in the other, ever ruled with so total an absence of Heart as the modern 'official', the Tyrants of the nineteenth century; whose rods are hobbies in the name of science miscalled, in the name of temperance perverted, in the name of progress backwards, in the name of education without food. It is time that the commonsense of society at large rose in revolution against it. Meantime dynamite.

This is a long digression: suppose while you have been reading it that Mr. Roberts has passed one of the two terrible nights, his faithful Bill at one end of the rickyard and himself at the other. The second night they took up their positions in the same manner as soon as it was dark. There was no moon, and the sky was overcast with those stationary clouds which often precede a great storm, so that the darkness was marked, and after they had parted a step or two they lost sight of each other. Worn with long wakefulness, and hard labour during the day, they both dropped asleep at their posts. Mr. Roberts awoke from the dead vacancy of sleep to the sensation of a flash of light crossing his eyelids, and to catch a glimpse of a man's neck with a red necktie illuminated by flame like a Rembrandt head in the centre of shadow. He leaped forward literally yelling – the incendiary he wholly forgot – his rick! his rick! He beat the side of the rick with his stick, and as it had but just caught he beat the flame out. Then he dropped senseless on the ground. Bill, awakened by Roberts' awful yell or shriek of excitement, started to his feet, heard a man rushing by in the darkness, and hurled his heavy stick in that direction. By the thud which followed and curse, he knew it had hit the object, but not with sufficient force to bring the scoundrel down. The fellow escaped; Bill went to his master and lifted him up; how he got Roberts home he did not know, but it was hours before Roberts could speak. Towards sunrise he recovered, and would go immediately to assure himself that the ricks were safe. There they found a man's hat – Bill's stick had knocked it off – and by that hat and the red necktie the incendiary was brought to justice. The hat was big Mat's; he always wore a red necktie.

Big Mat made no defence; he was simply stolidly indifferent to the whole proceedings. The only statement he made was that he had not fired four of the ricks, and he did not know who had done so. Example is contagious; some one had followed the dynamite lead, detection never took place, but the fires ceased. Mat, of course, went on the longest period of penal servitude the law allotted.

I should say that he did not himself know why he did it. That intense, brooding moroseness, that wormwood hatred, does not often understand itself. So much the more dangerous is it; no argument, no softening influence can reach it.

Faithful Bill, who had served Mr. Roberts almost all his life, and who probably would have served him till the end, received a money reward from the insurance office for his share in detecting the incendiary. This reward ruined him – killed him. Golden sovereigns in his pocket destroyed him. He went on the drink; he drank, and was enticed to drink, till in six weeks he died in the infirmary of the work-house.

Mat being in the convict prison, and Dolly near to another confinement, she could not support herself; she was driven to the same workhouse in which her brother had but just died. I am not sure, but believe that pseudo-science, the Torturer of these days, denied her the least drop of alcohol during her travail. If it did permit one drop, then was the Torturer false to his creed. Dolly survived but utterly broken, hollow-chested, a workhouse fixture. Still, so long as she could stand she had to wash in the laundry; weak as she was, they weakened her still further with steam and heat, and labour. Washing is hard work for those who enjoy health and vigour. To a girl, broken in heart and body, it is a slow destroyer. Heat relaxes all the fibres; Dolly's required bracing. Steam will soften wood and enable the artificer to bend it to any shape. Dolly's chest became yet more hollow; her cheek-bones prominent; she bent to the steam. This was the girl who had lingered in the lane to help the boy pick watercress, to gather a flower, to listen to a thrush, to bask in the sunshine. Open air and green fields were to her life itself. Heart miseries are always better borne in the open air. How just, how truly scientific, to shut her in a steaming wash-house!

The workhouse was situated in a lovely spot, on the lowest slope of hills, hills covered afar with woods. Meads at hand, corn-fields farther away, then green slopes over which broad cloud-shadows glided slowly. The larks sang in spring, in summer the wheat was golden, in autumn the distant woods were brown and red and yellow. Had you spent your youth in those fields, and your little drama of life been enacted in them, do you not think that you would like at least to gaze out at them from the windows of your prison? It was observed that the miserable wretches were always looking out of the windows in this direction. The windows on that side were accordingly built up and bricked in that they might not look out.

from *The Life of the Field*

Chapter 25

Shooting Poachers

The sport of shooting poachers, which comes in towards Christmas, is now in full swing (December 1884), some capital sport has already been obtained, and there appears to be plentiful supply of human game on hand. Bands of men go into the woods armed with guns, and bands of men carrying revolvers go to meet them. The savage encounters that ensue read like those with banditti in the days of Königsmark the Robber. Indeed, while our expedition toils up the Nile (to rescue Gordon) and correspondents have little to describe beyond hard rowing, another war is proceeding at home, accompanied with serious bloodshed. If a 'special' were on the spot he would have to relate something like this. The keepers on a large preserve, by means of scouts and vedettes, ascertain the probable intentions of a gang of poachers, and settle themselves in ambush as the night approaches. They are well armed with breech-loading guns and revolvers, six-shooters, in American 'frontier' style, as if for a battle with Indians. The poachers, not having wealthy people to buy good weapons for them, generally have old muzzle-loading guns, and have not yet arrived at the civilization of the revolver. Heavy shadows settle in the hollow by the firs; it is night, and by-and-by a scout creeps up with the intelligence that the enemy is busy at the side of the plantation. Fetching a detour the 'frontier' men suddenly rush out from a gateway. There is a scuffle – curses – quick flashes or red flame light up the scene. On one side a curl of white smoke ascends from the barrel of a levelled gun. On the other a curl of smoke darts from a revolver extended by an arm in velveteen. Two more men are rolling over each other on the ground, bound up inextricably in a great net into which they have fallen and drawn round them. Another lies twisted in a heap, doubled up, hard hit; a pheasant projects from his coat-pocket. Bang! bang! There are groans, curses, a lantern is turned on, and the fight is over. Next morning, if you visited the spot early, you might see scene two. On the wet grass, stained cartridge-cases; marks of heavy iron-shod boots dug deeply into the soil in the struggle; a broken pipe; a hare wire; blood on the grass and on the crushed bunch of rushes, blood which remains though a fine rain is falling, and drip, dripping from the still trees. Some pheasant feathers lie scattered by the ditch. Away in a shed a stiff and human carcass is extended under a sheet. Other human game, wounded but not mortally, is bagged in the cells at the nearest town. Cold and wet the grey winter's morning casts its chill over the view: this is the time to think of the fatherless children and the widow. Is not this a noble sport for Christmas-tide? A grand subject here for the next Academy Exhibition, two panels – (1) 'The Battle': (2) 'Next Morning'.

'The right to kill!' A fresh addition to the rights of man, invented when Madame Clovis Hugues shot M. Morin. In Paris you may avenge your honour – at least, a lady may; these are privileged cases. In England – moral England, which expressed such horror – everybody has a right to kill – a poacher. A keeper is a licensed killer; he shoots cats, weasels, crows, poachers, and other vermin equally. It is his royal pleasure – the keeper *s'amuse*. The boast of our civilization is the high value we set upon human life. Never, never before in the whole history of man was life so sacred as it is now. The tribunals hold that even starvation does not justify homicide. What, then, can justify this shooting of poachers? Of course a poacher is engaged in an unlawful act, but is that act sufficiently unlawful to render it right to kill him? He is not a burglar, he does not enter a house and put the lives of the inmates in danger. He is not a garrotter – he does not attack people with violence in the street. A wood is not a house – nor even a garden. The argument that he goes by night is merely a legal quibble – poaching by night is the same in this respect as poaching by day; neither by day nor night is there any assault. The poacher, in short, is simply a thief who steals rabbits and pheasants instead of watches from a shop window. It is not nearly so much an assault upon the person as stealing without violence, from the pocket. A man has his pocket picked at Charing-Cross Station; Policeman B. witnesses the robbery, runs up and seizes the thief; suppose Policeman B. drew a revolver from his breast and shot the thief instead? Would that be justifiable? It even remains a moot point what does and what does not justify one in shooting a burglar. Only a poacher may be shot with impunity.

But a poacher goes armed, true, but with the purpose of shooting pheasants. The keeper does not shoot pheasants at night, nor at any time, with revolvers; such weapons are intended to be used upon man. Those who have had any experience of the combative instincts of rude men know very well that there are many keepers – and others – who go to these brutal encounters with delight. Cases have been seen even of young farmers joining the keeper's gang to enjoy the battle. It is altogether nonsense to suppose that they go out armed with revolvers with the purely virtuous intention of protecting property. They like the row; they like to 'do' for somebody. Good keepers are perfectly well acquainted with various ways and means of tracking and identifying poachers, and if the present be not sufficient some one should invent a portable electric lantern to be suddenly turned on, and so, by making the covers as light as day, afford a view. Poachers would dread a bright light – which means identification – far more than gunpowder. The truth is that these bloodthirsty affairs are a disgrace to our boasted humanity. We have just had an outburst of indignation against keepers shooting cats; but shooting a poacher is nothing – it does not happen in Bulgaria, and is no atrocity. The truth also is that these bloodthirsty businesses are part and parcel of a marked change of tone in the population, they belong to the same class of sentiment that promotes prize-fighting, now so much on the increase. It is downright brutality, and nothing else. It is most injurious to the interest of sport, against which it must ultimately create a prejudice. Shooting doves from a trap became a fashionable atrocity a short while since; rank and fashion arrayed themselves on the side of the poor doves. But the poacher is an outlaw, outside the pale of humanity, far below a pigeon. If a man be privy to a murder, though he be not actually present, he is in law an accomplice; if a man sanction his keeper 'going for' poachers with revolvers, what is his position? His conscience at all events cannot be at ease, if slaughter ensues. Poaching is no new thing, but years ago before we became so humane it was the custom to 'go for' poachers armed with good stout cudgels, and with those good stout cudgels many a gang of poachers was captured. Then every consideration was in favour of the keepers; now, by using revolvers, they place themselves obviously in as bad a moral position as the poachers. Nor is suspicion wanting that when these local shooting cases come before local magnates the keepers are usually discharged. The whole thing has a bad odour – a very bad odour. Much blame lies in the law which visits night-poaching with penalties of ridiculous severity, not much better than the old plan of hanging for sheep-stealing. On the one hand, the poacher thinks he may as well be hung (so to say) for a sheep as a lamb; on the other hand, the keeper, knowing that the law is so heavily on his behalf, thinks himself fighting on the 'side of the angels', so that nothing he can do is wrong. It is scarcely possible now to pick up a newspaper without finding 'Serious Poaching Affray', 'Keepers Shot', 'Poachers Wounded', and so on ad nauseum. All this is most injurious to sport; as a champion of sport, a true believer in sport, I trust a stop will be put to it, or in time we shall get back to the days (and ways) of spring guns, steel man traps, bloodhounds, and similar amenities. Or shall we go forward and develop, as this is the age of evolution? We shall perhaps find that there are people better off than keepers and poachers who would like a 'brush' of this sort – the people who pay the money for prize fights. Here is a cutting from the sporting paper of the period:- 'The Hon. Jim Masher has a large party of guests staying at Pepperem Hall in anticipation of the Christmas Poacher Shooting. They are all armed with Winchester repeating rifles, and are looking anxiously to the full moon in order to take better aim. There is a very strong gang of poachers, and splendid sport is expected; they want decimating sadly. The poachers are said to have a big punt gun, carrying three pounds of shot, and place much reliance on this field-piece. The battue will probably come off in Lower Plantations, and will be a noisy affair. P.S. The J.P.s have been squared.'

from *Chronicles of the Hedges*

Chapter 26
The Story of Swindon

We have all of us passed through Swindon Station, whether *en route* to Southern Wales, to warm Devon – the fern-land – to the Channel Islands, or to Ireland. The ten minutes for refreshment, now in the case of certain trains reduced to five, have made thousands of travellers familiar with the name of the spot. Those who have not actually been there can recall to memory a shadowy tradition which has grown up and propagated itself, that here the soup skins the tongue, and that generally it is a near relative of the famous 'Mugby Junction.' Those who have been there retain at least a confused recollection of large and lofty saloons, velvet sofas, painted walls, and long semicircular bars covered with glittering glasses and decanters. Or it may be that the cleverly executed silver model of a locomotive under a glass case lingers still in their memories. At all events Swindon is a well-known oasis, familiar to the travelling public. Here let us do an act of justice. Much has been done of late to ameliorate many of the institutions which formerly led to bitter things being said against the place. The soup is no longer liquid fire, the beer is not lukewarm, the charges are more moderate; the lady manager has succeeded in substituting order for disorder, comfort and attention in place of lofty disdain. Passengers have not got to cross the line for a fresh ticket or to telegraph; the whole place is reformed. So much the better for the traveller. But how little do these birds of passage imagine the varied interest of the strange and even romantic story which is hidden in this most unromantic spot, given over, as it seems, to bricks and mortar!

Not that it ever had a history in the usual sense. There is but a faint, dim legend that the great Sweyn halted with his army on this hill – thence called Sweyn's dune, and so Swindon. There is a family here whose ancestry goes back to the times of the Vikings; which was in honour when Fair Rosamond bloomed at Woodstock; which fought in the great Civil War. Nothing further. The real history, written in iron and steel, of the place began forty years ago only. Then a certain small party of gentlemen sat down to luncheon on the greensward which was then where the platform is now. The furze was in blossom around them; the rabbits frisked in and out of their burrows; two or three distant farm-houses, one or two cottages, these were all the signs of human habitation, except a few cart-ruts indicating a track used for field purposes. There these gentlemen lunched, and one among them, ay, two among them, meditated great things, which the first planned, and the second lived to see realize the most sanguine anticipations. These two gentlemen were Isambard Brunel and Daniel Gooch. Driven away from the original plan, which was to follow the old coach-road, they had come here to survey and reconnoitre a possible track

Brunel

running in the valley at the northern edge of the great range of Wiltshire Downs. They decided that here should be their junction and their workshop. Immense sacrifices, enormous expenditure, the directors of the new railway incurred in their one great idea of getting it finished! They could not stay to cart the earth from the cuttings to the places where it was required for embanking, so where they excavated thousands of tons of clay they purchased land to cast it upon out of their way; and where they required an embankment they purchased a hill, and boldly removed it to fill up the hollow. They could not stay for the seasons, for proper weather to work in, and in consequence of this their clay embankment, thrown up wet and saturated, swelled out, bulged at the sides, and could not be made stable, till at last they drove rows of piles on each side, and chained them together with chain-cables, and so confined the slippery soil. They drove these piles, tall beech-trees, 20 feet into the earth, and at this day every train passes over tons of chain-cables hidden beneath the ballast. The world yet remembers the gigantic cost of the Box Tunnel, and how heaven and earth were moved to get the line open; and at last it was open, but at what cost! – a cost that hung like a millstone round the neck of the company, till a man rose into power who had the talent of administration, and that man was the very companion of Brunel whom we saw lunching among the furze-bushes. Reckless as the expenditure was, one cannot but admire the determination which overcame every obstacle. For the great line a workshop was needed, and that workshop was built at Swindon. The green fields were covered with forges, the hedges disappeared to make way for cottages for the workmen. The workmen required food – tradesmen came and supplied that food – and Swindon rose as Chicago rose, as if by magic. From that day to this additions have been made, and other departments concentrated upon this one spot, till at the present time the factory covers a space equal to that of a moderate farm, and employs nearly four thousand workmen to whom three hundred thousand pounds are yearly paid, whereby to purchase their

Gooch

daily bread. But at the early stage the difficulty was to find experienced workmen, and still greater to discover men who could superintend them. For these it was necessary to go up into the shrewd North, which had already foreseen the demand that must arise, and had partially educated her children in the new life that was about to dawn on the world; and so it is that to this time the names of those who are in authority over this army of workers carry with them in their sound a strong flavour of the heather and the brae, and seem more in accordance with ideas of 'following the wild deer' than of a dwelling in the midst of the clangour and smoke.

All these new inhabitants of the hitherto deserted fields had to be lodged, and in endeavouring to solve this problem the company were induced to try an experiment which savoured not a little of communism, though not so intended. A building was erected which was locally called the 'barracks,' and it well deserved the name, for at one time as many as perhaps five hundred men found shelter in it. It was a vast place, with innumerable rooms and corridors. The experiment did not altogether answer, and was in time abandoned, when the company built whole streets, and even erected a covered market-place for their labourers. They went further, and bore the chief expense in building a church. A reading-room was started, and grew and grew till a substantial place was required for the accommodation of the members. Finally, the 'barracks' was converted into a place of worship for a Dissenting body, and a grand hall it afforded when the interior was removed and only the shell left. But by this time vast changes had taken place, and great extensions had arisen through private energy. This land was the poorest in the neighbourhood; low-lying, shallow soil on top of an endless depth of stiff clay, worthless for arable purposes, of small value for pasture, covered with furze, rushes, and rowen; so much so that when a certain man with a little money purchased a good strip of it, he was talked of as a fool, and considered to have commited a most egregious error. How vain is human wisdom! In a few years the railway came. Land rose in price, and this very strip brought its owner thousands; so that the fool became wise, and the wise was deemed of no account. Private speculators, seeing the turn things were taking, ran up rows of houses; building societies stepped in and laid out streets; a whole town seemed to start into being at once. Still the company continued to concentrate their works at the junction, and at last added the culminating stroke by bringing the carriage department here, which was like planting a new colony. A fresh impulse was given to building; fresh blocks and streets arose; companies were formed to burn bricks – one of these makes bricks by steam, and can burn a quarter of a million at once in their kiln. This in a place where previously the rate of building was five new houses in twenty years! Sanitary districts were mapped out; boards of control elected; gas companies; water companies – who brought water out of the chalk hills three miles distant: all the distinctive characteristics of a city arose into being. Lastly came a sewage farm, for so great was the sewage that it became a burning question how to dispose of it, and on this sewage farm some most extraordinary results have been obtained, such as mangolds with leaves four feet in length – a tropical luxuriance of growth. One postman had sufficed, then two, then three, till a strong staff had to be organized, in regular uniform, provided with bull's-eye lanthorns to pick their way in and out of the dark and dirty back-streets. One single constable had sufficed, and a dark hole had done duty as a prison. Now a superintendent and other officers, a full staff, and a complete police-station, with cells, justice-room, all the paraphernalia were required; and so preposterous did this seem to other towns, formerly leading towns in the country, but which had remained stagnant while Swindon went ahead, that they bitterly resented the building, and satirized it as a 'Palace of Justice,' though, in good truth, sorely needed. A vast corn exchange, a vaster drill-hall for the workmen – who had formed a volunteer corps – to drill in, chapels of every description, and some of really large size – all these arose.

The little old town on the hill a mile from the station felt the wave of progress strongly. The streets were paved; sewers driven under the town at a depth of 40 feet through solid stone, in order to dispose of the sewage on a second sewage farm of over 100 acres. Shops, banks, and, above all, public-houses, abounded and increased apace, especially in the new town, where every third house seemed to be licensed premises. The cart-track seen by the luncheon-party in the furze was laid down and macadamized, and a street erected, named after the finest street in London, full of shops of all descriptions. Every denomination, from the Plymouth Brethren to the Roman Catholics, had their place of worship. Most of the tradesmen had two branches, one in the upper and one in the lower town, and the banks followed their example. Not satisfied with two railways, two others are now in embryo – one a link in the long-talked-of through communication between North and South, from

Manchester to Southampton, the other a local line with possible extensions. A population of barely 2,000 has risen to 15,000, and this does not nearly represent the real number of inhabitants, for there is a large floating population, and, in addition, five or six villages surrounding the town are in reality merely suburbs, and in great part populated by men working in the town. These villages have shared in the general movement, and some of them have almost trebled in size and importance. This population is made up of the most incongruous elements: labouring men of the adjacent counties who have left the plough and the sickle for the hammer and the spade; Irish in large numbers; Welshmen, Scotch, and North of England men; stalwart fellows from York and places in a similar latitude. Yet, notwithstanding all the building that has been going on, despite the rush of building societies and private speculators, the cry is still, 'More bricks and mortar,' for there exists an enormous amount of overcrowding. The high rents are almost prohibitory, and those who take houses underlet them and sublet them, till in six rooms three families may be living. The wages are good, ranging from 18s. for common labourers to 30s, 36s., 40s., and more for skilled mechanics, and the mode in which they live affords an illustrative contrast to the agricultural population immediately surrounding the place. As if to complete the picture, that nothing might be wanting, a music hall has been opened, where for threepence the workman may listen to the dulcet strains of 'London artistes' while he smokes his pipe.

Can a more striking, a more wonderful and interesting spectacle be seen than this busy, Black-Country-looking town, with its modern associations, its go-ahead ways, in the midst of a purely agricultural country, where there are no coal or iron mines, where in the memory of middle-aged men there was nothing but pasture-fields, furze, and rabbits? In itself it affords a perfect epitome of the spirit of the nineteenth century.

And much, if not all, of this marvellous transformation, of this abounding life and

vigorous vitality, is due to the energy and the forethought, the will of one man. It is notorious that the Swindon of today is the creation of the companion of Brunel at the lunch in the furze-bushes. Sir Daniel Gooch has had a wonderful life. Beginning literally at the beginning, he rose from stage to stage, till he became the responsible head of the vast company in whose service he had commenced life. In that position he did not forget the place where his early years were passed, but used his influence to enrich it with the real secret of wealth, employment for the people. In so doing, time has proved that he acted for the best interests of the company, for, apart from monetary matters, the mass of workmen assembled at this spot are possessed of overwhelming political power, and can return the man they choose to Parliament. Thus the company secures a representative in the House of Commons.

Among the institutions which the railway company fostered was the primitive reading-room which has been alluded to. Under their care this grew and grew, until it became a Mechanics' Institute, or, rather, a department of science and art, which at the present day has an intimate connection with South Kensington. Some hundred prizes are here annually distributed to the numerous students, both male and female, who can here obtain the very best instruction, at the very smallest cost, in almost every branch of learning, from sewing to shorthand, from freehand drawing to algebra and conic sections. On one occasion, while distributing the prizes to the successful competitors, Sir Daniel Gooch laid bare some of his early struggles as an incentive to the youth around him. He admitted that there was a time, and a dark hour, when he all but gave up hopes of ultimate success, when it seemed that the dearest wish of his heart must for ever go without fulfilment. In this desponding mood he was slowly crossing a bridge in London, when he observed an inscription upon the parapet – *Nil Desperandum* (Never despair). How he took heart at this as an omen, and went forth and persevered till – The speaker did not complete the sentence, but all the world knows what ultimately happened, and remembers the man who laid the first Atlantic cable. The great lesson of perseverance, of patience, was never drawn with better effect.

In the Eastern tales of magicians one reads of a town being found one day where there was nothing but sand the day before. Here the fable is fact, and the potent magician is Steam. Here is, perhaps, the greatest temple that has ever been built to that great god of our day. Taking little note of its immense extent, of the vast walls which enclose it, like some fortress, of the tunnel which gives entrance, and through which three thousand workmen pass four times a day, let us enter at once and go straight to the manufacture of those wheels and tires and axles of which we have heard so much since the tragedy at Shipton. To look at a carriage-wheel, the iron carriage-wheel, one would imagine that it was all one piece, that it was stamped out at a blow, so little sign is there of a junction of parts. The very contrary is the fact: the wheel is made of a large number of pieces of iron welded together, and again and again welded together, till at last it forms one solid homogeneous mass. The first of these processes consists in the manufacture of the spokes, which are made out of fine iron. The spoke is made in two pieces, at two different forges, and by two distinct gangs of men. A third forge and a third gang are constantly employed in welding these two detached parts in one continuous piece, forming a spoke. One of these parts resembles a T with the downward stroke very short, and the cross stroke at the top slightly bent, so as to form a section of a curve. The other piece is about the same length, but rather thicker, and at its larger end somewhat wedge-shaped. This last piece forms that part of the spoke which goes nearest to the centre of the wheel. These two parts, when completed, are again heated to a red heat, and in that ductile state hammered with dexterous blows into one, which then resembles the same letter T, only with the downward stroke disproportionately long. Eight or more of these spokes, according to the size of the wheel, and whether it is intended for a carriage, an engine, or tender, are then arranged together on the ground, so that the wedge-shaped ends fit close together, and in that position are firmly fixed by the imposition above them of what is called a 'washer,' a flat circular piece of iron, which is laid red-hot on the centre of the embryo wheel, and there hammered into cohesion. The wheel is then turned over, and a second 'washer' beaten on, so that the partially molten metal runs, and joins together with the particles of the spokes, and the whole is one mass. In the ordinary cart-wheel or gig-wheel the spokes are placed in mortise-holes made in a solid central block; but in this wheel before us, the ends of the spokes, well cemented together by the two washers, form the central block or boss. The ends of the spokes do not quite touch each other, and so a small circular space is left which is subsequently bored to fit the axle. The wheel now presents a curiously incomplete appearance, for the top strokes of the T's do not touch each other. There is a space between each, and these spaces have now to be filled with pieces of red-hot iron well welded and hammered together. To the uninitiated it would seem that all this work is superfluous; that the wheel might be made much more quickly in two or three pieces, instead of all these, and that it would be stronger. But the practical men engaged in the work say differently. It is their maxim that the more iron is hammered, the stronger and better it becomes; therefore all this welding adds to the strength of the wheel. In practice it is found quicker and more convenient to thus divide the labour than to endeavour to form the wheel of fewer component parts. The wheel is now taken to the lathe, and a portion is cut away from its edge, till a groove is left so as to dovetail into the tyre.

The tyres, which are of steel, are not made here; they come ready to be placed upon the wheel, and some care has to be taken in moving them, for, although several inches in thickness and of enormous strength, it has occasionally happened that a sudden jar from other solid bodies has fractured them. One outer edge of the tyre is prolonged, so to say, and forms the projecting flange which holds the rails and prevents the carriage from running off the road. So important a part requires the best metal and the most careful manufacture, and accordingly no trouble or expense is spared to secure suitable tyres. One of the inner edges of the tyre, on the opposite side to the flange, is grooved, and this groove is intended to receive the edge of the wheel itself; they dovetail together here. The tyre is now made hot, and the result of that heating is an expansion of the metal, so that the circle of the tyre becomes larger. The wheel is then driven into the tyre, which fits round it like a band. As it grows cool the steel tyre clasps the iron wheel with enormous force, and the softer metal is driven into the groove of the steel. But this is not all. The wheel is turned over, and the iron wheel is seen to be some little distance sunk, as it were, beneath the surface of the tyre. Immediately on a level with the iron wheel there runs round the steel tyre another deeper groove. The wheel is again heated – not to redness, for the steel will not bear blows if too hot – and when the tyre is sufficiently warm, a long, thin strip of iron is driven into this groove, and so shuts the iron wheel into the tyre as with a continuous wedge. Yet another process has to follow – yet another safeguard against accident. The tyre, once more heated, is attacked with the blows of three heavy sledge-hammers, wielded by as many stalwart smiths, and its inner edge, by their well-directed blows, bent down over the narrow band of iron, or continuous wedge, so that this wedge is closed in by what may be called a continuous rivet. The wheel is now complete, so far as its body is concerned, and to look at, it seems very nearly impossible that any wear or tear, or jar or accident, could disconnect its parts – all welded, overlapped, dovetailed as they are. Practically it seems the perfection of safety; nor was it to a wheel of this character that *the* accident happened. The only apparent risk is that there may be some slight undiscovered flaw in the solid steel which, under the pressure of unforeseen circumstances, may give way. But the whole design of the wheel is to guard against the ill-effects that would follow the snapping of a tyre. Suppose a tyre to 'fly' the result would be a small crack; supposing there were two cracks, or ten cracks, the speciality of this wheel is that not one of those pieces could come off – that the wheel would run as well and as safely with a tyre cracked through in a dozen places as when perfectly sound. The reason of this is that every single quarter of an inch of the tyre is fixed irremovably to the outer edge of the iron wheel, by the continuous dovetail, by the continuous wedge, and by the continuous overlapping. So that under no condition could any portion of the tyre fly off from the wheel. Close by this wheel thus finished upon this patent process there was an old riveted wheel which had been brought in to receive a new tyre on the new process. This old wheel aptly illustrates the advantages of the new one. Its tyre is fixed to the wheel by rivets or bolts placed at regular intervals. Now, the holes made for these bolts to some extent weaken both tyre and wheel. The bolt is liable, with constant shaking, to wear loose. The bolt only holds a very limited area of tyre to the wheel. If the tyre breaks in two places between the bolts, it comes off. If a bolt breaks, or the tyre breaks at the bolt, it flies. The tyre is, in fact, only fixed on in spots with intervals between. The new fastening leaves no intervals, and instead of spots is fixed everywhere. This is called the Gibson process, and was invented by an employee of the company. Latterly another process has partially come into vogue, particularly for wooden wheels, which are preferred sometimes on account of their noiselessness. By this (the Mansell) process, the tyres, which are similar, are fastened to the wheels by two circular bands which dovetail into the tyre, and are then bolted to the wood.

To return to the wheel – now really and substantially a wheel, but which has still to be turned so as to run perfectly true upon the metals – it is conveyed to the wheel lathe, and affixed to what looks like another wheel, which is set in motion by steam-power, and carries our wheel round with it. A workman sets a tool to plane its edge, which shaves off the steel as if it were wood, and reduces it to the prescribed scale. Then, when its centre has been bored to receive the axle, the genesis of the wheel is complete, and it enters upon its life of perpetual revolution. How little do the innumerable travellers who are carried to their destination upon it imagine the immense expenditure of care, skill, labour, and thought that has been expended before a perfect wheel was produced.

Next in natural order come the rails upon which the wheel must run. The former type of rail was a solid bar of iron, whose end presented a general resemblance to the letter T, which was thick at the top and at the bottom, and smaller in the middle. It was thought that this rail was not entirely satisfactory, for reasons that cannot be enumerated here, and accordingly a patent was taken out for a rail which, it is believed, can be more easily and cheaply manufactured, with a less expenditure of metal, and which can be more readily attached to the sleepers. In reality it is designed upon the principle of the arch, and the end of these rails somewhat resembles the Greek letter Ω, for they are hollow, and formed of a thin plate of metal rolled into this shape. Coming to this very abode of the Cyclops, the rail-mill, the first machine that appears resembles a pair of gigantic scissors, which are employed day and night in snipping off old rails and other pieces of iron into lengths suitable for the manufacture of new rails.

These scissors, or, perhaps, rather pincers, are driven by steam-power, and bite off the solid iron as if it were merely strips of ribbon. There is some danger in this process, for occasionally the metal breaks and flies, and men's hands are severely injured. At a guess, the lengths of iron for manufacture into rails may be about four feet long, and are piled up in flat pieces eight or nine inches or more in height. These pieces are carried to the furnace, heated to an intense heat, and then placed under the resistless blows of a steam-hammer, which welds them into one solid bar of iron, longer than the separate pieces were. The bar then goes back to the furnace, and again comes out white-hot. The swinging-shears seize it, and it is swung along to the rollers. These rollers are two massive cylindrical iron bars which revolve rapidly one over the other. The end of the white-hot metal is placed between these rollers, and is at once drawn out into a long strip of iron, much as a piece of dough is rolled out under the cook's rolling-pin. It is now perfectly flat, and entirely malleable. It is returned to the furnace heated, brought back, and placed in a second pair of rollers. This second pair have projections upon them, which so impress the flat strip of iron that it is drawn out into the required shape. The rail passes twice through these rollers, once forwards, then backwards. Terrible is the heat in this fiery spot. The experienced workman who guides the long red-hot rails to the mouth of the rollers is protected with a mask, with iron-shod shoes, iron greaves on his legs, an iron apron, and even further, with a shield of iron. The very floor beneath is formed of slabs of iron instead of slabs of stone, and the visitor very soon finds this iron floor too hot for his feet. The perfect rail, still red-hot or nearly, is run back to the circular saw, which cuts it off in regular lengths; for it is not possible to so apportion the iron in each bundle as to form absolutely identical strips. They are proportioned so as to be a little longer than required, and then sawn off to the exact length. While still hot, a workman files the sawn ends so that they may fit together closely when laid down on the sleepers. The completed rails are then stacked for removal on trucks to their destination. The rollers which turn out these rails in so regular and beautiful a manner are driven by a pair of engines of enormous power. The huge fly-wheel is twenty feet in diameter, and weighs, with its axle, thirty-five tons. When these rails were first manufactured, the rollers were driven direct from the axle of the fly-wheel, and the rails had to be lifted right over the roller – a difficult and dangerous process – and again inserted between them on the side at which it started. Since then an improvement has been effected, by which the rails are sent backwards through the rollers thus avoiding the trouble of lifting them over. This is managed by reversing the motion of the rollers, which is done in an instant by means of a 'crab.'

Immediately adjacent to these rail-mills are the steam-hammers, whose blows shake the solid earth. The largest descends with the force of seventy tons, yet so delicate is the machinery that visitors are shown how the same ponderous mass of metal and the same irresistible might can be so gently administered as to crush the shell of a nut without injuring the kernel. These hammers are employed in beating huge masses of iron into cranks for engines, and other heavy work which is beyond the unaided strength of man. Each of the hammers has its own steam-boiler and its furnace close at hand, and over head there are travelling cranes which convey the metal to and fro. These boilers may be called vertical, and with the structure on which they are supported have a dome-like shape. Hissing, with small puffs of white steam curling stealthily upwards, they resemble a group of volcanoes on the eve of an eruption. This place presents a wonderful and even terrible aspect at night, when the rail-mill and steam-hammers are in full swing. The open doors of the glaring furnaces shot forth an insupportable beam of brilliant white light, and out from among the glowing fire comes a massive bar of iron, hotter, whiter than the fire itself – barely to be looked upon. It is dragged and swung along under the great hammer; Thor strikes, and the metal doubles up, and bends as if of plastic clay, and showers of sparks fly high and far. What looks like a long strip of solid flame is guided between the rollers, and flattened and shaped, till it comes out a dull-red-hot rail, and the sharp teeth of the circular saw cut through it, throwing out a circle of sparks. The vast fly-wheel whirls round endless shaftings, and drums are revolving overhead, and the ear is full of a ceaseless overpowering hum, varied at intervals with the sharp scraping, ringing sound of the saw. The great boilers hiss, the furnaces roar, all around there is a sense of an irresistible power, but just held in by bars and rivets, ready in a moment to rend all asunder. Masses of glowing iron are wheeled hither and thither in wheelbarrows; smaller blocks are slid along the iron floor. Here is a heap of red-hot scraps hissing. A sulphurous hot smell prevails, a burning wind, a fierce heat, now from this side, now from that, and ever and anon bright streaks of light flow out from the open furnace doors, casting grotesque shadows upon the roof and walls. The men have barely a human look, with the reflection of the fire upon them; mingling thus with flame and heat, toying with danger, handling, at it seems, red-hot metal with ease. The whole scene suggests the infernal regions. A mingled hiss and roar and thud fill the building with reverberation, and the glare of the flames rising above the chimneys throws a reflection upon the sky, which is visible miles away, like that of a conflagration.

Stepping out of this pandemonium, there are rows upon rows of gleaming forges, each with its appointed smiths, whose hammers rise and fall in rhythmic strokes, and who manufacture the minor portions of the incipient locomotive. Here is a machine the central part of which resembles a great corkscrew or spiral constantly revolving. A weight is affixed to its inclined plane, and is carried up to the required height by the revolution of the screw, to be let fall upon a piece of red-hot iron, which in that moment becomes a bolt, with its projecting head or cap. Though they do not properly belong to our subject, the great marine boilers in course of construction in the adjoining department cannot be overlooked, even if only for their size – vast cylinders of twelve feet diameter. Next comes the erecting shop, where the various parts of the locomotive are fitted together, and it is built up much as a ship from the keel. These semi-completed engines have a singularly helpless look – out of proportion, without limbs, and many mere skeletons. Close by is the department where engines out of repair are made good. Some American engineer started the idea of a railway thirty feet wide, an idea which in this place is partially realized. The engine to be repaired is run on to what may be described as a turn-table resting upon wheels and this turn-table is bodily rolled along, like a truck, with the engine on it, to the place where tools and cranes and all the necessary gear are ready for the work upon it. Now by a yard, which seems one vast assemblage of wheels of all kinds – big wheels, little wheels, wheels of all sizes, nothing but wheels; past great mounds of iron, shapeless heaps of scrap, and then, perhaps, the most interesting shop of all, though the least capable of description, is entered. It is where the endless pieces of metal of which the locomotive is composed are filed and planed and smoothed into an accurate fit; an immense building, with shafting overhead and shafting below in endless revolution, yielding an incessant hum like the sound of armies of bees – a building which may be said to have a score of aisles, up which one may walk with machinery upon either side. Hundreds of lathes of every conceivable pattern are planing the solid steel and the solid iron as if it were wood, cutting off with each revolution a more or less thick slice of the hard metal, which curls up like a shaving of deal. So delicate is the touch of some of these tools, so good the metal they are employed to cut, that shavings are taken off three or more feet long, curled up like a spiral spring, and which may be wound round the hand like string. The interiors of the cylinders, the bearings, those portions of the engines which slide one upon the other, and require the most accurate fit, are here adjusted by unerring machinery, which turns out the work with an ease and exactness which the hand of man, delicate and wonderful organ as it is, cannot reach. From the smallest fitting up to the great engine cranks, the lathes smooth them all – reduce them to the precise size which they were intended to be by the draughtsman. These cranks and larger pieces of metal are conveyed to their lathes and placed in position by a steam crane, which glides along upon a single rail at the will of the driver, who rides on it, and which handles the massive metal almost with the same facility that an elephant would move a log of wood with his trunk. Most of us have an inherent idea that iron is exceedingly hard, but the ease with which it is cut and smoothed by these machines goes far to remove that impression.

The carriage department does not offer so much that will strike the eye, yet it is of the highest importance. To the uninitiated it is difficult to trace the connection between the various stages of the carriage, as it is progressively built up, and finally painted and gilded and fitted with cushions. Generally, the impression left from an inspection is that the frames of the carriages are made in a way calculated to secure great strength, the material being solid oak. The brake-vans especially are made strong. The carriages made here are for the narrow gauge, and are immensely superior in every way to the old broad-gauge carriage, being much more roomy, although not so wide. Over the department there lingers an odour of wood. It is common to speak of the scented woods of the East and the South, but even our English woods are not devoid of pleasant odour under the carpenter's hands. Hidden away amongst the piles of wood there is here a triumph of human ingenuity. It is an endless saw which revolves around two wheels, much in the same way as a band revolves around two drums. The wheels are perhaps three feet in diameter, and two inches in thickness at the circumference. They are placed – one as low as the workman's feet, another rather above his head – six or seven feet apart. Round the wheels there stretches an endless narrow band of blue steel, just as a ribbon might. This band of steel is very thin, and almost half an inch in width. Its edge towards the workman is serrated with sharp deep teeth. The wheels revolve by steam rapidly, and carry with them the saw, so that, instead of the old up and down motion, the teeth are continually running one way. The band of steel is so extremely flexible that it sustains the state of perpetual curve. There are stories in ancient chronicles of the wonderful swords of famous warriors made of such good steel that the blade could be bent till the point touched the hilt, and even till the blade was tied in a knot. These stories do not seem like fables before this endless saw, which does not bend once or twice, but is incessantly curved, and incessantly in the act of curving. A more beautiful machine cannot be imagined. Its chief use is to cut out the designs for cornices, and similar ornamental work in thin wood; but it is sufficiently strong to cut through a two-inch plank like paper. Every possible support that can be afforded by runners is given to the saw; still, with every aid, it is astonishing to see metal, which we have been taught to believe rigid, flexible as indiarubber. Adjoining are frame saws, working up and down by steam, and cutting half a dozen or more boards at the same time. It was in this department that the Queen's carriage was built at a great expenditure of skill and money – a carriage which is considered one of the masterpieces of this particular craft.

There rises up in the mind, after the contemplation of this vast workshop, with its endless examples of human ingenuity, a conviction that safety in railway travelling is not only possible, but probable, and even now on the way to us. No one can behold the degree of excellence to which the art of manufacturing material has been brought, no one can inspect the process by which the wheel, for instance, is finally welded into one compact mass, without a firm belief that, where so much has been done, in a little time still more will be done. That safer plans, that better designs, that closer compacted forms will arise seems as certain and assured a fact as that those forms now in use arose out of the rude beginnings of the past; for this great factory, both in its machine tools and in its products, the wheels and rails and locomotives is standing proof of the development which goes on in the mind of man when brought constantly to bear upon one subject. As with the development of species, so it is with that of machinery: rude and more general forms first, finer and

'The starling pours forth a flood of eloquence'
(*Nature and Eternity*)

'Goldfinches'
(*Nature and Eternity*)

more specialized forms afterwards. There is every reason to hope, for this factory is proof of the advance that has been made. It would seem that the capability of metal is practically infinite.

But what an enormous amount of labour, what skill, and what complicated machinery must be first employed before what is in itself a very small result can be arrived at! In order that an individual may travel from London to Oxford, see what innumerable conditions have to be fulfilled. Three thousand men have to work night and day that we may merely seat ourselves and remain passive till our destination is reached.

This small nation of workers, this army of the hammer, lathe, and drill, affords matter for deep meditation in its sociological aspect. Though so numerous that not one of them can be personally acquainted with more than a factional part, yet there is a strong *esprit de corps,* a spirit that ascends to the highest among them; for it is well known that the chief manager has a genuine feeling of almost fatherly affection for these his men, and will on no account let them suffer, and will, if possible, obtain for them every advantage. The influence he thereby acquires among them is principally used for moral and religious ends. Under these auspices have arisen the great chapels and places of worship of which the town is full. Of the men themselves, the majority are intelligent, contrasting strongly with the agricultural poor around them, and not a few are well educated and thoughtful. This gleaning of intellectual men are full of social life, or, rather, of an interest in the problems of social existence. They eagerly discuss the claims of religion *versus* the allegations of secularism; they are shrewd to detect the weak points of an argument; they lean, in fact, towards an eclecticism: they select the most rational part of every theory. They are full of information on every subject – information obtained not only from newspapers, books, conversation, and lectures, but from travel, for most have at least been over the greater part of England. They are probably higher in their intellectual life than a large proportion of the so-called middle classes. One is, indeed, tempted to declare, after considering the energy with which they enter on all questions, that this class of educated mechanics forms in reality the protoplasm, or living matter, out of which modern society is evolved. The great and well-supplied reading-room of the Mechanics' Institute is always full of readers; the library, now an extensive one, is constantly in use. Where one book is read in agricultural districts, fifty are read in the vicinity of the factory. Social questions of marriage, of religion, of politics, sanitary science, are for ever on the simmer among these men. It would almost seem as if the hammer, the lathe, and the drill would one day bring forth a creed of its own. A characteristic of all classes of these workmen is their demand for meat, of which great quantities are consumed. Nor do they stay at meat alone, but revel in fish and other luxuries at times, though the champagne of the miner is not known here. Notwithstanding the number of public-houses, it is a remarkable fact that there is very little drunkenness in proportion to the population, few crimes of violence, and, what is more singular still, and has been often remarked, very little immorality. Where there are some hundreds, perhaps thousands, of young uneducated girls, without work to occupy their time, there must of course exist a certain amount of lax conduct; but never, or extremely rarely, does a girl apply to the magistrates for an affiliation order, while from agricultural parishes such applications are common. The number of absolutely immoral women openly practising infamy is also remarkably small. There was a time when the workmen at this factory enjoyed an unpleasant notoriety for mischief and drunkeness, but that time has passed away, a most marked improvement having taken place in the last few years.

There appears, however, to be very little prudence amongst them. The man who receives some extra money for extra work simply spends it on unusual luxuries in food or drink; or, if it be summer, takes his wife and children a drive in a hired conveyance. To this latter there can be no objection ; but still, the fact remains prominent that men in the receipt of good wages do not save. They do not put by money; this is, of course, speaking of the majority. It would almost seem to be a characteristic of human nature that those who receive wages for work done, so much per week or fortnight, do not contract saving habits. The small struggling tradesman, whose income is very little more that that of the mechanic, often makes great exertions and practises much economy to put by a sum to assist him in difficulty or to extend his business. It may be that the very certainty of the wages acts as a deterrent – inasmuch as the mechanic feels safe of his weekly money, while the shopkeeper runs much risk. It is doubtful whether mechanics with good wages save more than agricultural labourers, except in indirect ways – ways which are thrust upon them. First of all, there is the yard club, to which all are compelled to pay by their employers, the object being to provide medical assistance in case of sickness. This is in some sense a saving. Then there are the building societies, which offer opportunities of possessing a house, and the mechanic who becomes a member has to pay for it by instalments. This also may be called an indirect saving, since the effect is the same. But of direct saving – putting money in a bank, or investing it – there is scarcely any. The quarter of a million annually paid in wages mostly finds its way into the pockets of the various trades-people, and at the end of the year the mechanic is none the better off. This is a grave defect in his character. Much of it results from a generous, liberal disposition: a readiness to treat a friend with a drink, to drive the family out into the country, to treat the daughter with a new dress. The mechanic does not set a value upon money in itself.

The effect of the existence of this factory upon the whole surrounding district has been marked. A large proportion of the lower class of mechanics, especially the factory labourers, are drawn from the agricultural poor of the adjacent villages. These work all day at the factory, and return at night. They daily walk great distances to secure this employment: three miles to and three miles back is common, four miles not uncommon, and some have been known to walk six or twelve miles per day. These carry back with them into the villages the knowledge they insensibly acquire from their better informed comrades, and exhibit an independent spirit. For a radius of six miles round the poorer class are better informed, quicker in perception, more ready with an answer to a question, than those who dwell farther back out of the track of modern life. Wages had materially risen long before the movement among the agricultural labourers took place.

Where there was lately nothing but furze and rabbits there is now a busy human population. Why was it that for so many hundreds of years the population of England remained nearly stationary? and why has it so marvellously increased in this last forty years? The history of this place seems to answer that interesting question. The increase is due to the facilities of communication which now exist, and to the numberless new employments in which that facility of communication took rise, and which it in turn adds to and fosters.

from *The Hills and the Vale*

Chapter 27

Nature and Eternity

The goldfinches sing so sweetly hidden in the topmost boughs of the apple-trees that heart of man cannot withstand them. These four walls, though never so well decorated with pictures, this flat white ceiling, feels all too small, and dull and tame. Down with books and pen, and let us away with the goldfinches, the princes of the birds. For thirty of their generations they have sung and courted and built their nests in those apple-trees, almost under the very windows – a time in their chronology equal to a thousand years. For they are so very busy, from earliest morn till night – a long summer's day is like a year. Now flirting with a gaily-decked and coy lady-love, chasing her from tree to tree; now splashing at the edge of a shallow stream till the golden feathers glisten and the red topknot shines. Then searching in and out the hedgerow for favourite seeds, and singing, singing all the while, verily a 'song without an end'. The wings never still, the bill never idle, the throat never silent, and the tiny heart within the proud breast beating so rapidly that, reckoning time by change and variety, an hour must be a day. A life all joy and freedom, without thought, and full of love. What a great god the sun must be to the finches from whose wings his beams are reflected in glittering gold! The abstract idea of a deity apart, as they feel their life-blood stirring, their eyelids opening, with the rising sun; as they fly to satisfy their hunger with those little fruits they use; as they revel in the warm sunshine, and utter soft notes of love to their beautiful mates, they cannot but feel a sense, unnamed, indefinite, of joyous gratitude towards that great orb which is very nearly akin to the sensual worship of ancient days. Darkness and cold are Typhon and Ahriman, light and warmth, Osiris and Ormuzd, indeed to them; with song they welcome the spring and celebrate the awakening of Adonis. Lovely little idolaters, my heart goes with them. Deep down in the mysteries of organic life there are causes for the marvellously extended grasp which the worship of light once held upon the world, hardly yet guessed at, and which even now play a part unsuspected in the motives of men. Even yet, despite our artificial life, despite railroads, telegraphs, printing-press, in the face of firm, monotheistic convictions, once a year the old, old influence breaks forth, driving thousands and thousands from cities and houses out into field and forest, to the seashore and mountain-top, to gather fresh health and strength from the Sun, from the Air – Jove – and old Ocean. So the goldfinches rejoice in the sunshine, and who can sit within doors when they sing?

Foolish fashion has banished the orchard from the mansion – the orchard which Homer tells us kings once valued as part of their demesne – and has substituted curious evergreens to which the birds do not take readily. But this orchard is almost under the windows, and in summer the finches wake the sleeper with their song, and in autumn the eye looks down upon the yellow and rosy fruit. Up the scaling bark of the trunks the brown tree-climbers run, peering into every cranny, and few are the insects which escape those keen eyes. Sitting on a bench under a pear-tree, I saw a spider drop from a leaf fully nine feet above the ground, and disappear in the grass, leaving a slender rope of web, attached at the upper end to a leaf, and at the lower to a fallen pear. In a few minutes a small white caterpillar, barely an inch long, began to climb this rope. It grasped the thread in the mouth and drew up its body about a sixteenth of an inch at a time, then held tight with the two fore-feet, and lifting its head, seized the rope a sixteenth higher; repeating this operation incessantly, the rest of the body swinging in the air. Never pausing, without haste and without rest, this creature patiently worked its way upwards, as a man might up a rope. Let anyone seize a beam overhead and attempt to lift the chest up to a level with it, the expenditure of strength is very great; even with long practice, to 'swarm' up a pole or rope to any distance is the hardest labour the human muscles are capable of. This despised 'creeping thing', without the slightest apparent effort, without once pausing to take breath, reached the leaf overhead in rather under half an hour, having climbed a rope fully 108 times its own length. To equal this a man must climb 648 feet, or more than half as high again as St.Paul's. The insect on reaching the top at once commenced feeding, and easily bit through the hard pear-leaf: how delicately then it must have grasped the slender spider's web, which a touch would destroy! The thoughts which this feat call forth do not end here, for there was no necessity to go up the thread; the insect could to all appearance have travelled up the trunk of the tree with ease, and it is not to be supposed that its mouth and feet were specially adapted to climb a web, a thing which I have never seen done since, and which was to all appearance merely the result of the *accident* of the insect coming along just after the spider had left the thread. Another few minutes, and the first puff of wind would have carried the thread away – as a puff actually did soon afterwards. I claim a wonderful amount of *original* intelligence – as opposed to the ill-used term instinct – of patience and perseverance for this creature. It is so easy to imagine that because man is big, brain power cannot exist in tiny organizations; but even in man the seat of thought is so minute that it escapes discovery, and his very life may be said to lie in the point of contact of two bones of the neck. Put the mind of man within the body of the caterpillar – what more could it have done? Accustomed to bite and eat its way through hard leaves, why did not the insect snip off and destroy its rope? These are matters to think over dreamily while the finches sing overhead in the apple-tree.

They are not the only regular inhabitants, still less the only visitors. As there are wide plains even in thickly populated England where man has built no populous city, so in bird-life there are fields and woods almost deserted by the songsters, who at the same time congregate thickly in a few favourite resorts, where experience gathered in slow time has shown them they need fear nothing from human beings. Such a place, such a city of the birds and beasts, is this old orchard. The bold and handsome bullfinch builds in the low hawthorn hedge which bounds it upon one side. In the walls of the arbour formed of thick ivy and flowering creepers, the robin and thrush hide their nests. On the topmost branches of the tall pear-trees the swallows rest and twitter. The noble blackbird, with full black eye, pecks at the decaying apples upon the sward, and takes no heed of a footstep. Sometimes the loving pair of squirrels who dwell in the fir-copse at the end of the meadow find their way down the hedges – staying at each tree as an inn by the road – into the orchard, and play their fantastic tricks upon the apple-boughs. The flycatchers perch on a branch clear from the tree, and dart at the passing flies. Merriest of all, the tomtits chatter and scold, hanging under the twigs, head downwards, and then away to their nest in the crumbling stone wall which encloses one side of the orchard. They have worked their way by a cranny deep into the thick wall. On the other side runs the king's highway, and ever and anon the teams go by, making music with their bells. One day a whole nation of martins savagely attacked this wall. Pressure of population probably had compelled them to emigrate from the sand quarry, and the chinks in the wall pleased their eyes. Five-and-thirty brown little birds went to work like miners at twelve or fourteen holes, tapping at the mortar with their bills, scratching out small fragments of stone, twittering and talking all the time, and there undoubtedly they would have founded a colony had not the jingling teams and now and then a barking dog disturbed them. Resting on the bench and leaning back against an apple-tree, it is easy to watch the eager starlings on the chimney-top, and see them tear out the straw of the thatch to form their holes. They are all orators born. They live in a democracy, and fluency of speech leads the populace. Perched on the edge of the chimney, his bronze-tinted wings flapping against his side to give greater emphasis – as a preacher moves his hands – the starling pours forth a flood of eloquence, now rising to screaming-pitch, now modulating his tones to soft persuasion, now descending to deep, low, complaining, regretful sounds – a speech without words – addressed to a dozen birds gravely listening on the ash-tree yonder. He is begging them to come with him to a meadow where food is abundant. In the ivy close under the window there, within reach of the hand, a water-wagtail built its nest. To this nest one lovely afternoon came a great bird like a hawk, to the fearful alarm and intense excitement of all the bird population. It was a cuckoo, and after three or four visits, despite a curious eye at the window, there was a strange egg in that nest. Inside that window, huddled fearfully in the darkest corner of the room, there was once a tiny heap of blue and yellow feathers. A tomtit straying through the casement had been chased by the cat till it dropped exhausted, and the cat was fortunately frightened by a foot step. The bird was all but dead – the feathers awry and ruffled, the eyelids closed, the body limp and helpless – only a faint fluttering of the tiny heart. When placed tenderly on the ledge of the casement, where the warm sunshine fell and the breeze came softly, it dropped listlessly on one side. But in a little while the life-giving rays quickened the blood, the eyelids opened, and presently it could stand perched upon the finger. Then, lest with returning consciousness fear should again arise, the clinging claws were transferred from the finger to a twig of wall-pear. A few minutes more, and with a chirp the bird was gone into the flood of sunlight. What intense joy there must have been in that little creature's heart as it drank the sweet air and felt the loving warmth of its great god Ra, the Sun!

Throwing open the little wicket-gate, by a step the greensward of the meadow is reached. Though the grass has been mown and the ground is dry, it is better to carry a thick rug, and cast it down in the shadow under the tall horse-chestnut-tree. It is only while in a dreamy, slumbrous, half-mesmerized state that nature's ancient papyrus roll can be read – only when the mind is at rest, separated from care and labour; when the body is at ease, luxuriating in warmth and delicious languor; when the soul is in accord and sympathy with the sunlight, with the leaf, with the slender blades of grass, and can feel with the tiniest insect which climbs up them as up a mighty tree. As the genius of the great musicians, without an articulated word or printed letter, can carry with it all the emotions, so now, lying prone upon the earth in the shadow, with quiescent will, listening, thoughts and feelings rise respondent to the sunbeams, to the leaf, the very blade of grass. Resting the head upon the hand, gazing down upon the ground, the strange and marvellous inner sight of the mind penetrates the solid earth, grasps in part the mystery of its vast extension upon either side, bearing its majestic mountains, its deep forests, its grand oceans, and almost feels the life which in ten thousand thousand forms revels upon its surface. Returning upon itself, the mind joys in the knowledge that it too is a part of this wonder – akin to the ten thousand thousand creatures, akin to the very earth itself. How grand and holy is this life! how

sacred the temple which contains it!

Out from the hedge, not five yards distant, pours a rush of deep luscious notes, succeeded by the sweetest trills heard by man. It is the nightingale, which tradition assigns to the night only, but which in fact sings as loudly, and to my ear more joyously, in the full sunlight, especially in the morning, and always close to the nest. The sun has moved onward upon his journey, and this spot is no longer completely shaded, but the foliage of a great oak breaks the force of his rays, and the eye can even bear to gaze at his disc for a few moments. Living for this brief hour at least in unalloyed sympathy with nature, apart from all disturbing influences, the sight of that splended disc carries the soul with it till it feels as eternal as the sun. Let the memory call up a picture of the desert sands of Egypt – upon the kings with the double crown, upon Rameses, upon Sesostris, upon Assurbanipal the burning beams of this very sun descended, filling their veins with tumultuous life, three thousand years ago. Lifted up in absorbing thought, the mind feels that these three thousand years are in truth no longer past than the last beat of the pulse. It throbbed – the throb is gone: their pulse throbbed, and it seems but a moment since, for to thought, as to the sun, there is no time. This little petty life of seventy years, with its little petty aims and hopes, its despicable fears and contemptible sorrows, is no more the life with which the mind is occupied. This golden disc has risen and set, as the graven marks of man alone record, full eight thousand years. The hieroglyphs of the rocks speak of a fiery sun shining inconceivable ages before that. Yet even this almost immortal sun had a beginning – perhaps emerging as a ball of incandescent gas from chaos: how long ago was that? And onwards, still onwards goes the disc, doubtless for ages and ages to come. It is time that our measures should be extended; these paltry divisions of hours and days and years – aye, of centuries – should be superseded by terms conveying some faint idea at least of the vastness of space. For in truth, when thinking thus, there is no time at all. The mind loses the sense of time and reposes in eternity. This hour, this instant is eternity; it extends backwards, it extends forwards, and we are in it. It is a grand and an ennobling feeling to know that at this moment illimitable time extends on either hand. No conception of a supernatural character formed in the brain has ever or will ever surpass the mystery of this endless existence as exemplified – as made manifest by the physical sun – a visible sign of immortality. This hour is part of the immortal life. Reclining upon this rug under the chestnut-tree, while the graceful shadows dance, a passing bee hums and the nightingale sings, while the oak foliage sprinkles the sunshine over us, we are really and in truth in the midst of eternity. Only by walking hand in hand with nature, only by a reverent and loving study of the mysteries for ever around us, is it possible to disabuse the mind of the narrow view, the contracted belief that time is now and eternity tomorrow. Eternity is today. The goldfinches and the tiny caterpillars, the brilliant sun, if looked at lovingly and thoughtfully, will lift the soul out of the smaller life of human care that is of selfish aims, bounded by seventy years, into the greater, the limitless life which has been going on over universal space from endless ages past, which is going on now, and which will for ever and for ever, in one form or another, continue to proceed.

Dreamily listening to the nightingale's song, let us look down upon the earth as the sun looks down upon it. In this meadow how many millions of blades of grass are there, each performing wonderful operations which the cleverest chemist can but poorly indicate, taking up from the earth its sap, from the air its gases, in a word living, living as much as ourselves, though in a lower form? On the oak-tree yonder, how many leaves are doing the same? Just now we felt the vastness of the earth – its extended majesty, bearing mountain, forest, and sea. Not a blade of grass but has its insect, not a leaf; the very air as it softly woos the cheek bears with it living germs, and upon all those mountains, within those forests; and in every drop of those oceans, life in some shape moves and stirs. Nay, the very solid earth itself, the very chalk and clay and stone and rock has been built up by once living organisms. But at this instant, looking down upon the earth as the sun does, how can words depict the glowing wonder, the marvellous beauty of all the plant, the insect, the animal life, which presses upon the mental eye? It is impossible. But with these that are more immediately around us – with the goldfinch, the caterpillar, the nightingale, the blades of grass, the leaves – with these we may feel, into their life we may in part enter, and find our own existence thereby enlarged. Would that it were possible for the heart and mind to enter into all the life that glows and teems upon the earth – to feel with it, hope with it, sorrow with it – and thereby to become a grander, nobler being. Such a being, with such a sympathy and larger existence, must hold in scorn the feeble, cowardly, selfish desire for an immortality of pleasure only, whose one great hope is to escape pain! No. Let me joy with all living creatures; let me suffer with them all – the reward of feeling a deeper, grander life would be amply sufficient.

What wonderful patience the creatures called 'lower' exhibit! Watch this small red ant travelling among the grass-blades. To it they are as high as the oak-trees to us, and they are entangled and matted together as a forest overthrown by a tornado. The insect slowly overcomes all the difficulties of its route – now climbing over the creeping roots of the buttercups, now struggling under a fallen leaf, now getting up a bennet, up and down, making one inch forward for three vertically, but never pausing, always onwards at racing speed. A shadow sweeps rapidly over the grass – it is that of a rook which has flown between us and the sun. Looking upwards into the deep azure of the sky, intently gazing into space and forgetting for a while the life around and beneath, there comes into the mind an intense desire to rise, to penetrate the height, to become part and parcel of that wondrous infinity which extends overhead as it extends along the surface. The soul full of thought grows concentrated in itself, marvels only at its own destiny, labours to behold the secret of its own existence, and, above all, utters without articulate words a prayer forced from it by the bright sun, by the blue sky, by bird and plant: – Let me have wider feelings, more extended sympathies, let me feel with all living things, rejoice and praise with them. Let me have deeper knowledge, a nearer insight, a more reverent conception. Let me see the mystery of life – the secret of the sap as it rises in the tree – the secret of the blood as it courses through the vein. Reveal the broad earth and the ends of it – make the majestic ocean open to the eye down to its inmost recesses. Expand the mind till it grasps the idea of the unseen forces which hold the globe suspended and draw the vast suns and stars through space. Let it see the life, the organisms which dwell in those great worlds, and feel with them their hopes and joys and sorrows. Ever upwards, onwards, wider, deeper, broader, till capable of all – all. Never did vivid imagination stretch out the powers of deity with such a fulness, with such intellectual grasp, vigour, omniscience as the human mind could reach to, if only its organs, its means, were equal to its thought. Give us, then, greater strength of body, greater length of days; give us more vital energy, let our limbs be mighty as those of the giants of old. Supplement such organs with nobler mechanical engines – with extended means of locomotion; add novel and more minute methods of analysis and discovery. Let us become as demi-gods. And why not? Whoso gave the gift of the mind gave also an infinite space, an infinite matter for it to work upon, an infinite time in which to work. Let no one presume to define the boundaries of that divine gift – that mind – for all the experience of eight thousand years proves beyond a question that the limits of its powers will never be reached, though the human race dwell upon the globe for eternity. Up, then, and labour: and let that labour be sound and holy. Not for immediate and petty reward, not that the appetite or the vanity may be gratified, but that the sum of human perfection may be advanced; labouring as consecrated priests, for true science is religion. All is possible. A grand future awaits the world. When man has only partially worked out his own conceptions – when only a portion of what the mind foresees and plans is realized – then already earth will be as a paradise.

Full of love and sympathy for this feeble ant climbing over grass and leaf, for yonder nightingale pouring forth its song, feeling a community with the finches, with bird, with plant, with animal, and reverently studying all these and more – how is it possible for the heart while thus wrapped up to conceive the desire of crime? For ever anxious and labouring for perfection, shall the soul, convinced of the divinity of its work, halt and turn aside to fall into imperfection? Lying thus upon the rug under the shadow of the oak and horse-chestnut-tree, full of the joy of life – full of the joy which all organisms feel in living alone – lifting the eye far, far above the sphere even of the sun, shall we ever conceive the idea of murder, of violence, of aught that degrades ourselves? It is impossible while in this frame. So thus reclining, and thus occupied, we require no judge, no prison, no law, no punishment – and, further, no army, no monarch. At this moment, did neither of these institutions exist our conduct would be the same. Our whole existence at this moment is permeated with a reverent love, an aspiration – a desire of a more perfect life; if the very name of religion was extinct, our hopes, our wish would be the same. It is but a simple transition to conclude that with more extended knowledge, with wider sympathies, with greater powers – powers more equal to the vague longings of their minds, the human race would be as we are at this moment in the shadow of the chestnut-tree. No need of priest and lawyer; no need of armies or kings. It is probable that with the progress of knowledge it will be possible to satisfy the necessary wants of existence much more easily than now, and thus to remove one great cause of discord. And all these thoughts because the passing shadow of a rook caused the eye to gaze upwards into the deep azure of the sky. There is no limit, no number to the thoughts which the study of nature may call forth, any more than there is a limit to the number of the rays of the sun.

This blade of grass grows as high as it can, the nightingale there sings as sweetly as it can, the goldfinches feed to their full desire and lay down no arbitrary rules of life; the great sun above pours out its heat and light in a flood unrestrained. What is the meaning of this hieroglyph, which is repeated in a thousand thousand other ways and shapes, which meets us at every turn? It is evident that all living creatures, from the zoophyte upwards, plant, reptile, bird, animal, and in his natural state – in his physical frame – man also, strive with all their powers to obtain as perfect an existence as possible. It is the one great law of their being, followed from birth to death. All the efforts of the plant are put forth to obtain more light, more air, more moisture – in a word, more food – upon which to grow, expand, and become more beautiful and perfect. The aim may be unconscious, but the result is evident. It is equally so with the animal; its lowest appetites subserve the one grand object of its advance. Whether it be eating, drinking, sleeping, procreating, all tends to one end, a fuller development of the individual, a higher condition of the species; still further, to the production of new races capable of additional progress. Part and parcel as we are of the great community of living beings, indissolubly connected with them from the lowest to the highest by a thousand ties, it is impossible for us to escape from the operation of this law; or if, by the exertion of the will, and the resources of the intellect, it is partially suspended, then the individual may perhaps pass away unharmed, but the race must suffer. It is, rather, the province of that inestimable gift, the mind, to aid nature, to smooth away the difficulties, to assist both the physical and mental man to increase his powers and widen his influence. Such efforts have been made from time to time, but unfortunately upon purely empirical principles, by arbitrary interference, without a long previous study of the delicate organization it was proposed to amend. If there is one thing our latter-day students have demonstrated beyond all reach of cavil, it is that both the physical and the mental man are, as it were, a mass of inherited structures – are built up of partially absorbed rudimentary organs and primitive conceptions, much as the trunks of certain trees are formed by the absorption of the leaves. He is made up of the Past. This is a happy and an inspiriting discovery, insomuch as it holds out a resplendent promise that there may yet come a man of the future made out of our present which will then be the past. It is a discovery which calls upon us for new and larger moral and physical exertion, which throws upon us wider and nobler duties, for upon us depends the future. At one blow this new light casts aside those melancholy convictions which, judging from the evil blood which seemed to stain each new generation alike, had elevated into a faith the depressing idea that man could not advance. It explains the causes of that stain, the reason of those imperfections, not necessary parts of the ideal man, but inherited from a lower order of life, and to be gradually expunged.

But this marvellous mystery of inheritance has brought with it a series of mental instincts, so to say; a whole circle of ideas of moral conceptions, in a sense belonging to the Past – ideas which were high and noble in the rudimentary being, which were beyond the capacity of the pure animal, but which are now in great part merely obstructions to advancement. Let these perish. We must seek for enlightenment for progress, not in the dim failing traditions of a period but just removed from the time of the rudimentary or primeval man – we must no longer allow the hoary age of such traditions to blind the eye and cause the knee to bend – we must no longer stultify the mind by compelling it to receive as infallible what in the very nature of things must have been fallible to the highest degree. The very plants are wiser far. They seek the light of today, the heat of the sun which shines at this hour; they make no attempt to guide their life by the feeble reflection of rays which were extinguished ages ago. This slender blade of grass, beside the edge of our rug under the chestnut-tree, shoots upwards in the fresh air today; its roots draw nourishment from the moisture of the dew which heaven deposited this morning. If it does make use of the past – of the soil, the earth that has accumulated in centuries – it is to advance its present growth. Root out at once and for ever these primeval, narrow, and contracted ideas; fix the mind upon the sun of the present, and prepare for the sun that must rise tomorrow. It is our duty to develop both mind and body and soul to the utmost: as it is the duty of this blade of grass and this oak-tree to grow and expand as far as their powers will admit. But the blade of grass and the oak have this great disadvantage to work against – they can only labour in the lines laid down for them, and unconsciously; while man can think, foresee, and plan. The greatest obstacle to progress is the lack now beginning to be felt all over the world, but more especially in the countries most highly civilized, of a true ideal to work up to. It is necessary that some far-seeing master-mind, some giant intellect, should arise, and sketch out in bold, unmistakable outlines the grand and noble future which the human race should labour for. There have been weak attempts – there are contemptible makeshifts now on their trial, especially in the new world – but the whole of these, without exception, are simply diluted reproductions of systems long since worn out. These can only last a little while; if anything, they are worse than the prejudices and traditions which form the body of wider-spread creeds. The world cries out for an intellect which shall draw its inspiration from the unvarying and infallible laws regulating the universe; which shall found its faith upon the teaching of grass, of leaf, of bird, of beast, of hoary rock, great ocean, star and sun; which shall afford full room for the development of muscle, sense and above all of the wondrous brain; and which without fettering the individual shall secure the ultimate apotheosis of the race. No such system can spring at once, complete, perfect in detail, from any one mind. But assuredly when once a firm basis has been laid down, when an outline has been drawn, the converging efforts of a thousand thousand thinkers will be brought to bear upon it, and it will be elaborated into something approaching a reliable guide. The faiths of the past, of the ancient world, now extinct or feebly lingering on, were each inspired by one mind only. The faith of the future, in strong contrast, will spring from the researches of a thousand thousand thinkers, whose minds, once brought into a focus, will speedily burn up all that is useless and worn out with a fierce heat, and evoke a new and brilliant light. This converging thought is one of the greatest blessings of our day, made possible by the vastly extended means of communication, and almost seems specially destined for this very purpose. Thought increases with the ages. At this moment there are probably as many busy brains studying, reflecting, collecting scattered truths, as there were thinkers – effectual thinkers – in all the recorded eighty centuries gone by. Daily and hourly the noble army swells its numbers, and the sound of its mighty march grows louder; the inscribed roll of its victories fills the heart with exultation.

There is a slight rustle among the bushes and the fern upon the mount. It is a rabbit who has peeped forth into the sunshine. His eye opens wide with wonder at the sight of us; his nostrils work nervously as he watches us narrowly. But in a little while the silence and stillness reassure him; he nibbles in a desultory way at the stray grasses on the mound, and finally ventures out into the meadow almost within reach of the hand. It is so easy to make the acquaintance – to make friends with the children of Nature. From the tiniest insect upwards they are so ready to dwell in sympathy with us – only be tender, quiet, considerate, in a word, gentlemanly, towards them and they will freely wander around. And they have all such marvellous tales to tell – intricate problems to solve for us. This common wild rabbit has an ancestry of almost unsearchable antiquity. Within that little body there are organs and structures which, rightly studied, will throw a light upon the mysteries hidden in our own frames. It is a peculiarity of this search that nothing is despicable; nothing can be passed over – not so much as a fallen leaf, or a grain of sand. Literally everything bears stamped upon it characters in the hieratic, the sacred handwriting, not one word of which shall fall to the ground.

Sitting indoors, with every modern luxury around, rich carpets, artistic furniture, pictures, statuary, food and drink brought from the uttermost ends of the earth, with the telegraph, the printing-press, the railway at immediate command, it is easy to say, 'What have I to do with all this? I am neither an animal nor a plant, and the sun is nothing to me. This is my life which I have created; I am apart from the other inhabitants of the earth.' But go to the window. See – there is but a thin, transparent sheet of brittle glass between the artificial man and the air, the light, the trees, and grass. So between him and the other innumerable organisms which live and breathe there is but a thin feeble crust of prejudice and social custom. Between him and those irresistible laws which keep the sun upon its course there is absolutely no bar whatever. Without air he cannot live. Nature cannot be escaped. Then face the facts, and having done so, there will speedily arise a calm pleasure beckoning onwards.

The shadows of the oak and chestnut-tree no longer shelter our rug; the beams of the noonday sun fall vertically on us; we will leave the spot for a while. The nightingale and the goldfinces, the thrushes and blackbirds, are silent for a time in the sultry heat. But they only wait for the evening to burst forth in one exquisite chorus, praising this wondrous life and the beauties of the earth.

from *The Hills and the Vale*

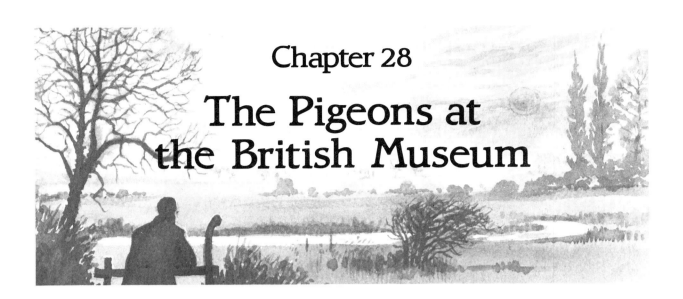

Chapter 28
The Pigeons at the British Museum

The front of the British Museum stands in the sunlight clearly marked against the firm blue of the northern sky. The blue appears firm as if solid above the angle of the stonework, for while looking towards it – towards the north – the rays do not come through the azure, which is therefore colour without life. It seems nearer than the southern sky, it descends and forms a close background to the building; as you approach you seem to come nearer to the blue surface rising at its rear. The dark edges of sloping stone are distinct and separate, but not sharp; the hue of the stone is toned by time and weather, and is so indefinite as to have lost its hardness. Those small rounded bodies upon the cornice are pigeons resting in the sun, so motionless and neutral-tinted that they might be mistaken for some portion of the carving. A double gilt ring, a circle in a circle, at the feet of an allegorical figure gleams brightly against the dark surface. The sky already seems farther away seen between the boles of stone, perpetual shade dwells in their depth, but two or three of the pigeons fluttering down are searching for food on the sunlit gravel at the bottom of the steps.

To them the building is merely a rock, pierced with convenient caverns; they use its exterior for their purpose, but penetrate no farther. With air and light, the sunlit gravel, the green lawn between it and the outer railings – with these they are concerned, and with these only. The heavy roll of the traffic in Oxford Street, audible here, is nothing to them; the struggle for money does not touch them, they let it go by. Nor the many minds searching and re-searching in the great Library, this mental toil is no more to them than the lading of waggons in the street. Neither the tangible product nor the intellectual attainment is of any value – only the air and light. There are idols in the galleries within upon whose sculptured features the hot Eastern sun shone thousands of years since. They were made by human effort, however mistaken, and they were the outcome of human thought and handiwork. The doves fluttered about the temples in those days, full only of the air and light. They fluttered about the better temples of Greece and round the porticos where philosophy was born. Still only the light, the sunlight, the air of heaven. We labour on and think, and carve our idols and the pen never ceases from its labour; but the lapse of the centuries has left us in the same place. The doves who have not laboured nor travailed in thought possess the sunlight. Is not theirs the preferable portion?

The shade deepens as I turn from the portico to the hall and vast domed house of books. The half-hearted light under the dome is stagnant and dead. For it is the nature of light to beat and throb; it has a pulse and undulation like the swing of the sea. Under the trees in the woodlands it vibrates and lives; on the hills there is a resonance of light. It beats against every leaf, and, thrown back, beats again; it is agitated with the motion of the grass blades; you can feel it ceaselessly streaming on your face. It is renewed and fresh every moment, and never twice do you see the same ray. Stayed and checked by the dome and book-built walls, the beams lose their elasticity, and the ripple ceases in the motionless pool. The eyes, responding, forget to turn quickly, and only partially see. Deeper thought and inspiration quit the heart, for they can only exist where the light vibrates and communicates its tone to the soul. If any imagine they shall find thought in many books, certainly they will be disappointed. Thought dwells by the stream and sea, by the hill and in the woodland, in the sunlight and free wind, where the wild dove haunts. Walls and roof shut it off as they shut off the undulation of light. The very lightning cannot penetrate here. A murkiness marks the coming of the cloud, and the dome becomes vague, but the firece flash is shorn to a pale reflection, and the thunder is no more than the rolling of a heavier truck loaded with tomes. But in closing out the sky, with it is cut off all that the sky can tell you with its light, or in its passion of storm.

Sitting at these long desks and trying to read, I soon find that I have made a mistake; it is not here I shall find that which I seek. yet the magic of books draws me here time after time, to be as often disappointed. Something in a book tempts the mind as pictures tempt the eye; the eye grows weary of pictures, but looks again. The mind wearies of books, yet cannot forget that once when they were first opened in youth they gave it hope of knowledge. Those first books exhausted, there is nothing left but words and covers. It seems as if all the books in the world – really books – can be bought for £10. Man's whole thought is purchaseable at that small price, for the value of a watch, of a good dog. For the rest it is repetition and paraphrase. The grains of wheat were threshed out and garnered two thousand years since. Except the receipts of chemists, except specifications for the steam-engine, or the electric motor, there is nothing in these millions of books that was not known at the commencement of our era. Not a thought has been added. Continual threshing has widened out the heap of straw and spread it abroad, but it is empty. Nothing will ever be found in it. Those original grains of true thought were found beside the stream, the sea, in the sunlight, at the shady verge of woods. Let us leave this beating and turning over of empty straw; let us return to the stream and the hills; let us ponder by night in view of the stars.

It is pleasant to go out again into the portico under the great columns. On the threshold I feel nearer knowledge than when within. The sun shines, and southwards above the houses there is a statue crowning the summit of some building. The figure is in the midst of the light; it stands out clear and white as if in Italy. The southern blue is luminous – the beams of light flow through it – the air is full of the undulation and life of light. There is rest in gazing at the sky: a sense that wisdom does exist and may be found, a hope returns that was taken away among the books. The green lawn is pleasant to look at, though it is mown so ruthlessly. If they would only let the grass spring up, there would be a thought somewhere entangled in the long blades as a dewdrop sparkles in their depths. Seats should be placed here, under the great columns or by the grass, so that one might enjoy the sunshine after books and watch the pigeons. They have no fear of the people, they come to my feet, but the noise of a door heavily swinging-to in the great building alarms them; they rise and float round, and return again. The sunlight casts a shadow of the pigeon's head and neck upon his shoulder; he turns his head, and the shadow of his beak falls on his breast. Iridescent gleams of bronze and green and blue play about his neck; blue predominates. His pink feet step so near, the red round his eye is visible. As he rises vertically, forcing his way in a straight line upwards, his wings almost meet above his back and again beneath the body; they are put forth to his full stroke. When his flight inclines and becomes gradually horizontal, the effort is less and the wing tips do not approach so closely.

They have not laboured in mental searching as we have; they have not wasted their time looking among empty straw for the grain that is not there. They have been in the sunlight. Since the days of ancient Greece the doves have remained in the sunshine; we who have laboured have found nothing. In the sunshine, by the shady verge of woods, by the sweet waters where the wild dove sips, there alone will thought be found.

from *The Life of the Fields*

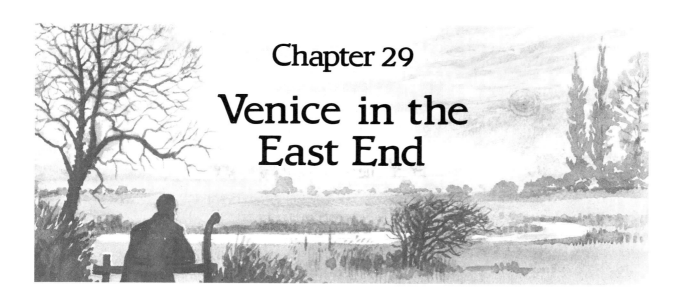

Chapter 29

Venice in the East End

The great red bowsprit of an Australian clipper projects aslant the quay. Stem to the shore, the vessel thrusts an outstretched arm high over the land, as an oak in a glade pushes a bare branch athwart the opening. This beam is larger than an entire tree divested of its foliage, such trees, that is, as are seen in English woods. The great oaks might be bigger at the base where they swell and rest themselves on a secure pedestal. Five hundred years old an oak might measure more at six feet, at eight, or ten feet from the ground; after five hundred years, that is, of steady growth. But if even such a monarch were taken, and by some enormous mechanic power drawn out, its substance elongated into a tapering spar, it would not be massive enough to form this single beam. Where it starts from the stem of the vessel it is already placed as high above the level of the quay as it is from the sward to the first branch of an oak. At its root it starts high overhead, high enough for a trapeze to be slung to it upon which grown persons could practise athletic exercises. From its roots, from the forward end of the deck, the red beam rises at a regular angle, diminishing in size with altitude till its end in comparison with the commencement may be called pointed, though in reality blunt. To the pointed end it would be a long climb; it would need a ladder. The dull red of the vast beam is obscured by the neutral tint of the ropes which are attached to it; colour generally gives a sense of lightness by defining shape, but this red is worn and weatherbeaten, rubbed and battered, so that its uncertain surface adds to the weight of the boom.

It hangs, an immense arm thrust across the sky; it is so high it is scarcely noticed in walking under it; it is so great and ponderous, and ultra in size, that the eye and mind alike fail to estimate it. For it is a common effect of great things to be overlooked. A moderately large rock, a moderately large house, is understood and mentally put down, as it were, at a certain figure, but the immense – which is beyond the human – cannot enter the organs of the senses. The portals of the senses are not wide enough to receive it; you must turn your back on it and reflect, and add a little piece of it to another little piece, and so build up your understanding. Human things are small; you live in a large house, but the space you actually occupy is very inconsiderable; the earth itself, great as it is, is overlooked, it is too large to be seen. The eye is accustomed to the little, and cannot in a moment receive the immense. Only by slow comparison with the bulk of oak trees, by the height of a trapeze, by the climbing of a ladder, can I convey to my mind a true estimate and idea of this gigantic bowsprit. It would be quite possible to walk by and never see it because of its size, as one walks by bridges or travels over a viaduct without a thought.

The vessel lies with her bowsprit projecting over the quay, moored as a boat run ashore on the quiet sandy beach of a lake, not as a ship is generally placed with her broadside to the quay wall or to the pier. Her stern is yonder – far out in the waters of the dock, too far to concern us much as we look from the verge of the wall. Access to the ship is obtained by a wooden staging running out at the side; instead of the ship lying beside the pier, a pier has been built out to fit the ship. This plan, contrary to preconceived ideas, is evidently founded on good reason, for if such a vessel were moored broadside to the quay

how much space would she take up? There would be, first, the hull itself, say eighty yards, and then the immense bowsprit. Two or three such ships would, as it were, fill a whole field of water; they would fill a whole dock; it would not require many to cover a mile. By placing each stem to the quay they only occupy a space equal to their breadth instead of to their length. This arrangement, again, tends to deceive the eye; you might pass by, and, seeing only the bow, casually think there was nothing particular in it. Everything there is on so grand a scale that the largest component part is diminished; the quay, broad enough to build several streets abreast; the square, open stretches of gloomy water; and beyond these the wide river. The wind blows across these open spaces in a broad way – not as it comes in sudden gusts around a street corner, but in a broad open way, each puff a quarter of a mile wide. The view of the sky is open overhead, masts do not obstruct the upward look; the sunshine illumines or the cloud-shadows darken hundreds of acres at once. It is a great plain; a plain of enclosed waters, built in and restrained by the labour of man, and holding upon its surface fleet upon fleet, argosy upon argosy. Masts to the right, masts to the left, masts in front, masts yonder above the warehouses; masts in among the streets as steeples appear amid roofs; masts across the river hung with dropping half-furled sails; masts afar down thin and attenuated, mere dark straight lines in the distance. They await in stillness the rising of the tide.

It comes, and at the exact moment – foreknown to a second – the gates are opened, and the world of ships moves outwards to the stream. Downwards they drift to the east, some slowly that have as yet but barely felt the pull of the hawser, others swiftly, and the swifter because their masts cross and pass the masts of inward-bound ships ascending.

Two lines of masts, one raking one way, the other the other, cross and puzzle the eye to separate their weaving motion and to assign the rigging to the right vessel. White funnels aslant, dark funnels, red funnels rush between them; white steam curls upwards; there is a hum, a haste, almost a whirl, for the commerce of the world is crowded into the hour of the full tide. These great hulls, these crossing masts a-rake, the intertangled rigging, the background of black barges drifting downwards, the lines and ripple of the water as the sun comes out, if you look too steadily, daze the eyes and cause a sense of giddiness. It is so difficult to realise so much mass – so much bulk – moving so swiftly, and in so intertangled a manner; a mighty dance of thousands of tons – gliding, slipping, drifting onwards, yet without apparent effort. Thousands upon thousands of tons go by like shadows, silently, as if the ponderous hulls had no stability or weight; like a dream they float past, solid and yet without reality. It is a giddiness to watch them.

This happens, not on one day only, not one tide, but at every tide and every day the year through, year after year. The bright summer sun glows upon it; the red sun of the frosty hours of winter looks at it from under the deepening canopy of vapour; the blasts of the autumnal equinox howl over the vast city and whistle shrilly in the rigging; still at every tide the world of ships moves out into the river. Why does not a painter come here and place the real romance of these things upon canvas, as Venice has been placed? Never twice alike, the changing atmosphere is reflected in the hue of the varnished masts, now gleaming, now dull, now dark. Till it has been painted, and sung by poet, and described by writers, nothing is human. Venice has been made human by poet, painter, and dramatist, yet what was Venice to this – this, the Fact of our own day? Two of the caravels of the Doge's fleet, two of Othello's strongest war-ships, could scarcely carry the mast of my Australian clipper. At a guess it is four feet through; it is of iron, tubular; there is room for a winding spiral staircase within it; as for its height, I will not risk a guess at it. Could Othello's

185

war-ships carry it they would consider it a feat, as the bringing of the Egyptain obelisk to London was thought a feat. The petty ripples of the Adriatic, what were they? This red bowsprit at its roots is high enough to suspend a trapeze; at its head a ladder would be required to mount it from the quay; yet by-and-by, when the tide at last comes, and its time arrives to move outwards in the dance of a million tons, this mighty bowsprit, meeting the Atlantic rollers in the Bay of Biscay, will dip and bury itself in foam under the stress of the vast sails aloft. The forty-feet billows of the Pacific will swing these three or four thousand or more tons, this giant hull which must be moored even stem to shore, up and down and side to side as a handful in the grasp of the sea. Now, each night as the clouds part, the north star looks down upon the deck; then, the Southern Cross will be visible in the sky, words quickly written, but half a globe apart. What was there in Venice to arouse thoughts such as spring from the sight of this red bowsprit? In two voyages my Australian-clipper shall carry as much merchandise as shall equal the entire commerce of Venice for a year.

Yet it is not the volume, not the bulk only; cannot you see the white sails swelling, and the proud vessel rising to the Pacific billows, the north star sinking, and the advent of the Southern Cross; the thousand miles of ocean without land around, the voyage through space made visible as sea, the far, far south, the transit around a world? If Italian painters had had such things as these to paint, if poets of old time had had such things as these to sing, do you imagine they would have been contented with crank caravels and tales thrice told already? They had eyes to see that which was around them. Open your eyes and see those things which are around us at this hour.

from *The life of the Fields*

Chapter 30
The Lions in Trafalgar Square

The lions in Trafalgar Square are to me the centre of London. By those lions began my London work; from them, as spokes from the middle of a wheel, radiate my London thoughts. Standing by them and looking south you have in front the Houses of Parliament, where resides the mastership of England; at your back is the National Gallery – that is art; and farther back the British Museum – books. To the right lies the wealth and luxury of the West End; to the left the roar and labour, the craft and gold, of the City. For themselves, they are the only monument in this vast capital worthy of a second visit as a monument. Over the entire area covered by the metropolis there does not exist another work of art in the open air. There are many structures and things, no other art. The outlines of the great animals, the bold curves and firm touches of the master hand, the deep indents, as it were, of his thumb on the plastic metal, all the *technique* and grasp written there, is legible at a glance. Then comes the *pose* and expression of the whole, the calm strength in repose, the indifference to little things, the resolute view of great ones. Lastly, the soul of the maker, the spirit which was taken from nature, abides in the massive bronze. These lions are finer than those that crouch in the cages at the Zoological Gardens; these are truer and more real, and, besides, these are lions to whom has been added the heart of a man. Nothing disfigures them; smoke and, what is much worse, black rain – rain which washes the atmosphere of the suspended mud – does not affect them in the least. If the choke-damp of fog obscures them, it leaves no stain on the design; if the surfaces be stained, the idea made tangible in metal is not. They are no more touched than Time itself by the alternations of the seasons. The only noble open-air work of native art in the four-million city, they rest there supreme and are the centre. Did such a work exist now in Venice, what immense folios would be issued about it! All the language of the studios would be huddled together in piled-up and running-over laudation, and curses on our insular swine-eyes that could not see it. I have not been to Venice, therefore I do not pretend to a knowledge of that mediaeval

potsherd; this I do know, that in all the endless pictures on the walls of the galleries in London, year after year exposed and disappearing like snow somewhere unseen, never has there appeared one with such a subject as this. Weak, feeble, mosaic, gimcrack, coloured tiles, and far-fetched compound monsters, artificial as the graining on a deal front door, they cannot be compared; it is the gingerbread gilt on a circus car to the column of a Greek temple. This is pure open air, grand as Nature herself, because it is Nature with, as I say, the heart of a man added.

But if any one desire the meretricious painting of warm light and cool yet not hard shade, the effect of colour, with the twitching of triangles, the spangles glittering, and all the arrangement contrived to take the eye, then he can have it here as well as noble sculpture. Ascend the steps to the National Gallery, and stand looking over the balustrade down across the square in summer hours. Let the sun have sloped enough to throw a slant of shadow outward; let the fountains splash whose bubbles restless speak of rest and leisure, idle and dreamy; let the blue-tinted pigeons nod their heads walking, and anon crowd through the air to the roof-tops. Shadow upon the one side, bright light upon the other, azure above the swallows. Ever rolling the human stream flows, mostly on the south side yonder, near enough to be audible, but toned to bearableness. A stream of human hearts, every atom a living mind filled with what thoughts? – a stream that ran through Rome once, but has altered its course and wears away the banks here now and triturates its own atoms, the hearts, to dust in the process. Yellow omnibuses and red cabs, dark shining carriages, chestnut horses, all rushing,and by their motion mixing their colours so that the commonness of it disappears and the hues remain, a streak drawn in the groove of the street – dashed hastily with thick camel's hair. In the midst the calm lions, dusky, unmoved, full always of the one grand idea that was infused into them. So full of it that the golden sun and the bright wall of the eastern houses, the shade that is slipping towards them, the sweet swallows and the azure sky, all the human stream holds of wealth and power and coroneted panels – nature, man, and city – pass as naught. Mind is stronger than matter. The soul alone stands when the sun sinks, when the shade is universal night, when the van's wheels are silent and the dust rises no more.

At summer noontide, when the day surrounds us and it is bright light even in the shadow, I like to stand by one of the lions and yield to the old feeling. The sunshine glows on the dusky creature, as it seems, not on the surface, but under the skin, as if it came up from out of the limb. The roar of the rolling wheels sinks and becomes distant as the sound of a waterfall when dreams are coming. All the abundant human life is smoothed and levelled, the abruptness of the individuals lost in the flowing current, like separate flowers drawn along in a border, like music heard so far off that the notes are molten and the theme only remains. The abyss of the sky over and the ancient sun are near. They only are close at hand, they and immortal thought. When the yellow Syrian lions stood in old time of Egypt, then, too, the sunlight gleamed on the eyes of men, as now this hour on mine. The same consciousness of light, the same sun, but the eyes that saw it and mine, how far apart! The immense lion here beside me expresses larger nature – cosmos – the ever-existent thought which sustains the world. Massiveness exalts the mind till the vast roads of space which the sun tramples are as an arm's-length. Such a moment cannot endure long; gradually the roar deepens, the current resolves into individuals, the houses return – it is only a square.

But a square potent. For London is the only *real* place in the world. The cities turn towards London as young partridges run to their mother. The cities know that they are not real. They are only houses and wharves, and bricks and stucco; only outside.

The minds of all men in them, merchants, artists, thinkers, are bent on London. Thither they go as soon as they can. San Francisco thinks London; so does St. Petersburg.

Men amuse themselves in Paris; they work in London. Gold is made abroad, but London has a hook and line on every napoleon and dollar, pulling the round discs hither. A house is not a dwelling if a man's heart be elsewhere. Now, the heart of the world is in London, and the cities with the simulacrum of man in them are empty. They are moving images only; stand here and you are real.

from *The Toilers of the Field*

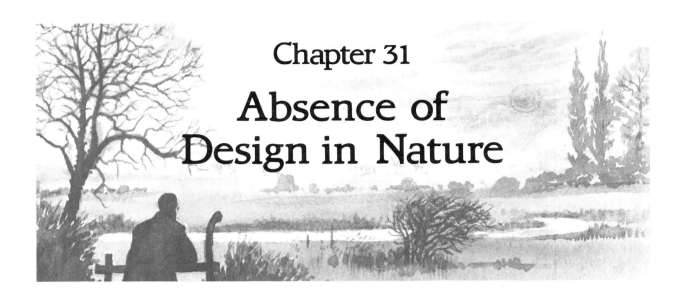

Chapter 31

Absence of Design in Nature

In the parlour to which I have retired from the heat there is a chair and a table, and a picture on the wall: the chair was made for an object and a purpose, to sit in; the table for a purpose, to write on; the picture was painted for a purpose, to please the eye. But outside, in the meadow, in the hedge, on the hill, in the water; or, looking still farther, to the sun, the moon, and stars, I see no such chair, or table, or picture.

Pondering deeply and for long upon the plants, the living things (myself, too, as a physical being): upon the elements, on the holy miracle, water; the holy miracle, sunlight; the earth, and the air, I come at last – and not without, for a while, sorrow – to the inevitable conclusion that there is no object, no end, no purpose, no design, and no plan; no anything, that is.

By a strong and continued effort, I compelled myself to see the world mentally: with my mind, as it were, abstracted; hold yourself, as it were, apart from it, and there is no object, and no plan; no law, and no rule.

From childhood we build up for ourselves an encyclopaedia of the world, answering all questions: we turn to Day, and the reply is Light; to Night, and the reply is Darkness. It is difficult to burst through these fetters and to get beyond Day and Night: but, in truth, there is no Day and Night; the sun always shines. It is our minds which supply the purpose, the end, the plan, the law, and the rule. For the practical matters of life, these are sufficient – they are like conventional agreements. But if you wish to really know the truth, there is none. When you first realize this, the whole arch of thought falls in; the structure the brain has reared, or, rather, which so many minds have reared for it, becomes a crumbling ruin, and there seems nothing left. I felt crushed when I first saw that there was no chair, no table, no picture, in nature: I use 'nature' in the widest sense; in the cosmos then. Nothing especially made for man to sit on, to write on, to admire – not even the colour of the buttercups or the beautiful sun-gleam which had me spellbound glowing on the water in my hand in the rocky cell.

The rudest quern ever yet discovered in which the earliest man ground his wheat did not fall from the sky; even that poor instrument, the mere hollowed stone, was not thrown to him prepared for use; he had to make it himself. There neither is, nor has been, nor will be any chair, or table, or picture, or quern in the cosmos. Nor is there any plan even in the buttercups themselves, looked at for themselves: they are not geometrical, or mathematical; nor precisely circular, nor anything regular. A general pattern, as a common colour, may be claimed for them, a pattern, however, liable to modification under cultivation; but, fully admitting this, it is no more than saying that water is water: that one crystal is always an octahedron, another a dodecahedron; that one element is oxygen and another hydrogen; that the earth is the earth; and the sun, the sun. It is only stating in the simplest way the fact that a thing *is:* and, after the most rigid research, that is, in the end, all that can be stated.

To say that there is a general buttercup pattern is only saying that it is not a bluebell or violet. Perhaps the general form of the buttercup is not absolutely necessary to its existence; many birds can fly equally well if their tails be removed, or even a great part of their wings. There are some birds that do not fly at all. Some further illustrations presently will arise; indeed, nothing could be examined without affording some. I had forgotten that the parlour, beside the chair and table, had a carpet. The carpet has a pattern: it is woven; the threads can be discerned, and a little investigation shows beyond doubt that it was designed and made by a man. It is certainly pretty and ingenious. But the grass of my golden meadow has no design, and no purpose: it is beautiful, and more; it is divine.

When at last I had disabused my mind of the enormous imposture of a design, an object, and an end, a purpose or a system, I began to see dimly how much more grandeur, beauty and hope there is in a divine chaos – not chaos in the sense of disorder or confusion but simply the absence of order – than there is in a universe made by pattern. This draught-board universe my mind had laid out: this machine-made world and piece of mechanism; what a petty, despicable, micro-cosmus I had substituted for the reality.

Logically, that which has a design or purpose has a limit. The very idea of a design or a purpose has since grown repulsive to me, on account of its littleness. I do not venture, for a moment, even to attempt to supply a reason to take the place of the exploded plan. I simply deliberately deny, or, rather, I have now advanced to that stage that to my own mind even the admission of the subject to discussion is impossible. I look at the sunshine and feel that there is no contracted order: there is divine chaos, and, in it, limitless hope and possibilities.

from *The Old House at Coate*

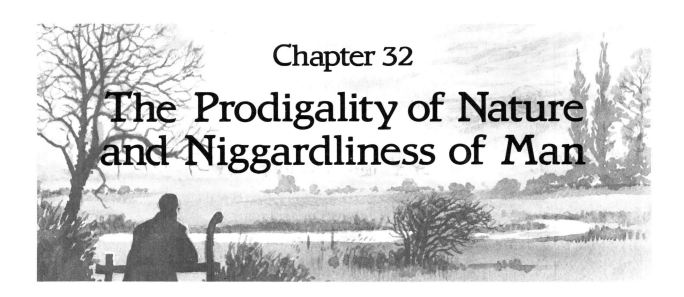

Chapter 32
The Prodigality of Nature and Niggardliness of Man

Without number, the buttercups crowd the mead: not one here and there, or sufficient only to tint the sward. There is not just enough for some purpose: there they are without number, in all the extravagance of uselessness and beauty. The apple bloom – it is falling fast now as the days advance – who can count the myriad blossoms of the orchard? There are leaves upon the hedges which bound that single meadow on three sides (the fourth being enclosed by a brook) enough to occupy the whole summer to count; and before it was half done they would be falling. But that half would be enough for shadow – for use.

Half the rain that falls would be enough. Half the acorns on the oaks in autumn, more than enough. Wheat itself is often thrown into the sty. Famines and droughts occur, but whenever any comes it is in abundance – sow a grain of wheat, and the stalk, one stalk alone, of those that rise from it will yield forty times.

There is no *enough* in nature. It is one vast prodigality. It is a feast. There is no economy: it is all one immense extravagance. It is all giving, giving, giving: no saving, no penury; a golden shower of good things is for ever descending. I love beyond all things to contemplate this indescribable lavishness – I would it could be introduced into our human life. I know, none better, having gone through the personal experience myself, that it is at the present moment impossible to practise it: that each individual is compelled, in order to exist, to labour, to save, and to economize. I know, of course, as all do who have ever read a book, that attempts to distribute possessions, to live in community of goods, have each failed miserably. If I rightly

192

judge, the human race would require a century of training before even an approximation to such a thing were possible. All this, and much more to the same effect, I fully admit. But still the feeling remains and will not be denied. I dislike the word economy: I detest the word thrift; I hate the thought of saving. Maybe some scheme in the future may be devised whereby such efforts may be turned to a general end. This alone I am certain of: there is no economy, thrift, or saving, in nature; it is one splendid waste. It is that waste which makes it so beautiful, and so irresistible! Now nature was not made by man, and is a better exemplar than he can furnish: each thread in this carpet goes to form the pattern; but go out into my golden mead and gather ten thousand blades of grass, and it will not destroy it.

Perhaps there never were so many houses upon the face of the earth as at the present day: so luxuriously appointed, so comfortable, so handsomely furnished. Yet, with all this wealth and magnificence, these appointments and engineering: with all these many courses at dinner and array of wines, it has ever seemed to me a mean and penurious age. It is formal and in order; there is no heart in it. Food should be broadcast, open, free: wine should be in flagons, not in tiny glasses; in a word, there should be genial waste. Let the crumbs fall: there are birds enough to pick them up.

The greatest proof of the extreme meanness of the age is the long list of names appended to a subscription for a famine or fashionable charity. Worthy as are these objects, the donors write down their own unutterable meanness. There are men in their warehouses, their offices, on their lands, who have served them honourably for years and have received for their wage just exactly as much as experience has proved can be made to support life. No cheque with a great flourishing signature has ever been presented to them.

I say that the entire labouring population – some skilled trades excepted as not really labouring – is miserably underpaid, not because there is a pressure or scarcity, a trouble, a famine, but from pure selfishness. This selfishness, moreover, is not intentional, but quite unconscious; and individuals are not individually guilty, because they are within their rights. A man has a hundred thousand pounds: he eats and drinks and pleases his little whims – likely enough quite innocent little whims – but he never gives to a friend, or a relation; never assists, does nothing with it. This is commercially right, but it is not the buttercups in the golden mead; it is not the grain of wheat that yielded forty times. It is not according to the exemplar of nature. Therefore I say that although I admit all attempts to adjust possessions have been and for the age at least must prove failures, yet my feeling remains the same. Thrift, economy, accumulation of wealth, are inventions; they are not nature. As there are more than enough buttercups in this single meadow for the pleasure of all the children in the hamlet, so too it is a fact, a very stubborn fact, that there is more than enough food in the world for all its human children. In the year 1880, it was found, on careful calculation made for strictly commercial purposes, that there was surplus grain production of* bushels. That is to say, if every buttercup in this meadow represented a bushel of wheat, there would be all that over and above what was necessary. This is a very extraordinary fact. That the wheat has to be produced, to be distributed; that there are a thousand social complications to be considered, is, of course, incontrovertible. Still, there was the surplus; bushels of golden grain as numerous as the golden buttercups.

But that does not represent the capacity of the earth for production: it is not possible to gauge that capacity – so practically inexhaustible is it.

Thrift and economy and accumulation, therefore, represent a state of things contrary to the exemplar of nature, and in individual life they destroy its beauty. There is no pleasure without waste: the banquet is a formality; the wine tasteless, unless the viands and the liquor are in prodigal quantities. Give me the lavish extravagance of the golden mead!

from *The Old House at Coate*

A Checklist of Published Works by Richard Jefferies

Compiled by Colin Laurie McKelvie

Reporting, Editing and Authorship. London: John Snow, 1873

Jack Brass, Emperor of England. London: T Pettitt, 1873

A Memoir of the Goddards of North Wilts, Complied from Ancient Records, Registers and Family Papers. London: Simmons and Botten, 1873

The Scarlet Shawl: A Novel. London: Tinsley, 1874

Restless Human Hearts. 3 vols. London: Tinsley, 1875

Suez-cide!! Or How Miss Britannia Bought a Dirty Puddle and Lost Her Sugar-plums. London: John Snow, 1876

World's End: A Story in Three Books. 3 vols. London: Tinsley, 1877.

The Gamekeeper at Home; or, Sketches of Natural History and Rural Life. London: Smith Elder, 1878.

Wild Life in a Southern County. London: Smith Elder, 1879 (American reprint 1903, 1904 was re-titled *An English Village*).

The Amateur Poacher. London: Smith Elder, 1879.

Greene Ferne Farm. London: Smith Elder, 1880.

Hodge and His Masters. 2 vols. London: Smith Elder, 1880 (English reprint 1946 retitled *A Classic of English Farming*).

Round About a Great Estate. London: Smith Elder, 1880.

Wood Magic: A Fable. 2 vols. London: Cassell, 1881 (American abridgement 1899-1900 entitled *Sir Bevis: A Tale of the Fields*).

Bevis: The Story of a Boy. 3 vols. London: Sampson Low, 1882 (English abridgements were entitled *Bevis at Home* 1937 and *Bevis and Mark* 1940).

Nature Near London, London: Chatto & Windus, 1883.

Society Novelettes. By Various Authors. 2 vols. London: Vizetelly, 1883 (Jefferies contributed two short stories, *'Kiss and Try'* in volume I, *'Out of the Season'* in volume II. Volume I reprinted in 1886 as *No Rose Without a Thorn, and Other Tales,* volume II as *The Dove's Nest, and Other Tales*).

The Story of My Heart: My Autobiography. London: Longmans, 1883.

Red Deer. London: Longmans, 1884.

The Life of the Fields. London: Chatto & Windus, 1884.

The Dewy Morn. 2 vols. London: Bentley, 1884

After London; or, Wild England. London: Cassell, 1885

The Open Air. London: Chatto & Windus, 1885

White, Gilbert. *The Natural History of Selborne* With an introduction by Richard Jefferies. London: Walter Scott, 1887.

Amaryllis at the Fair. London: Sampson Low, 1887.

Field and Hedgerow: Being the Last Essays of Richard Jefferies, Collected by His Widow. London: Longmans, 1889.

The Toilers of the Field. London: Longmans, 1892.

Thoughts from the Writings of Richard Jefferies. Selected by H.S.H. Waylen. London: Longmans, 1896.

The Early Fiction of Richard Jefferies. Edited by Grace Toplis. London: Simpkin, Marshall, 1896.

Jefferies' Land: A History of Swindon and Its Environs. Edited by Grace Toplis. London: Simpkin, Marshall, 1896.

T.T.T. Wells: A. Young, 1896 (short story).

Jefferies' Nature Thoughts. Edited by Thomas Coke Watkins. Portland, Marine: T. Mosher, 1904.

Passages from the Nature Writings of Richard Jefferies. Selected by A.H. Hyatt. London: Chatto & Windus, 1905 (the third impression was entitled *The Pocket Richard Jefferies* Anthology,1911).

The Hills and the Vale. With an introduction by Edward Thomas. London: Duckworth 1909.

Selections from Richard Jefferies. Made by F.W. Tickner. London: Longmans, 1909.

Out-of-Doors with Richard Jefferies. Edited by Eric Fitch Daglish. London: Dent, 1935.

Richard Jefferies: Selections of His Work, with details of His Life and Cirumstance, His Death and Immortality. Edited with an introduction by Henry Williamson. London: Faber, 1937.

Jefferies' England. Edited by Samuel J. Looker. London: Constable, 1937.

Readings from Richard Jefferies. Edited by Ronald Hook. London: Macmillian, 1940.

The Nature Diaries and Notebooks of Richard Jefferies, with an Essay "A Tangle of Autumn', now printed for the first time. Edited by Samuel J. Looker. Billericay. Essex: Grey Walls Press, 1941.

Jefferies' Countryside. Edited by Samuel J. Looker. London: Constable, 1944.

Richard Jefferies' London. Edited by Samuel J. Looker. London: Lutterworth Press, 1944.

A Richard Jefferies Anthology. Selected by George Prattinsh. London: Collins, 1945.

The Spring of the Year. Edited by Samuel J. Looker. London: Lutterworth Press, 1946.

Summer in the Woods. A selection from the works of Richard Jefferies, with four drawings by S.H. de Roos. Amsterdam: Type Foundry, 1947.

The Essential Richard Jefferies. With an introduction by Malcolm Elwin. London: Johnathan Cape, 1948.

The Jefferies Companion. Edited by Samuel J. Looker. London: Phoenix House, 1948.

Beauty is Immortal (Felise of the Dewy Morn), with *Some Hitherto Uncollected Essays and Manuscripts*. Edited by Samuel J. Looker. Worthing: Aldridge Brothers, 1948.

The Old House at Coate, and Other Hitherto Unprinted Essays. Edited by Samuel J. Looker. London: Lutterworth press, 1948.

The Nature Diaries and Note-Books of Richard Jefferies. Edited by Samuel J. Looker. London: Grey Walls Press, 1948.

Chronicles of the Hedges, and Other Essays, Edited by Samuel J. Looker. London: Phoenix House, 1948.

Field and Farm: Essays Now First Collected, With Some from MSS Edited by Samuel J. Looker. London: Phoenix House, 1957.

Jefferies Unpublished Manuscripts by Samuel J. Looker in Victor Bonham-Carter (edit), *The Bryanston Miscellany*, Bryanston School, Dorset: 1958.

Richard Jefferies: Man of the Fields, a Biography and Letters by Samuel J. Looker and

Crichton Porteous. London: John Baker, 1965.

Serialized Writings.

The Amateur Poacher, in Pall Mall Gazette. (1877: Nov. 16); 1879: March 1,8,14,25,29;
April 3,10,16,23,26; May 6,10,17,23,31; June 10,18,21,25; July 1,5,7.

The Gamekeeper at Home, in Pall Mall Gazette. (1877: Dec. 12,14,29); 1878: Jan.
4,9,12,18,22,26,31; Feb. 2,8,12,16,23; March 2,12,15,19,26,28; April 1,5,9,12,17,24.

Green Ferne Farm, in Time. April 1879 to February 1880.

History of Cirencester, in Wilts and Gloucestershire Standard 1870: March 12,26;
April 4; May 7,28; June 11; July 2,9,30; Aug. 6; Oct. 29.

History of Malmesbury, in North Wilts Herald 1867: April 20,27; May 4,11,25; June
1,15,22,29; July 6,13,20,27; Aug. 3,10,24,31; Sept. 14,21,28.

History of Swindon and Its Environs in North Wilts Herald 1867: Oct. 5,12,19, 26;
Nov. 2,9; 1868: Jan. 4; Feb. 29. Published as *Jefferies' Land: A History of*
Swindon   and Its Environs 1896).

Hodge and His Masters, in The Standard (1878: Sept. 24; Oct. 9,17,30; Nov. 14); Nov.
19, 26; Dec. 4,12,19,25; 1879: Jan. 2,8,17,28; Feb, 4; (March 3; April 15); Aug.
16,22,26; Sept. 2,8,15,23,30; Oct. 7,14,21,28; Nov. 4, 12,18; Dec. (16), 26,30; 1880:
Jan 5,12. (Published in *The Standard* as two serials: *Hodge at His Work,* Nov. 19,
1878 to Feb. 4, 1879; *Hodge's Masters,* Aug. 16, 1879 to Jan. 12, 1880.)

The Rise of Maximin, Emperor of the Occident, in *New Monthly Magazine.* 1876:
Oct., Nov., Dec.; 1877: Jan., Feb., March, April two pieces, May, June, July.

Round About a Great Estate in *Pall Mall Gazette* 1880: Jan. 13,19,21,24,29; Feb.
5,11,14,18,24; March 2.11,17,22,29; April 2,10,,14,26,28.

Wild Life in a Southern County, in Pall Mall Gazette. 1878: May 9,13,17,22,28; June
1,6,11,14,19,21,27; July 1,6,10,16,19,22,27; Aug. 1,6,10,13,16,21,23,26; Sept.
5,7,11,14,19,21,25,20; Oct. 7,12,16,19,24,28; Nov. 2,9,16,25; Dec. 4.

Essays and other short pieces

Listed alphabetically under title, followed by place and date of first publication.

'About the Hedges.' *Standard,* Oct 9, 1878 (Incorporated into *Hodge and His*
Masters.)

'Acorn-Gather, The.' (*See* 'Bits of Oak-Bark')

'After the Country Franchise' *Longman's Magazine,* Feb. 1884 *(The Hills and the*
Vale.)

'Agricultural Affairs.' *Pall Mall Gazette,* June 5, 1880.

'Agricultural Book-Keeping.' *St. James's Gazette,* Aug. 15, 1884.

'Agricultural 'Capital Account', The.' *Live Stock Journal,* Sept, 7, 1877.

'Agricultural Heraldry.' *Live Stock Journal,* Dec. 7, 1877 *(Field and Farm.)*

'Agricultural Labour.' Letter to *Wilts and Gloucester Standard,* March 9, 1872
(Landscape and Labour.)

'Agricultural   abourer's Vote, The.' *Pall Mall Gazette,* May 24, 1877.

'Agricultural Side of the Water Question, The.' *Live Stock Journal,* April 5, 1878.

'Agricultural and the Water Congress.' *Live Stock Journal,* May 31, 1878.

'America and the Meat Market.' *Live Stock Journal,* Jan. 5, 1877.

'American Views on the Meat Traffic.' *Live Stock Journal,* March 2, 1877.

'Among the Nuts.' *Standard,* Aug.23, 1886 *(Field and Hedgerow.)*

'April Gossip.' *St. James's Gazette,* April 19, 1886. *(Field and Hedgerow).*

'Art of Shooting, The' *The Field,* March 15, 1947. *(Field and Farm.)*

'August Out-of-doors.' *Pall Mall Gazette,* Aug 28, 1879. *(Chronicles of the Hedges.)*

"Autonomy' and What It Means.' *Cassell's Family Magazine,* Feb. 1877.

'Autumn Fairs, The.' *Live Stock Journal,* Oct. 19, 1877.

'Average of Beauty, The.' *World* April 26, 1876.

'Average Servant, The.' *Cassell's Family Magazine,* Jan. 1878.

'Backwoods, The.' *(Beauty is Immortal.)*

'Backwoods of London.' *Globe* Sept. 21, 1877 *(Chronicles of the Hedges.)*

'Bad Harvests in Sussex.' *The Times,* Sept. 21, 1881. *(Chronicles of the Hedges.)*

'Barn, A.' *Standard,* Sept. 23, 1880. *(Nature Near London.)*

'Bathing Season, The.' *Pall Mall Gazette,* July 28 and Aug. 8, 1884. *(The Open Air.)*

'Bath Show Yard, The.' *Live Stock Journal,* June 15,1877.

'Battle of 1866, The.' (poem). *North Wilts Herald,* June 30, 1866. *(The Early Fiction of Richard Jefferies.)*

'Beatrice and the Centaur' (See Samuel J. Looker, *Jefferies Unpublished Manuscripts.)*

'Beauty in the Country. *(The Open Air.)*

'Beauty of the Fields, The.' (See *Notes on Landscape Painting.)*

'Beauty of the Trees, The' (See *Fir, Larch and Sycamore, Near London.)*

'Benediction of the Light, The.' (See *Thoughts in the Fields.)*

'Ben Tubbs' Adventures.' Not published. (See *Times Literary Supplement,* May 29, 1959. The MS. was sold at Hodgson's, April 1959.)

'Bill-Hook, The.' (See *Chronicles of the Hedges.)*

'Bird Catchers.' *Pall Mall Gazette,* Oct. 26, 1880.

'Birds Notes in June' *(Field and Farm.)*

'Birds Climbing the Air.' *St. James's Gazette* July 28, 1883. *(The Life of the Fields.)* (Published in *St. James's Gazette* as *'Climbing the Air.')*

'Birds of Spring.' *Chambers' Journal,* March 1, 1884. *(The Hills and the Vales.)*

'Birds of Swindon. *'Letter to Swindon Advertiser,* April 24, 1871. *(Landscape and Labour.)*

'Birds' Nests.' *St. James's Gazette,* April 19, 1884. *(Field and Hedgerow.)*

'Bits of Oak Bark.' *Longman's Magazine,* March 1883. (*The Life of the Fields.* This includes *'The Acorn-Gatherer,' 'The Legend of a Gateway,* and *'A Roman Brook.')*

'Both Sides of the Meat Question.' *Live Stock Journal,* Feb. 9. 1887.

'Breeze on Beachy Head, The.*' Standard,* Sept.6, 1881. *(Nature Near London.)*

'Brook, A.' *Standard,* Sept. 30, 1880 *(Nature Near London.)*

'Buckhurst Park.' *Standard,* Aug. 19, 1886. *(Field and Hedgerow.)*

'Butterfly Corner.' *Standard,* Aug. 23, 1887 *(Landscape and Labour.)*

'By the Exe.' *Standard,* Sept, 25, 1883. *The Life of the Fields.* (In the collected version, 'The Otter in Somerset' and a passage concerning otters are added to the orginal text.

'Castle Shed at Coate, The.' *Countrygoer,* Winter 1948. *(Field and Farm.)*

'Chaffinch, The.' (See *'Chronicles of the Hedges.')*

'Changes in Country Habits.'*Pall Mall Gazette,* Aug. 28, 1877. *(Field and Farm)*

'Cheese.' *Pall Mall Gazette,* Nov. 30, 1877.

'Cheese-Making in the West.' *Globe,* Oct.9, 1877. *(Landscape and Labour.)*

'Choosing a Gun.' *The Hills and the Vale.* (Some used in the final chapter of *The Amateur Poacher.)*

'Christmas: Then and Now.' *Live Stock Journal Literary Supplement,* Dec. 21, 1877 *(Field and Farm.)*

'Chronicles of the Hedges.' Land, Feb. 12,19,26; March 19; April 2,23; May 14,21, 1881 (*Chronicles of the Hedges* This included 'The Bill-Hook,' 'The Chaffinch,' and 'The Meadow Gateway.')

'Clematis Lane.' *Standard,* Sept. 12, 1883. *(The Life of the Fields.)*

'Climbing the Air.' *See* 'Birds Climbing the Air.'

'Coming of Summer, The.' *Long*man's Magazine, *Dec. 1891. (The Toilers of the*

Field.)

'Coming Woman, The.' *World,* June 18, 1876.

'Commonest Thing in the World, The.' *Graphic,* Aug. 11. 1877. *(Landscape and Labour.)*

'Conforming to Environment.' *St. James's Gazette,* June 24, 1886.

'Contents of Ten Acres – May, The.' *Forestry,* May, 1883 *(Landscape and Labour.)*

'Contrast Between Town and Country' (editor's title). *(Chronicles of the Hedges.)*

'Cost of Agricultural Labour in 1875, The.' *Standard,* Oct. 1, 1875.

'Cottage Ideas.' Chambers' *Journal,* May 8, 1886 *(Field and Hedgerow.)*

'Cottage Society and Country Suffrage.' *Pall Mall Gazette,* Nov. 6, 1877. *(Field and Farm.)*

'Country Curate, The.' *Standard,* Dec. 16, 1879. (Included in *Hodge and His Masters.)*

'Country Girls.' *Standard,* Oct. 30, 1878. (Included in *Hodge and His Masters.)*

'Country Literature.' *Pall Mall* Gazette, Oct.22,,29; Nov. 5,22,30, 1881. *(The Life of the Fields.)*

'Country Places.' *Manchester Guardian,* Jan 4,11, 1887. *(Field and Hedgerow.)*

'Country Readers.' *Pall Mall Gazette,* Dec. 22, 1877. *(Field and Farm.)*

'Countryside: Sussex, The.' *Manchester Guardian,* Aug. 24,31, 1886. *(Field and Hedgerow.)*

'Country Sunday, The.' *Longman's Magazine,* June 1887 *(Field and hedgerow.)*

'Crows, The.' *Standard,* Nov. 12, 1880. *(Nature Near London.)*

'Dairy District, A.' *Live Stock Journal,* Oct. 5, 1877. *(Field and Farm.)*

'Dairy Factory System, The.' *Live Stock Journal,* Feb. 15, 1878.

'Danger to Dairymen, A.' *Live Stock Journal,* Nov. 9, 1877. *(Field and Farm)*

'Danger of Hunting, The.' *Live Stock Journal.* Jan 12, 1877.

'Dawn, The.' *(The Hills and the Vale.)*

'Decline of Breeding, The.' *Live Stock Journal,* Jan. 4, 1878.

'Decline of Partridge Shooting.' *Pall Mall Gazette,* Aug. 31, 1878. *(Chronicles of the Hedges.)*

'Defence of Sport, A.' National Review Aug. 1883. *(Chronicles of the Hedges.* (Part of this, omitted from *Chronicles of the Hedges,* previously published as *'Sport and Science'* in *The Life of the Fields.)*

'Dinner at the Farm.' *The Bryanston Miscellany.* Samuel J. Looker, *'Jefferies Unpublished Manuscripts.*

'Ditch and the Pool, The.' *(Chronicles of the Hedges.)*

'Domestic Rook, The.' *Live Stock Journal,* Feb. 1, 1878 *(Chronicles of the Hedges.)*

'Downs.' *The Times,* Sept. 21, 1881. *The Open Air.* (Published in *The Times* as *'Some Uncultivated Country: Downs.')*

'Dreams of Landseer's Lions, A.' (An early draft of 'The Lions in Trafalgar Square.' See Samuel J. Looker, 'Jefferies Unpublished Manuscripts.')

'Early Autumn.' *Pall Mall Gazette,* Oct. 20, 1879. *(Chronicles of the Hedges.)*

'Early in March.' *Standard,* March 31, 1879. Included in *Hodge and His Masters.)*

'Earth Prayer, The' *(Chronicles of the Hedges.)*

'Eggs and Poultry.' *St. James's Gazette,* Nov. 17, 1880.

'Economic Value of Game, The.' *Live Stock Journal,* Nov. 30, 1877.

'English Agricultural Chemists.' *Live Stock Journal,* May 17, 24, 1878.

'English Animals Abroad.' *Live Stock Journal,* April 20, 1877. *(Field and Farm.)*

'English Deerpark, An.' *Century Illustrated Magazine,* Oct. 1888. *(Field and Hedgerow.)*

'English Homestead, An.' *Fraser's Magazine* Nov. 1876. *(The Toilers of the Field.)*

'Entered at Stationer's Hall.' *Cassell's Family Magazine,* Oct. 1877.

'Essay on Instinct.' (*See* Samuel J. Looker, *'Jefferies Unpublished Manuscripts.*)

'Extinct Race, An.' *Longman's Magazine,* June 1891. (*The Toilers of the Field.*)

'Fallacy of Prices, The.' *Live Stock Journal,* May 4, 1877.

'Farmer at Home, The.' *Fraser's Magazine,* Aug. 1874. (*The Toilers of the Field.*)

'Farmer's Stores in London: An Opening for Young Agriculturists.' *Live Stock Journal,* July 12, 1878.

'Farm Prospects in the West of England.' *St. James's Gazette,* May 5, 1881.

'Farms Out of Cultivation.' *The Times,* Sept. 3, 1881. (*Field and Farm.*)

'February Day in Stanmer Park, A.' *St. James's Gazette,* Feb. 17, 1883. (*Chronicles of the Hedges.*)

'Fictitious Manure.' *Live Stock Journal,* April 18, 1878.

'Field and Farm.' *St. James's Gazette,* March 30, 1883. (*Field and Farm.*)

'Field-Faring Women.' *Fraser's Magazine,* Sept. 1875. (*The Toilers of the Field.*)

'Field-Play, The.' *Time,* Dec. 1883. (*The Life of the Fields.*)

'Field Sports in Art.' *Art Journal,* April 1885. (*Field and Hedgerow.*)

'Field Words and Ways.' *Pall Mall Gazette,* Nov. 25, 1886. (*Field and Hedgerow.*)

'Fields in April, The." *Pall Mall Gazette,* May 2, 1879. (*Chronicles of the Hedges* - this forms Part 2 of 'In the Fields. April.')

'Fields in May, The.' *Pall Mall Gazette,* June 3, 1879. (*Chronicels of the Hedges.*)

'Fine Lady Farmer, The.' *Standard,* Oct. 17, 1878. (Included in *Hodge and His Masters.*)

'Fir, Larch, and Sycamore, near London.' *The Field,* June 7, 1947 (*Chronicles of the Hedges.*)

'Flocks of Birds.' *Standard,* Nov. 18, 1880 (*Nature Near London.*)

'Flowers and Fruit.' *Globe,* July 19, 1877 (*Landscape and Labour.*)

'Flower of the Grass (*Chronicles of the Hedges.*)

'Flying Dutchman, The (A Legend of the Great Western Railway.) (Manuscript for sale by a USA book dealer 1970.)

'Footpaths.' *Standard,* Nov.3, 1880 (*Nature Near London.*)

'Forest.' *The Times,* Sept 24, 1881. (*The Open Air* published in *The Times* as 'Some Uncultivated Country: Forest.')

'Future of Country Society, The.' *New Quarterly,* July 1877. (*Landscape and Labour.*)

'Future of Farming, The *Fraser's Magazine,* Dec. 1873 (*Landscape and Labour.*)

'Future of the Dairy, The.' *Live Stock Journal Almanack,* 1879.

'Game and Tenants' Leases.' *Live Stock Journal,* Oct. 11, 1878.

'Game as Property.' *Live Stock Journal,* March 8, 1878 (*Field and Farm.*)

'Game for Bicycles, A.' (See Samuel J. Looker, *Jefferies Unpublished Manuscripts.*)

'Game Question, The.' *Live Stock Journal,* March 1, 1878.

'Gaudy as a Garden.' *Graphic,* Aug. 26, 1876 (*Chronicles of the Hedges.*)

'Genesis of The Story of My Heart' (*Field and Farm.*)

'Gentleman Farmer, The.' *World* , Nov. 21, 1877. (*Landscape and Labour.*)

'Getting to Market.' *Live Stock Journal,* June 29, 1877.

''Gilt-Edged' Butter.' *Live Stock Journal,* Nov.23, 1877.

'Gold-Crested Wren, The.' *Longman's Magazine* June 1891. (*The Toilers of the Field.*)

'Golden Brown.' *Pall Mall Gazette,* Aug. 27, 1884. (*The Open Air.*)

'Great Agricultural Opportunity, A.' *Live Stock Journal.* Aug. 9, 1878.

'Great Agricultural Problem, A.' *Fraser's Magazine,* March 1878.

'Greater Gardens.' *Globe,* April 19, 1877.

'Great Grievance, A.' *Live Stock Journal,* March 8, 1878. (*Field and Farm.*)

'Great Snow, The' *The Field,* March 22, 1847. (*Beauty is Immortal.*)

'Green Corn, The.' Good Words, May 1883. *The Open Air.* (In *The Open Air* this essay is the final paragraphs of 'Out of Doors in February.'

'Grouse and Partridge Poaching.' *Pall Mall Gazette,* Aug. 13, 1880.

'Harvest, The.' *Pall Mall Gazette,* Aug. 23, 1880.

'Harvest Field, The.' *Live Stock Journal,* Aug. 16, 1878.

'Haunt of the Hare, The.' *Standard,* Nov. 14, 1884. *(The Open Air.)*

'Haunts of the Lapwing.' *Good Words,* Jan. and March 1883. *(The Open Air –* part of this essay is also the first part of 'Vignettes from Nature')

'Hay Harvest Notes.' *Live Stock Journal,* June 15, 1877. *(Chronicles of the Hedges.)*

'Haymaking by Aritificial Heat.' *Live Stock Journal,* July 5, 1878.

'Heart of England, The., or The Farmer and His Man.'
  (A fragment of a proposed book. See 'Richard Jefferies: Man of the Fields'.

'Heathlands.' *Standard,* Dec 23, 1880 (*Nature Near London* Published in *The Standard* as 'Rural London: Anthills. Adders.')

'Hedge and the Smell of Hops, The' *(Chronicles of the Hedges.)*

'Hedge Miners.' *Land,* Aug. 6 1881 *(Chronicles of the Hedges.)*

'Hedgerow Sportsman, The.' *St. James's Gazette,* Jan 28, 1882 *(Chronicles of the Hedges.)*

'Henrique Beaumont' *North Wilts Herald,* July 21, 28; Aug. 4, 1866. *(The early Fiction of Richard Jefferies.)*

'Herbs.' *Standard,* Oct. 15, 1880 (Nature Near London.)

'High-Pressure Agriculture.' *Fraser's Magazine,* August 1876. *(Landscape and Labour.)*

'Horse as a Social Force, The.' *Live Stock Journal,* July 20, 1877 *(Field and Farm.)*

'Horses in Relation to Art.' *Magazine of Art,* May and October 1878 *(Beauty is Immortal.)*

'Hours of Spring.' *Longman's Magazine,* May 1886 *(Field and Hedgerow.)*

'House Martins.' *(Field and Hedgerow.)*

'Hovering of the Kestrel, The.' *St. James's Gazette,* Feb. 22, 1883. *(The Life of the Fields.)*

'How to Read Books.' *Cassell's Family Magazine,* Aug. 1876. *(Beauty is Immortal.)*

'Humanity and Natural History.' *Knowledge,* Jan.5, 1883.

'Hyperion' *(Beauty is Immortal.)*

'Idle Earth, The.' *Longman's Magazine,* Dec. 1894. *(The Hills and the Vale.)*

'Imitation Cheeses.' *St. James's Gazette,* June 17, 1882.

'Improved Cars for Cattle.' *Live Stock Journal,* June 28, 1878.

'In a Pine-Wood.' *Graphic,* May 19,1877. *(Landscape and Labour.)*

'In Brighton' (editor's title). *(Beauty is Immortal.)*

'Increasing Importance of Horse-Breeding.' *Live Stock Journal,* July 13, 1877.

'In Summer Fields.' *St. James's Gazette,* June 7, 1886.

'Intermixed Agriculture.' *Live Stock Journal,* Nov. 2, 1877.

'In the Fields: April.' *St. James's Gazette,* April 20, 1881. *(Chronicles of the Hedges.)*

'In the Fields. March.' *St. James's Gazette,* March 12, 1881.*(Chronicles of the Hedges.)*

'In the Hop-Gardens.' *St. James's Gazette,* Sept. 23, 1880. *(Chronicles of the Hedges.)*

Introduction to Gilbert White's *Natural History of Selborne.* Camelot Classics, 1887. *(The Spring of the Year.)*

'January in the Sussex Woods.' *Standard,* Jan. 22, 1884. *(The Life of the Fields.)*

'January Notes.' *Pall Mall Gazette,* Jan. 31, 1880.

'Jockeying Pheasant Preserves.' *Live Stock Journal,* June 1, 1877.

'John Smith's Shanty.' *Fraser's Magazine,* Feb. 1874. *(The Toilers of the Field)*

'Joint-Stock Agriculture.' *Pall Mall Gazette*, March 16, 1877.

'Joy of the Wind, The.' *(Chronicles of the Hedges.)*

'July Grass, The.' *Pall Mall Gazette*, July 24, 1886. *(Field and Hedgerow.)*

'Just Before Winter.' *Chambers 'Journal*, Dec. 18, 1886 *(Field and Hedgerow.)*

'Kilburn Show, The.' *Pall Mall Gazette*, July 4, 1879. *(Field and Farm.)*

'King of Acres, A.' *Chambers' Journal*, Jan. 5,12, 1884. *(The Hills and the Vale.)*

'Kiss and Try' *London Society*, Feb. 1877. *(Society Novelettes I.)*

'Labourer and His Hire, The.' *Live Stock Journal*, Aug. 30, 1878.

'Labourer's Daily Life, The.' *Fraser's Magazine*, Nov. 1874. *(The Toilers of the Field.)*

'Larger Thought of London, The.' *(Chronicles of the Hedges.)*

'Last of a London Trout, The.'*(The Old House at Coate.)*

'Lawn Preserves.' *Globe*, May 9, 1877.

'Leafy November, A.' *Pall Mall Gazette*, Nov. 25, 1879. *(Chronicles of the Hedges.)*

'Left Out in the Cold.' *St. James's Gazette*, Dec. 30, 1884. *(Field and Farm.)*

'Legend of a Gateway, The.' *(See* 'Bits of Oak-Bark.)

'Leicester Square.' *(Chronicles of the Hedges.)*

'Lesser Birds, The.' *(See* 'Thoughts in the Fields.')

'Lesson in Lent, A.' *Live Stock Journal*, March 30, 1877. *(Chronicles of the Hedges.)*

'Less Stock, Less Wheat.' *Live Stock Journal*, Oct. 26, 1877.

'Let Me Think.' *Cassell's Family Magazine*, Oct. 1876. *(Beauty is Immortal.)*

'Life of the Soul, The.' (editor's title). *(The Old House at Coate.)*

'Lions in Trafalgar Square, The.' *Longman's Magazine*, March 1892. *(The Toilers of the Field.)*

'Locality and Nature.' *Pall Mall Gazette*, Feb. 17, 1887. *(Field and Hedgerow.)*

'Local Taxation' *Wilts and Gloucestershire Standard*, Jan. 1, 1876.

'London Bridge Station.' *(Chronicles of the Hedges.)*

'London Contrasts' *(Chronicles of the Hedges.)*

'London Mud' *(Chronicles of the Hedges.)*

'London Reflections' *The Field*, Sept. 27, Oct 4, 1947 *(Chronicles of the Hedges.)*

'London Scents and Colours' *(Chronicles of the Hedges.)*

'London Selfishness' *(Chronicle of the Hedges.)*

'London Trout, A.' *(Nature Near London.)*

'Lonely Common, The.' *(Field and Farm.)*

'Machiavelli: A Study.' *Nineenth Century and After*, Sept. 1948.

'Magic of the Night.' *(Chronicle of the Hedges.)*

'Magpie Fields.' *(Nature Near London.)*

'Makers of Summer, The.' *Chambers' Journal*, May 28, 1887. *(Field and Hedgerow.)*

'Man of the Future, The.' *Swindon Advertiser*, June 19, 1871.

'March Notes.' *St. James's Gazette*, March 6, 1883. *(Chronicles of the Hedges.)*

'Market Gardening.' *St. James's Gazette*, Oct. 20, 1880.

'Marlborough Forest.' *Graphic*, Oct. 23, 1875. *(The Hills and the Vale.)*

'Masked' (short story). *North Wilts Herald*, Oct. 13,20,27, 1866. *(The Early Fiction of Richard Jefferies.)*

'Meadow Gateway, The.' *(See* 'Chronicles of the Hedges.')

'Meadow Thoughts.' *Graphic*, April 5, 1884. *(The Life of the Fields.)*

'Midsummer 1879.' *Pall Mall Gazette*, July 12, 1879 *(Chronicles of the Hedges.)*

'Midsummer Hum, The.' *Graphic*, July 15, 1876 *(Chronicles of the Hedges.)*

'Midsummer Pests.' *Live Stock Journal*, June 22, 1877 *(Chronicles of the Hedges.)*

'Mind Under Water; or Fishes as They Really Are. *Graphic*, May 19, 1883. *(The Life of the Fields.)*

'Minor Sources of Income.' *Live Stock Journal*, March 16, 1877.

'Minute Cultivation – A Silver Mine.' *Live Stock Journal,* July 26, 1878. *(Chronicles of the Hedges.)*

'Mixed Days of May and December.' *Pall Mall Gazette,* May 13, 1887. *(Field and Hedgerow.)*

'Modern Sporting Guns.' *Pall Mall Gazette,* Nov. 17, 1879. *(Chronicles of the Hedges.)*

'Modern Thames, The.' *Pall Mall Gazette,* Sept. 6, 1884. The Open Air.

'Monkebourne Mystery, The' *New Monthly Magazine,* Jan. 1876.

'More About Butter.' *Live Stock Journal* Jan. 11, 1878.

'Mowers and Reapers: Recent Improvements.' *Live Stock Journal,* April 26 and May 10, 1878.

'Mr. Mechi's Budget.' *Live Stock Journal,* April 27, 1877.

'Mulberry Tree, The.' (*See* 'The Tree of Life.')

'My Chaffinch (poem). *Pall Mall Gazette,* March 18, 1887. *(Field and Hedgerow.)*

'My Old Village.' *Longman's Magazine,* Oct. 1887 *(Field and Hedgerow.)*

'Mystery of Offal, The.' *Live Stock Journal,* April 12, 1878.

'Natural History of Beautiful Women, The.' *(Field and Farm.)*

'Natural System of National Defence. A' *Swindon Advertiser,* June 26; July 3, 10, 1871.

'Nature and Books.' *Fortnightly Review,* May 1887. *(Field and Hedgerow.)*

'Nature and Eternity.' *Longman's Magazine,* May 1895. *(The Hills and the Vale.)*

'Nature and the Gamekeeper.' *St James's Gazette,* March 13, 1883. *(The Life of the Fields.)*

'Nature in the Louvre.' *Magazine of Art,* Sept. 1887. *(Field and Hedgerow.)*

'Nature Near Brighton.' *Standard,* Aug. 28, 1883. *(The Life of the Fields.)*

'Nature on the Roof.' *Chambers' Journal,* June 21, 1884. *(The Open Air.)*

'Neglected Pig, The.' Live Stock Journal, Feb. 22, 1878. *(Field and Farm.)*

'New Facts in Landscape.' (*See* 'Notes on Landscape Painting.)

'Nightingale Road.' *Standard,* Nov. 26, 1880. *(Nature Near London.)*

'Nightingales.' *St. James's Gazette,* April 10, 1886. *(Chronicles of the Hedges.)*

'Noontide in the Meadow' *(Greene Ferne Farm.)* (Later printed separately by Samuel J. Looker in notes to the Collector's edition of *Field and Hedgerow,* 1948.)

'Notes A-Field.' *St. James's Gazette,* July 28, 1885.

'Notes on Landscape Painting.' *Magazine of Art,* March and November 1882. *(The Life of the Fields.)*

'Novelty in Literature.' (*See* Samuel J. Looker, *'Jefferies Unpublished Manuscripts.'*)

'November Days.' *Standard,* Nov. 14, 1878 (Included in *Hodge and His Masters.*)

'Nude in London, The.' *World,* June 12, 1878.

'Nutty Autumn.' *Standard,* Sept. 30, 1881. *(Nature Near London.)*

'Oak Bark.' (*See* 'Thoughts in the Fields.)

'October.' *The Bryanston Miscellany.* Samuel J. Looker, *'Jefferies Unpublished Manuscripts.'* (Extract from an early draft of *Bevis.*)

'Old House at Coate, The.' *(The Old House at Coate.)*

'Old Keeper, The.' *(Field and Farm.)*

'Old Mill, The.' *Graphic,* Feb 9, 1878.*(Landscape and Labour)*

'On Allotment Gardens.' *New Quarterly,* April 1875.

'One of the New Voters.' *Manchester Guardian,* Jan. 24, and 31, 1885. *(The Open Air.)*

'On the Downs.' *Standard,* March 23, 1883. *(The Hills and the Vale.)*

'On the London Road,' *Pall Mall Gazette,* April 2, 1885. *(The Open Air.)* In the *Pall Mall Gazette* this was entitled *'Scenes on the London Road.')*

'Orchis Mascula.' *Longman's Magazine,* June 1891. *(The Toilers of the Field.)*

'Otter in Somerset, The.' *Manchester Guardian,* Aug. 27, 1883. *(The Life of the Fields.)*

'Our River: 1. Its Natural Denizens.' (*See* 'The Modern Thames.')

'Our Winter Food.' *Live Stock Journal,* Sept. 14, 1877.

'Out of Doors in February.' *Good Words,* Feb. 1882, May 1883. *(The Open Air.)*

'Out of the Season.' *London Society,* Sept. 1876. *(Society Novelettes II.)*

'Outside London.' *Chambers' Journal,* Jan 17, Feb. 21, 1885. *(The Open Air.)*

'Pageant of Summer, The.' *Longman's Magazine,* June 1883. *(The Life of the Fields.)*

'Paradox: Slow Progress of Science, The.' *The Field,* July 19, 1947. *(Beauty is Immortal* Published in *The Field* under the title 'Slow Progress of Science.')

'Parliamentary Measures Affecting the Grazier.' *Live Stock Journal,* Feb. 23, 1877.

'Partridge Hatching Season.' *St. James's Gazette,* June 27, 1883.

'Partridges in 1880.' *St. James's Gazette,* June 29, 1880.

'Pasture and Population.' *Pall Mall Gazette,* Oct. 25, 1877.

'Pasture and Stock.' *Live Stock Journal,* March 23, 1877.

''Patent' Butter.' *Live Stock Journal.* Feb. 8, 1878.

'Persecution of St. Partridge, The.' *Live Stock Journal,* June 8, 1877. *(Field and Farm.)*

'Pheasant Breeding.' *St. James's Gazette,* Oct. 3, 1882.

'Philosophy of Mayflies. The.' *The Field,* May 24, 1947 *(Field and Farm.)*

'Piccadilly.' *(Chronicle of the Hedges.)*

'Picture of April' *Pall Mall Gazette,* April 30, 1885. *(Chronicles of the Hedges.)*

'Picture of Men and Women Living Upon the Land.' (Early synopsis of *Hodge and His Masters. See* Samuel J. Looker, *Jefferies Unpublished Manuscripts.)*

'Pictures in the National Gallery' *(Chronicles of the Hedges.)*

'Pigeons at the British Museum, The.' *Pall Mall Gazette,* Jan 11 1884. *(The Life of the Fields.)*

'Pine Wood, The.' *Standard,* Sept. 3 1885 *(The Open Air.)*

'Place of Ambush, The.' *The Field,* April 26, 1947. *(Field and Farm.)*

'Plainest City in Europe, The.' *Pall Mall Gazette,* Oct. 20, 1883. *(The Life of the Fields.)*

'Plea for Pheasant Shooting, A.' *Live Stock Journal,* Sept. 28, 1887.

'Poaching as a Profession.' *Pall Mall Gazette,* Dec. 12,14, 1877. (Included in *The Gamekeeper at Home.)*

'Poetry of the Bible, The.' *Broad Churchman,* early 1873.

'Postion of the Grazier, The.' *Live Stock Journal,* Feb. 2, 1877.

'Power of the Farmers, The.' *Fortnightly Review,* June 1874.

'Preservation of Game in England, The.' *St. James's Gazette,* Oct. 25, 1881.

'Primrose Gold in Our Village.' *Pall Mall Gazette,* June 8, 1887. *(Field and Farm.)*

'Producers and Consumers.' *Live Stock Journal,* June 21, 1878.

'Professional Bird' Catcher, The.' *St. James's Gazette,* Aug. 4, 1885 *(Chronicles of the Hedges.)*

'Profit from Rabbits.' *Live Stock Journal,* Sept. 13, 1878.

'Prospects of the First, The.' *St. James's Gazette,* Sept. 1, 1882.

'Protection of Hunting, The.' *Live Stock Journal,* May 25, 1877.

'Protection of Nature, The.' *(Field and Farm.)*

'Queen's New Subjects, The.' *Cassell's Family Magazine,* Aug. 1877.

'Rabbits and Hares.' *Pall Mall Gazette,* Aug. 18, 1880.

'Rabbits as Food.' *Live Stock Journal,* Dec. 29, 1877.

'Rabbit Shooting.' *St. James's Gazette,* Feb. 3, 1882.

'Rabbit Warrens and the Returns.' *Live Stock Journal,* Jan. 4, 1878. *(Field and Farm.)*

'Railway Accidents Bill, A.' *Fraser's Magazine,* May 1874.

'Rats, Mice and Game Preserves.' *Live Stock Journal,* Sept. 27, 1878.

'Recapitulation' (poem,) *(Chronicle of the Hedges.)*

'Red Roofs of London.' *St. James's Gazette,* Aug. 2, 1884 (*The Open Air.* In the *St.. James's Gazette* this was published as 'The Roofs of London.')

'Reorganizing the Meat Supply.' *Live Stock Journal,* Jan 26, 1877. *(Field and Farm.)*

'River, The.' *Standard,* Sept. 10, 1880. *(Nature Near London.)*

'Roman Brook, A.' (*See* 'Bits of Oak Bark.')

'Rook Shooting.' *St. James's Gazette,* May 9, 1882.

'Rooks, The.' *(Chronicles of the Hedges.)*

'Round of London Copse.' *Standard,* Dec. 26, 1882. *(Nature Near London.)*

'Rural Dynamite.' *See* 'The Field Play.'

'Sacrifice to Trout, The.' S*t. James's Gazette,* March 17, 1883. *(The Life of the Fields.)*

'Saint Guido.' *English Illustrated Magazine,* Dec. 1884. *(The Open Air.)*

'Scarcity of Bacon Pigs, The.' *Live Stock Journal,* July 19, 1878.

'Scenes on the London Road.' *See* 'On the London Road.'

'Scientific Culture of Grasses and Clover.' *Live Stock Journal,* Nov. 16, 1877.

'Seasons in Surrey: Tree and Bird Life in the Copse, The.' *(The Old House at Coate.)*

'Sea, Sky, and Down.' *Standard,* Jan. 3, 1884. *(The Life of the Fields.)*

'Seed Inquisition, The.' *Live Stock Journal,* Dec. 21, 1877.

'Selling by Rule of Thumb.' *Live Stock Journal,* May 10, 1878.

'Shipton Accident, The.' *Fraser's Magazine,* Feb. 1875.

'Shooting' (*See* Samuel J. Looker, *Jefferies Unpublished Manuscripts.*)

'Shooting a Rabbit.' *Pall Mall Gazette,* June 25, 1880 *(Chronicles of the Hedges.)*

'Shooting Poachers.' *Pall Mall Gazette,* Dec. 13, 1884. *(Chronicles of the Hedges.)*

'Shortest Day Scene, A.' *St. James's Gazette,* Dec. 22, 1884. *(Chronicles of the Hedges.)*

'Shorthorn in France, The.' *Live Stock Journal,* June 7, 1878.

'Shorthorns on Arable Land.' *Live Stock Journal,* April 13, 1877.

'Shrinking of the Scene in Winter.' *(Chronicles of the Hedges.)*

'Sin and Shame, A.' (short story). *New Monthly Magazine,* Nov. 1875.

'Single Barrel Gun, The.' *St. James's Gazette,* Dec. 19 1884. *(The Open Air.)*

'Sipping the Season.' *World,* June 7, 1876.

'Size of Farms, The.' *New Quarterly,* Oct. 1874. *(Landscape and Labour.)*

'Skating.' *(The Hills and the Vale.)*

'Skating.' *(The Hills and the Vale.)*

'Sleight-of-Hand Poaching.' *Pall Mall Gazette,* Dec. 29, 1877. (Included in *The Gamekeeper at Home.*)

'Slow Progress of Science.' *See* 'The Paradox: Slow Progress of Science.'

'Small Birds.' *Pall Mall Gazette,* Dec. 30, 1878. *(Chronicles of the Hedges.)*

'Snipe and Moonlit Sport.' *Pall Mall Gazette,* Nov. 16, 1877. (Included in *The Amateur Poacher.*)

'Sold by Auction.' *St. James's Gazette,* Feb. 24, 1885. *(Field and Farm.)*

'Some April Insects.' *Pall Mall Gazette,* April 27. 1887. *(Field and Hedgerow.)*

'Some Triumphs of Poor Men.' *Cassell's Family Magazine,* April 1877. *(Beauty is Immortal.)*

'Southdown Shepherd, The.' *The Standard,* Aug. 31, 1881. *(Nature Near London.)*

'Speciality Cheese.' *Globe,* Oct. 15, 1877.

'Spirit of Modern Agriculture, The.' *New Quarterly,* July 1876.

'Sport and Science.' *National Review* Aug. 1883. *(The Life of the Fields:* includes only part of the original essay whose full title was 'A Defence of Sport' [q.v.].)

'Spring Notes.' *Pall Mall Gazette*, April 23, 1880. *(Chronicles of the Hedges.)*

'Spring of the Year, The.' *Longman's Magazine*, June 1894. *(The Hills and the Vale.)*

'Spring Prospects and Farm Work.' *Live Stock Journal*, March 22, 1878. *(Chronicles of the Hedges.)*

'Squire and the Land, The.' *(The Old House at Coate.)*

'Squire at Home. The.' (See Samuel J. Looker, *Jefferies Unpublished Manuscrips*.)

'Squire's Preserves, The.' *(Field and Farm.)*

'Stars Above the Elms, The.' *(Chronicles of the Hedges.)*

'State of Farming, The.' *St. James's Gazette*, Aug. 3,5,13, 1881. *(Field and Farm.)*

'Steam on Country Roads.' *Standard*, Sept. 13, 1881. *(Field and Hedgerow.)*

'Story of Furniture, The.' *Cassell's Family Magazine* June 1877. *(Beauty is Immortal.)*

'Story of Swindon, The.' *Fraser's Magazine*, May 1875. *(The Hills and the Vale.)*

'Strand, The.' *(Chronicles of the Hedges.)*

'Strange Story, A' (short story). *North Wilts Herald*, June 30, 1866. *(The Early Fiction of Richard Jefferies.)*

'Straw and Stock,' *Live Stock Journal*, Oct. 12, 1877.

'Strength of the English' *(The Old House at Coate.)*

'Study of Stock , The.' *Live Stock Journal*, May 11, 1877. *(Chronicles of the Hedges.)*

'Summer Day in Savernake Forest, A.' *Globe*, July 27, 1876. *(Landscape and Labour.)*

'Summer Evening, A.' *Pall Mall Gazette*, July 28, 1881. *(Chronicles of the Hedges.)*

'Summer in Somerset.' *English Illustrated Magazine*, Oct. 1887. *(Field and Hedgerow.)*

'Summer Meat Supply.' *Live Stock Journal*, May 17, 1878.

'Summer Notes., *Pall Mall Gazette*, July 6, 1880. *(Chronicles of the Hedges.)*

'Sun and the Brook, The.' *Knowledge*, Oct. 13, 1882. *(The Hills and the Vale.)*

'Sunlight in a London Square.' *Pall Mall Gazette*, Sept. 7, 1883. *(The Life of the Fields.)*

'Sunny Brighton.' *Longman's Magazine*, July 1884. *(The Open Air.)*

'Swallow Time.' *Standard*, Aug. 3, 1886. *(Field and Hedgerow.)*

'Swindon: Its History and Antiquities.' *Wilts Archaeological and Natural History Magazine*, March 1874.

'Tangle of Autumn, A.' *(Field and Farm.)*

'Thoughts in the Fields' *The Field*, Sept. 13, 1947. *(Chronicles of the Hedges.)*

'Thoughts on Cattle Feeding.' *Live Stock Journal*, May 24, 1878.

'Thoughts on the Labour Question.' *Pall Mall Gazette*, Nov. 10, 1891. *(Field and Farm)*

'Three Centuries at Home.' *(The Old House at Coate.)*

'Time of the Year, The.' *Pall Mall Gazette*, April 9, 1887. *(Field and Hedgerow.)*

'Tits and the Trees' *(Chronicles of the Hedges.)*

'To a Fashionable Bonnet' *North Wilts Herald*, June 30, 1866. *(The Early Fiction of Richard Jefferies.)*

'To Brighton.' *Standard*, Sept 15, 1880 *(Nature Near London.)*

'Too Much "Margin"' *Live Stock Journal*, Jan. 25 1878.

'Training Schools for Servants.' *Cassell's Family Magazine*, March 1878.

'Traits of the Olden Times.' *North Wilts Herald*, March 2, 1866. *(The Early Fiction of Richard Jefferies.)*

'Travelling Labour.' *Live Stock Journal*, July 6, 1877. *(Chronicles of the Hedges.)*

'Tree of Life, *The Scots' Observer*, Nov. 8, 1890 (Reprinted by Samuel J. Looker in the 1941 edition of the *Notebooks* and in the Collector's edition of *Field and Hedgerow*, 1948.)

'Trees About Town.' *Standard*, Sept. 28, 1881. *(Nature Near London.)*

'Trees and Birds of the Wood' *See* 'Thoughts in the Fields.'

'Trees in and Around London' *(The Old House at Coate.)*

'Trepass.' Live Stock Journal, Aug. 24, 1877. *(Chronicles of the Hedges.)*

'True Approach to Nature, The.' *(Chronicles of the Hedges.)*

'True Tale of a Wiltshire Labourer, A.' *(The Toilers of the Fields.)*

'T.T.T.' *North Wilts Herald,* Feb. 2, 1867 (Printed separately in 1896.)

'Typical Prize Farm, A.' *Live Stock Journal,* Aug. 23, 1878.

'Under the Acorns.' *Chambers Journal,* Oct. 18, 1884. *(The Open Air.)*

'Under the Snow.' *Pall Mall Gazette,* Jan 20, 1879. *(Chronicles of the Hedges.)*

'Under Tropical Rains.' *Live Stock Journal,* Jan. 19, 1877.

'Unequal Agriculture.' *Fraser's Magazine* May 1877. *(The Hills and the Vale.)*

'Untutored Love.' (*The Bryanston Miscellany.* Samuel J. Looker, *Jefferies
  Unpublished Manuscripts.)*

'Uptill-a-Thorn.' *See* 'The Field Play.'

'Utility of Birds.' *Live Stock Journal,* Aug. 3, 1887 *(Chronicles of the Hedges.)*

'Value of Grass,The.' *Live Stock Journal,* March 9, 1877.

'Value of Small Things, The.' *Live Stock Journal,* Jan. 18, 1878. *(Field and Farm.)*

'Varied Sounds' *(Chronicles of the Hedges.)*

'Venice in the East End.' *Pall Mall Gazette,* Nov. 5, 1883. *(The Life of the Fields.)*

'Vignettes from Nature.' *Longman's Magazine,* July 1895. *(The Hills and the Vale.)*

'Village Chruches.' *Graphic,* Dec. 4, 1875. *(The Hills and the Vale.)*

'Village Hunting.' *Globe,* Aug. 22, 1877 *(Landscape and Labour.)*

'Village Miners.' *Gentleman's Magazine* June 1883 *(The Life of the Fields.)*

'Village Organization.' *New Quarterly,* Oct. 1875. *(The Hills and the Vale.)*

'Walks in the Wheat-Fields.' *English Illustrated Magazine,* July & August 1887 *(Field
  and Hedgerow.)*

'War, The.' *Live Stock Journal,* May 18, 1877.

'Wasp-Flies or Hoverers' *(Chronicles of the Hedges.)*

'Water.' *Live Stock Journal,* April 6, 1877. *(Field and Farm.)*

'Water-Colley, The.' *Manchester Guardian,* Aug. 31, 1883. *(The Life of the Fields.)*

'Weather and Wages in the Country.' *Pall Mall Gazette,* July 26, 1879. *(Landscape and
  Labour.)*

'Weeds and Waste.' *Live Stock Journal,* Sept, 6, 1878. *(Chronicles of the Hedges.)*

'Wet Night in London.A.' *Pall Mall Gazette,* Dec. 31, 1884. *(The Open Air.)*

'Wheatfields.' *Standard,* Aug. 17, 1880 *(Nature Near London.)*

'Which is the Way?' *Cassell's Family Magazine,* Dec. 1876.

'Who Will Win? or, American Adventure.' *North Wilts Herald,* Aug. 25; Sept.
  1,8,15,22,29,1866 *(The Early Fiction of Richard Jefferies.)*

'Wild Flowers.' *Longman's Magazine,* July 1885. *(The Open Air.)*

'Wild Flowers and Wheat.' *Pall Mall Gazette,* July 20, 1881. *(Chronicles of the
  Hedges.)*

'Wild Fowl and Small Birds.' *Pall Mall Gazette,* April 18, 1877. *(Chronicles of the
  Hedges.)*

'Wild Fowling.' *St. James's Gazette,* Dec. 4, 1885.

'Wild Thyme of the Hills, The.' *See* 'Thoughts in the Fields.'

'Willow-Tide.' *Standard,* April 15, 1879. (Included in *Hodge and His Masters.)*

'Wiltshire Downs, The.' *Graphic,* June 30, 1877. *(Landscape and Labour.)*

'Wiltshire Labourer, The.' *Longman's Magazine,* Nov. 1883. *(The Hills and the Vale.)*

'Wiltshire Labourers.' Letters to *The Times,* Nov. 12,23,27, 1872. *(The Toilers of the
  Field.)*

'Window-Seat in the Gun-Room, The.' *The Bryanston Miscellany.* Samuel J. Looker,
  Jefferies Unpublished Manuscripts.

'Winds of Heaven.' *Chambers' Journal,* Aug. 7, 1886. *(Field and Hedgerow.)*

'Winter Scene, A' *(Field and Farm.)*
'Women in the Field.' *Graphic,* Sept. 11, 1875. *(Landscape and Labour.)*
'Woodlands.' *Standard,* Aug, 25, 1880. *(Nature Near London.)*